KORAN HIT
THE GENIUS OF GENTELMEN

S F RAHAMAN

First Published in March 2022

ISBN: 978-93-5611-035-9

BLUEROSE PUBLISHERS
www.BlueRoseONE.com
info@bluerosepublishers.com
+91 8882 898 898

Cover Design:
Geetika

Typographic Design:
Namrata Saini

Distributed by: BlueRose, Amazon, Flipkart

Preface

The image of the Qur'an, in general, is caught painfully at an ambiguous edge that lies somewhere between misconception and fear. The world is being constantly subjected to compulsive over-feeding on multitude of wrong information about Islam. The outcomes of the campaigns, needless to say, are extremely disturbing and can send a shudder of wide fear through the innocent hearts of Muslims and non-Muslims alike. Such outcomes benumb! Needless to say, the Qur'an is immured within the walls of fear and obscurity!

I am convinced that the Qur'an is the epitome of pure revelation, and its true soul should be explored the way it should be. Revealed for the whole humankind, the Qur'an is highly heralded as the last and final minister in the series of divine guidance. I believe that the Qur'an deserves a premium platform wherein its divine authorship, true flair must be discussed, argued and debated with due cogency. In this book, the spirit of questioning has been honoured and edified as the sublime moral-demand of human beings. Efforts have been made to impart a view-altering experience to readers who are in the search of exploring the insights of the Qur'an, and at the same time looking for disabusing themselves of the influence of wrong information about the Qur'an. Pivoting on the Qur'an, the book spans multiple aspects ranging from science to interfaith-discussion to history to geopolitics to many other important facets transpired during the course of debate.

The book wishes that peace and amity get established amongst the people of the world by understanding each other through the path of true enlightenment. The book wishes that the scatter pieces of humanity get joined together and enlivened forever like a perennially flowering tree whose blush brings hope. In it consists the book's satisfaction.

Acknowledgement

I am immensely indebted to my parents for standing by me in every respect.

I am also indebted to my wife, Fatema, who had been an incredible source of constant inspiration and steady support all the way to the last line of the book. She stood by me throughout the journey that demanded sheer perseverance and full engrossment.

I am grateful to Siddik, Jahir and Fardeen for their generous encouragements in authoring the book. I would like to give special thanks to Siddik for his perseverance in reviewing the book.

I extend my copious thankfulness to the ever-eager and incredibly professional team of the Bluerose Publishers who took up the job with sheer dedication required for an impressive performance. I thank them for their brightest efforts employed in giving a timely completeness to the book.

I thank you all!

Chapter 1

The sun was low in the western sky and sliding languidly towards the setting point. The fiery ball had already dissipated much of its ravening glare and cooled down into a mellow disposition. Having endured the angry glare of the sun, the landscapes sank down to have bathed in the mellowness of the pleasant glow. Meanwhile, the southerly breeze started blowing daintily placating the sunburnt things with her tender touches. I felt it flicking me fondly. Mild rays of golden shine were dancing upon the swaying heads of daffodils, goldenrods, and many other roadside flowers flaunting youthful exuberance full-jestingly.

Little away, my eyes swept across an enchanting sight of a flock of homebound herons gliding relaxedly along the margins of a hill. I watched them making the flight through tender rays of the sun dotting the green hill with colour white. My heart pranced and pulled me madly to climb the hill for a closer look. Up in the sky, a press of cumulus clouds was merrily floating through the comfortable sunshine over the landscapes. I wished I would lift into its fluffy chest and run fast over the rippling seas, the winding rivers, the rolling mountains, the rocky hills, across the lush prairies, the undulating meadows and the bald terrains of scablands. The moment exuded a shower of enchanting scenes that dewed me with lasting joy.

The generosity of the moment overpowered me, and the multitude of hospitality made me believe that I was the invite-only guest to that great company.

The sun was sinking and the evening was asked to descend. It tended silently to put a stop into the party!

We entered the service centre. The manager readily agreed to provide complete support for vehicle hospitality. Further, he assured us of giving all necessary supports required during the course of testing. The test was all about to validate engine misfire calibration by manipulating spark strength and fuel injection. It was our company authorised service centre, so hospitality was almost offered on a platter. The test vehicle was taken inside the premises and the mechanical snag associated with spark-path explained to the manager. He listened to it attentively and assured us of fixing the problem.

"By the way, would you like some coffee?" Kumaran suggested and I agreed on. The restaurant was near-by and reachable by walking.

On the way, after a little walk, Kumaran quizzed,

"Which state does the *Bay of Bengal* belong to?"

My questing mind hastily took an orthodox search towards geography. I *beat my brains out* for the answer but could not beat failure.

"It is in liquid state," Kumaran entertained with a wit.

"That's amusing really. It provokes laughter."

Next, I continued, "What is 114% of 50?"

"What's great in it? It's a flat calculation," Kumaran reacted innocently.

"Answer it in three seconds flat."

"Ah! Bit difficult," Kumaran said in a suppressed voice.

"Just move the '%' sign to '50' and calculate."

He loved the trick and offered me a cute curl of a half-smile.

"Does the sun rotate?" Kumaran quizzed.

"It's a gas-body unlike the earth. The fusion of the hydrogen into helium produces 'kinetics' that may result in certain rotational dynamics inside the sun. By the way, I sometimes wonder, does its rotation really matter?"

Kumaran looked at me in concordance and wagged his head.

Kumaran Muthuswamy, by profession, was a mechanical engineer and working in a service-providing organisation of great repute. I myself knew nothing about his faith, but to my glib guess, agnosticism commandeered greatly the space of his faculty. Still I would say, taking good anticipation on my side, it requires extraordinary insights to dig out his faith. Kumaran and myself were of same age. Kumaran's face belies his age and he ages in reverse.

We reached the restaurant and situated ourselves comfortably round a table placed fairly adjacent to the kitchen.

"Prejudiced! They will never change; they are frozen with the fear of religion!" a reactive, mildly agitated voice emerged like a projectile from the restaurant's kitchen. The clanger was set to *touch a raw nerve* of its intended prey.

Kumaran hailed the waiter and ordered two cups of coffee.

Kumaran's earlier visits made him somewhat familiar with the restaurant. With a wee of hesitation he inquired,

"Who are that prejudiced and who would never change?"

"Muslims!" the waiter responded with a complete disregard to hesitation.

"Reason?" Kumaran inquired. His voice was barely above a whisper.

"Ah! It centres around the 'Halal' factor. It seems to have become impossible for them to shackle off religious dogmas. The 'Halal' factor has made a deeper seepage into their psyches. Surprisingly, they pride themselves on being faithful to it. They keep the ‘non-vegetarian’ meals off dining table as to honour a stupid dogma of their religion.

The world has made many admiring leaps forward rejecting the potpourri of human manufactured class-customs, social-rituals, religious-dogmas to the care of hell, but Muslims, I think, have blissfully camped at the last depth of darkness. Someone should come forward and talk some sense into them,” described the waiter with unflappable cool.

The waiter rubbished Muslims and left hastily to attend another table placed at a good distance.

The waiter could not bear the variance in food habit of Muslims. To his wonder, how the nonsense ‘Halal’ could make Muslims love *vegetarian-meals* while away from home? It seemed, if he were given executive power, he would have perhaps imposed some ‘resolute laws’ on Muslims.

The mood of the moment went *into a spin*. The clanger dropped by the waiter vitiated the overall ambience and gave way to silence. I too tended to prefer silence.

The waiter combined mock and slander efficiently but wisdom, - yes, wisdom was seen nowhere.

Embarrassment was running across the face of Kumaran, but it failed to seize me. Instead, I managed to collect a fair measure of nerve while dealing with the clanger, and after a quick while, I pushed it with a great ease to the back of my mind for a late foster care. I beat embarrassment easily and maintained a calm pose, though maintaining a cool disposition at that moment was almost a challenge.

Silence was reigning the moment like a king and appeared as the only saviour that could have *turned the corner* to relieve us from the imposed uneasiness. The moment was weeping uneasiness quite profusely.

I myself loved the way the waiter presented himself upfront making a serious description of the food habit of Muslims. He, in all honesty, vented out the subject that was galling his innocent heart perhaps for a quite long time. He was unpretentious to himself, but the 'view' could make a raw Muslim flaming!

As birds use thermals to lift itself in the air so I intended to make the most of the moment in explaining Islam to my friend. The waiter gifted me an unmissable opportunity poised favourably to be 'exploited' in a big way. I wished I should *beat a path to gentleman's door* to present the excitingly the nice soul of the Qur'an. An opportunity was put in my way! I inhaled a lungful of air and released it in a deep sigh almost soundlessly.

As the silence was in its prime, I wished to spend the moment watching the beauty of a meadow adjacent to the restaurant. My glance fell upon a solitary quail swaggering through the swathe of a grassland –green and trimmed. The search was aggressive but classic and was full of unflagging energy. The quail seemed to be trying religiously, with all its elegance intact, to arrange a majestic meal. The glances were incisive and the spirit was indomitable to say precisely about it. With my enamoured heart, I watched it scuttling around with its quick but short steps scanning the land for the search of preys. The beautiful meadow with its gorgeous guest looked august and remarkably enjoyable. The disheartening side of the scene, I guessed, was the quail's regular vigilance on the surroundings. Perhaps, in the past, it had experienced lethality from a local cruel denizen.

"Look, I prodded Kumaran into agreement, how beautiful it is!"

"Yes…really… it is captivating," Kumaran nodded spontaneously.

Thc quail disappeared silently into a patch of wildflowers rubbing gently the drooping foliage. I was ostensibly content but wished to watch its magnificence for a longer while. It was a joy to behold! I dragged my heart from the scene somehow and suppressed its longing.

'Sir, coffee,' the waiter broke the silence and served the orders. He left making a soft tick on the surface of the table. Coffee was hot and giving off a haze of aroma-filled steam that curled up high misting slightly our faces.

Kumaran leaned back on the chair after the first sip and appeared laidback. A mild thudding noise emerged from the slat of the chair while the process of his leaning was in progress. It seemed that Kumaran was pondering over something discernibly serious.

"I would like to ask a few questions pertaining to Islam," Kumaran begged my permission discreetly.

Kumaran came out of his usual character of quizzing and bantering on almost every subject but religion. Never did he asked me, in friendship, any question that connects religion.

"It's a joy and in fact I am overjoyed to welcome you. Ask questions on Islam that might have been nagging in the back of your mind. Any question on Islam! I am offering you the rights equal to the rights that you rightfully claim on your mother's milk."

My intention was to discuss Islam in an open and amicable atmosphere. I do believe that the freedom of rational expression crowns democracy, and in the same vein, the freedom of intellectual-debate coerces ignorance into submission.

"Do you think I am secular and liberal?" Kumaran asked for my disposition with an apt anticipation of a positive reply. I came across a note of seriousness in his otherwise calm voice.

"Yes I do." I timed a quick nod.

The coffee shrieked for my attention. I took a short drag of aroma of the coffee that pulled me immediately to appreciate its richness in flavour. Kumaran induced a swirl into the cup to cool it faster.

"Though Hinduism and Islam are two great religions yet they do co-exist like water and oil, -why not like water and sugar?" Kumaran stated thoughtfully. I sensed his serious mood.

"Why do you stick to "Halal" food only?" Kumaran fired the first question that situated its context into religion. He stared at me with steady but inquisitive eyes. I felt a mild trepidation in his voice about the possible reply.

"My good man, this is the way of living prescribed by Islam."

"Though I do have a shallow knowledge on it, but still would like to ask you, do you really find presence of any sense in this prescription?" Kumaran inquired. The tone of his voice was pleasantly agreeable.

"Yes, much sense is present in the prescription.

Which of the following killing methods do you think lies adjacent to ethical treatment to animals? -

Pushing red-hot rod through the anus of an animal (killing wild boar);

An animal packed in gunnysack and thrown into deep water till its last breath (killing a pet pig);

Piercing spears into the lungs of an animal (killing a Yak in hilly areas);

Severing the head in a single quick shot;

Gagging or hitting violently on the head."

"No doubt these are grisly. But, how do you slaughter animals and how does it benefit you?" Kumaran inquired retaining the agreeable disposition.

"In Islamic slaughtering method the windpipe and the jugular veins of the animal are cut very quickly letting the blood to be gushed out. The animals thus killed die due to shortage of blood. Animals feel lesser pain than the pain that they generally experience in natural death. The Qur'an says:

"Forbidden to you (for food) are: dead meat, blood, the flesh of swine, and that on which hath been invoked The name of other than Allah; that which hath been killed by strangling, or by a violent blow, or by a headlong fall, or by being gored to death; …" [Qur'an: Maidah 5:3].

When an animal is killed by any of such methods other than the Islamic one, the animal invariably dies due to either internal injury, or damage of its any vital organ or sudden cardiac arrest. Importantly, the animal thus killed experiences severe pain. Furthermore, we do know that blood is potentially infectious and the meat thus procured is not good for health."

Kumaran snatched a placid glance at me.

I called the manager of the service centre and inquired about the status.

"The work is in progress," informed manager.

My boss called me and informed that Phillip would join the team by evening with another test vehicle. Boss instructed strongly that he would not accept any slip during the test, -his demand was on successful and seamless completion of the assignment.

Phillip Ravichandran is a German citizen of Indian origin. He travelled to India for the test as an expert in engine misfire calibration. He and Kumaran worked in the same organisation. Phillip was extremely outgoing by nature.

We visited the service centre to check the progress of the work. They had fixed the reported problem but were working on another problem found during the course of inspection. I requested the manager to expedite the work. He gave a good shake of his head in full agreement.

Meantime, we finalised the test plan.

"Sir, the problem is fixed…," manager informed in due time.

It was around the dusk and we were waiting for Phillip. Phillip informed us that it would take five minutes to reach the location. We were about to move to hotel.

"The vehicle just rectified would give somewhat less mileage, -it will drink more compared to the other."

"Why?" asked Kumaran.

"The vehicle is fitted with new engine and a set of new tyres. Raw engine friction and high tyre rolling resistance may effect the fuel economy."

Taking clue from the word 'drink', Kumaran proposed for a get-together at hotel. Evening 9 o'clock was fixed. We met at the hotel terrace.

"I am off alcohol. I shall go for coffee."

"I am not pressing you for a skinful drink, at least you can have a *Bear Can* of 500ml, -alcohol contain is very less. Believe me that much alcohol would not affect the *'neural plasticity'* of your hippocampus!" Kumaran took a class on neurophysiology. He fussed over the drink.

"You guys enjoy, I am here accompanying you, but...."

"Ah! Poor guy! Please deactivate your *olfactory bulb* till we are done, else it will inhale traces of alcohol.

See, I take it occasionally, you can too have it to *wind down*... it is good for health," Kumaran began in a lighter vein full of grace. The note of his voice was very passionate and outgoing.

"Yes I do know it does yield some benefits."

"Then, who stops you?" Kumaran almost implored in an honorific way.

"The sum of the harm is greater than that of the benefits. The Qur'an flags up the danger lies disguised in alcohol. It says:

"They ask thee concerning wine and gambling. Say: "In them is great sin, and some profit, for men; but the sin is greater than the profit ..." [Qur'an: Baqara 2: 219]

If I emphasise, alcohol has two disgraceful outcomes of indelible stigma. The most ignoble outcome of alcohol is the impaired moral judgement ...could not differentiate between wife and daughter."

"It stinks to high heaven! Are you in sense or you have *taken leave of your senses*?" Phillip scowled. He stared at me with a welling of disgust and appeared dismissive of my view.

"It is not out of the way. It is apposite to the moment.

Sense is alive and my sensibility is *going with a swing*. The Bible says that Prophet Lot (pbuh) had sex with his own daughters in drunken condition:

"*... That night they gave him wine to drink, and the older daughter had intercourse with him. But he was so drunk that he did not know it,*" [Bible: Genesis 19: 31-33].

The effect of alcohol is dreadful, and *more often than not* leads to anarchy, lawlessness and sometimes pushes the preys into committing even incest. Unfortunately, the Bible has dragged a wrong person into abomination, -a Prophet of God is dragged to incest! You should be ashamed of yourself for dragging a Prophet into such lowness!"

"It incenses me! What else could I expect from a person who campaigns for a 'conservative ideology'?

I know many bizarre emotions are welling up in you against the Bible. But the world knows what Islam is! 'Islam' and 'conservative' are a conjoined twin born in sand-caked Arabia. Islam is a drag on the progress of the civilisation, -it retards things," Phillip loathed Islam. Seemed, a viper slithered from an underbrush!

"I welcome with much appreciation the way you have unboxed your inmost feelings to my face. I am willingly offering you a liberty which is as long as a diameter. Thank you really for opening up.

By the way, what do you exactly mean by 'fundamentalist' and 'conservative'?"

"Why women in Islam are forced to wear *Burka*? Is not it a sign of subjugation? Is not it a sign of animal-treatment to women? I find in it a drag of Islam on the progressive pace of civilisation," Phillip almost blew a *tempest in a teacup*. His voice mildly quivered with disgust.

"Can you show me a single true religious Book in the whole world that says that women can walk on the streets wearing 'bikini', 'monokini' or 'tankini'?

Furthermore, why do you exhibit the statue of mother Mary dressed up in a modest Hijab?

The Bible too is intolerant to immodesty. Perhaps it will awaken you to a realisation:

"The Lord said, Look how proud the women of Jerusalem are! They walk along with their noses in the air. They are always flirting. They take dainty little steps and bracelets on their ankles jingle."

"But I will punish them—I will shave their heads and leave them bald." [Bible: Isaiah 3: 16-17]

The Bible has prescribed a *raw deal* only for women. The Bible, unlike the Qur'an, hardly prescribes anything about the modesty of men. The discrimination is brutal and *below the belt!*

One will find a clear difference between the Qur'an and the Bible on the matter of modesty. The stand of the Qur'an on modesty is impartial, honorific and highly distinguished. On modesty, the instruction of the Qur'an to men is preceded by the instruction given to women. It says:

"Say to the believing men that they should lower their gaze and guard their modesty:..."

"And say to the believing women that they should lower their gaze and guard their modesty;..." [Qur'an: Al Nur 24: 30-31]

Modesty gives birth to piety whereas nudity breeds sensuality. By the way, what sorts of benefits do you reap by scanting the dresses of women?"

"The answer does not satisfy the crux of my question. Just tell me, why women in Islam are forced to wear Burka?" Phillip insisted. His impatience climbed to a new height.

"Please apprise me, why women in western countries are reverting to Islam? The question will thrust a realisation into your mind.

But, why do you prefer that women should dress scantily?"

"It is a sign of refinement; it paces with modernity. Women too are free like air," Phillip said smoothly *like a knife through butter*.

"Do you think nudity and spirituality can go parallel? Do you recommend that a nude woman basking in beach can read the Bible to attain spirituality?"

"Why not?" replied Phillip swiftly.

"Then why do you display mother Mary in Hijab?"

"Time has changed, -it demands refinement and liberty. The time does not respect conservatism anymore," Phillip retorted by way of explanation.

"Why do women participating in *Beauty Contest* wear scanty dress? What purpose does it serve?"

"Do you think that they should wear *black Burka*?" Phillip mocked.

"Have you seen the beauty contest held in Indonesia (year 2014)? Did the contestants wear Burka?"

"Yes I did. The sparkles of beautiful 'figures' of women were buried deep beneath the dark layer of Burka. The Contest was a farce that sank their personalities!" Phillip went deeper in jibing to my face.

"To judge whether our own sisters are beautiful or not, should we dress them scantily? Should we expose them to check the presence of sensuality?"

"Squalid outlook! It *makes my skin crawl*! Your tongue needs refinement!" Phillip shrieked and gawked at me. As crashes resound, his voice rose fitfully to an unpleasant shrillness.

My view did not dissolve into his psyche rather it thrust an indignation into his mood.

"I know your blood is boiling because it has hurt the very sobriety of your '*sexopose*' theory applicable for all save your sister. Friend, sensual-desire is not tasted with tongue but with eyes, -your eyes need refinement!

Islam objects strongly to brutal objectification of women. Islam is modest and the women of Islam should be dressed modestly.

The Qur'an flags up the dangers lie dormant in exposing sensuality and showing off luscious body contour.

My view has got its support definitely from Mother Mary, the Noble Laureate Mother Teresa and the Noble Laureate from Yemen, Tawakul Karman.

When Tawakul was asked about her Hijaab by journalists and how it was not proportionate with her level of intellect and education, she replied:

"*Man in the early times was almost naked and as his intellect evolved he started wearing clothes. What I am today and what I am wearing represents the highest level of thought and civilisation that man has achieved, and is not regressive. It is the removal of clothes again that is regressive back to ancient time.*"

I looked at them, -they wore bland expressions. I paused and after a little reflection I continued, -

I do really appreciate your concern about the Burka clad 'repressed' Muslim women. In the same vein, I am asking you, do you show the same sober concern about the prostitutes languishing in ghettos of brothels and leading lives with distasteful means of livelihood? Are you proportionately concerned for them too?"

"It's an industry… they cater for the society," Kumaran manufactured a trail of frail logic.

"In our country, the male population has outnumbered significantly the female's, and yet the existence of "*red light area*" does not shame us? Do you still think that it is a sign of a progressive society?"

"Think about those who possess less than four wives, or do not possess any," Phillip lampooned.

"Intellectual solves problems, but genius prevents."

"Do you mean your Book is genius?" Phillip threw the query with a fiendish smile. His lips curved impishly and strived hard to disregard my view.

"Yes, the Qur'an is genius!"

"Marrying four women is an instruction of a genius? Is the sense with you?" Kumaran wondered and sniffed at me.

"I would reveal the wisdom behind the prescription.

I would request you to reflect on the following points. -

How many women died in WWI and WWII as compared to men?

How many women were killed in Crusades as compared to men?

How many women did Genghis Khan kill in comparison to men?

How many women did the Great Alexander kill in comparison to men?

How many women did Stalin put in *Gulag* concentration camp compared to men?

Certainly, the percentage of women killed in those wars, battles and camps was far lesser than that of men. Indisputably, societies had then excess numbers of women.

According to British press in 1939 in Britain only, twenty eight lakh and eighteen thousands female (28, 18,000) were in excess compared to the numbers of male. Gays were included in the male population.

Now I am asking you, what was the solution to that sex imbalance?"

"Those were exceptional situations, -the world was not at peace. Now suppose, peace prevails and foeticide is an absolute absence in society. Then, how the theory of the genius can convert intelligent people to agree? How then it could recommend 300 percent increase in women-consumption?" Phillip made a rational inquiry. He just evaded my question.

"The Qur'an does not give surface solution.

Friends, the situation occurred and persisted for a long-time. What was the most acceptable solution to that exceptional situation? Do you have any?"

"But they *rode out* the storm," Phillip replied. He again evaded my question cunningly.

"Prostitutes too do survive in harsh conditions. They strive to scrape up the cost of a meal! Do you think that they do need no solution to their plights?

Here, I'm asking for the solution to that massive sex imbalance. Do you have any?"

"Do you think every man should marry more than one woman to solve the crisis?" Phillip rebuked half-wittingly. He hinted at the solution that I was about to propose.

"Yes. There is no better alternative to that.

The Qur'an is genius and its every work has forced the world to reorganise its ongoing thoughts whose applications have incurred nothing but a heap of setbacks, discouragement and rejection."

"Does the solution stand the test when the world is at peace and foeticide is an absolute absence?" Kumaran raised the question that Phillip had raised.

"Friends, the vision of the genius is not insular, neither is short-sighted, -the solution does hold good for every situation be it normal or exceptional, ordinary or extraordinary, or whatsoever. You should not be quick to miscalculate the level of genius of the Qur'an.

You must be aware of the medical research conducted in 20th century by the University of Adelaide (Australia), University Tromso (Norway) and University of Stanford (America). If I summarise the research, it says:

"*With female babies, there is much higher expression of genes involved in placental development, the maintenance of pregnancy and maternal immune tolerance. The blood-clotting disorder hemophilia occurs almost exclusively in males. The disease is caused by a mutation in a gene on the X chromosome. Women, with two X chromosomes, have a back-up version of this gene, while men, with only one X chromosome, don't. The researchers took blood samples from male and female volunteers who were given a flu shot. Women had higher levels of immune system molecules circulating in their blood than men, and they produced more effective antibodies against the flu virus".*

The bottom line of the research is: 'Women are medically stronger than men'.

So, even in the peaceful and morally correct world, women would outnumber men. The genius says:

"If ye fear that ye shall not be able to deal justly with the orphans, Marry women of your choice, Two or three or four; but if ye fear that ye shall not be able to deal justly (with them), then only one, …." [Qur'an: Al Nisa 4: 3]

The Qur'an does permit to marry more than one woman depending on the situation, else marry only one."

"Ask women whether they would readily share their husbands?" Phillip inquired. He snatched a fugitive glance at me.

"Should I ask this question to those excess women deprived of husbands? Should I ask this question to a prostitute if she wants a husband? Should I ask this question to a widow if she wants a husband?

Here I shall narrate a harrowing 'obituary' of a surrogate mother. -

"The society responded to my indigence in a very unique way that left me mystified and forced me to wonder till I gasped my last breath. I seemed to have lost myself, but my trim looks and petite physique came forwards boldly and offered me a life-saving air pocket during the 'earth quake'!

I was constantly surrounded by the lewd glances of marauding beasts who were always ready to help me out in exchange of sex and surrogacy. Nothing of the world overpowered me except its extravagant passion for draining thick pockets for sexual gratification. They were always ready to run on their knees *at full tilt* and with thick pockets. The enthusiasm really amazed me and the generosity overpowered me greatly. I would like to recount a slice of my dark life.

The stint was of ten months and I agreeably acquiesced in the agreement. I consented for sex from the day one till the seventh month of pregnancy. Neither was he a nutcase about sex, nor did he believe to ravish someone for it, and I felt that I had had an association with a deferential person. He knew sex during menstrual period is something that is not permitted from medical perspective, and he obeyed that medical-observance with a fair strictness. He was out and out gentleman, as if someone thrust politeness into his heart.

Half of the payment was made in advance, the rest was paid off as soon as the womb had discharged the load. Honestly, the amount could fill perfectly a capacious pocket and satisfy elegantly a rapacious mind. In principle, fifteen days of breast-feeding was agreed upon, but if udder went dry, fifteen days could have been reduced to five days. Next entails the scene that marks the exit.

I got the first flavour of surrogacy. Apprehension could not overcome me as I knew the task was executable and had been accomplished successfully by the women race throughout the ages. And yes I was at the bloom of child-bearing age. After the drop of semen, my womb executed the task successfully. After the brilliant accomplishment, yes I executed the task with great fluency, I boarded the return flight leaving my new-born baby to his biological father. One warm hug and then I passed him to the arms of his father for a cosy cradle. Then, I took a reluctant bite on an elegant torte offered to me on a silver plate. The cake sweetened my tongue but failed to enliven the heart that rued. It denied delight to my downcast eyes that pleaded for tears. I nursed the cake for a longer while.

I gifted away my newborn baby whom I might never meet again. Labour pain and the final loudest screaming that rent the air of the delivery room remained with me as the souvenirs of the stint.

Devastation crept down to my heart…I sank. But sooner I steadied myself and I started behaving like a mechanical mother upon collecting mental assistance from the plights of the tyres attached to the landing gears of the hawkish plane. I saluted, in my conjecture, the unbeatable endurance of the hapless tyres that bear silently all the brunt of, without being melted and torn-apart, landings and take-offs. The plane made a perfect landing, but I was crushed to the core as my motherhood was tortured by some unseen and insolent directness of sentimental feelings that had thrown me into the abyss of despair. I felt my heart quickened, then thudded and I just crumbled succumbing to the rigour of the excruciating feelings! I paled and withered giving off much of my vigour and vitalities. At one point of time, seemed it, I was fitted with rusted iron-lungs and a disused heart overcome much by sorrows and sufferings!

'Sex and surrogacy' both remained my all-weather friends though I found myself *demi-monde*…quite maladjustive in the thick of refined society. As time went on, despair silently climbed further up a flight of steps allying itself with isolation. My person receded into darkness rendering me maladjusted to the normal mental standard of the society. I was sure that one of the above friends would accompany me even after my death albeit with name changed: '*phantom pregnancy*'! Good bye the civilised world of gentlemen!"

Do you think that she loved her life the way it should have been loved?"

"Can a woman practise polyandry? Can they too have four husbands?" asked Kumaran inquiringly.

"Do you want to be one of the husbands?"

"Yes, why not?" Kumaran replied with a fainter voice.

"Are you ready to visit brothel?"

"Brainless inquiry!" Kumaran fumed.

"Your question too is not of a brainiac!"

"Why?" Kumaran inquired in an overhaste.

"It is perfectly fine if amongst the four husbands three are gays, else it will result in a weird situation. It will be constantly threatened by the quirks of the situation.

Please count, how many days you could avail her fairly in a month.

Are you ready to visit medical centre for DNA test after the birth of every child?

Friend, if an offer of a reserved taxi is available on a platter, then why do you want to board an overloaded shared taxi? -

You must know that the suspensions of an overloaded vehicle behave like a solid body and this phenomenon makes the vehicle prone to accident."

"Why cannot you marry a woman of different religion without converting her to Islam?" Kumaran probed. He fixed his eyes on me. I turned my face after enduring it for a short while.

"Do women of different religions have blood of different colours?" Phillip tailgated his comment quickly.

"No, it is not the colour of blood but the faith mixed with the blood. 'Faith' is considered premier by Muslims. It cannot be compromised for anything even if our both hands are awarded with gold amounting to the size of the biggest celestial body. There is nothing in the Universe deemed as the worthy replacement of the 'Faith'.

For a Muslims, marrying women of different religion amounts to a risk."

"Risk…?" Phillip almost yelled snatching a simmering glance at me.

"Truly conservativeness has made a nasty seepage into your psyche. The word '*conservative*' is very thick with Islam and has been blooming smilingly in the same tub for the past 1400 years, or so. An antique of a perfect bond; an antique of a perfect co-existence; an antique of an absolute inseparability. As cape sticks into a sea, conservativeness sticks to Islam; as baby nestles snugly at chest, conservativeness finds warmth on the chest of

Islam. The phenomenon is hugely intriguing, the reason is inexplicable and the bond is inextricable.

I will draw a metaphor and hope that it will not thrust a pain into your heart…: 'as the 'scent gland' is to a wild skunk, the 'conservatism' is to a fanatic Muslim!'" Kumaran rode on the vortex of multifariously vituperative remarks. His tongue sliced through the layers of detestation.

"Hate and insults no longer are strangers to Islam. They follow Islam like shadows and try their every malicious bit to put Islam down. Surprisingly, they get perished when Islam directs its blazing light upon them."

"Islam has rigged your conscience!

Do you think that women of other religions possess different colour of blood? Or, do they have different class of taste, touch and smell? Please don't behave like a nutcase," groused Kumaran. The word 'risk' made him *blow his top*!

"This is not a question of look-alike.

If it is so, then do you think the blood and milk of a cow and a camel are the same?"

"What do you mean?" asked Kumaran with a tinge of curiosity.

"Unlike other mammals, the red blood cells of camels are oval. This facilitates the flow of red blood cells during dehydration and makes them better at withstanding high osmotic variation.

Like cow milk, the milk of camel cannot be made into butter by the traditional churning method. It requires certain additive.

Friends, -

Can you hitch a cow and a camel together for ploughing?

Would you prefer to fly an aeroplane having one wing of '*aerofoil*' cross-section and the other of '*blunt body*'?"

"It sounds nice. But what does the Koran say? We are waiting with ever-eager ears to hear from the genius," inquired Kumaran mockingly.

"The Qur'an prohibits us from marrying unbelievers. The Qur'an says:

"Do not marry unbelieving women, until they believe: A slave woman who believes is better than an unbelieving woman, even though she allures you. Nor marry (your girls) to unbelievers until they believe: A man slave who believes is better than an unbeliever, even though he allures you. Unbelievers do (but) beckon you to the Fire. ..." [Qur'an : Baqara 2: 221]

To us, a believing slave woman is a far better choice than a ravishingly beautiful and unbelievably rich unbelieving woman!

The outlook of an unbelieving woman is parochial and limited mainly to dreary boundaries of the worldly affairs. To her, everything starts here and everything is bound to perish on the face of the earth. Nothing goes beyond this, nor even her soul. She gets lured, tangled, trapped and outfoxed by the untidy complex labyrinth of beauty, glamour, amusement and riches. Life to her is nothing but a sort of rollicking play that compels her to strike thick relation with every modern vagary of life, even with *money to burn*. The coupling of the pompousness and the brag transitions to dominate her, and she tends to be articulate all the time about her high-class standard by displaying ostentation through small pathetic things of daily life, might it be even as trivial as an artichoke dessert that follows her majestic meal. She looks down upon the other side of the aisle flocked with commonplace. To her, the concept of '*Hereafter*' is a fairy tale promulgated by a bunch of unlettered or less-learned folks.

A believing woman, on the other hand, is an antipode to an unbelieving woman. The outlook of a believing woman transcends the narrow boundaries of the worldly affairs. She finds the purpose of life in leading it in the confines of the prescription drafted by none but the Almighty Himself. To her, the manifold of beauty, fame and fortune are conditional, fugitive by nature, and cannot be given premium placement as absolutists, nor be considered as the overarching principles in life. Because with the passage of time, they all sink in impermanence and fade away into futility. To her, all these are useless overhangs and can easily be buried under her persistent quests for attaining spiritual breakthroughs before the deadline as set by the life. She considers, life on the earth is just a passing event and can be deemed as a decent equivalent to a stint of a transient visitor. She steeps herself in modesty; her humbleness overshadows braggadocio and she extends gratitude to the Creator even after having a frugal meal. She looks up to the hungry side of the aisle and thanks her Creator for being blessed with a meal that stills hunger. In the pursuit, her spirituality transitions to an ascension, and she vanquishes easily the urges of whimsy and other pompous family of things. She aspires earnestly to achieve a blissful abode in the 'Hereafter'!"

"Scrap it!

The story does not provoke any curiosity in me at all. I think it could be regarded by the people whose souls are denied of grace and trapped in a desolate corner inhabited by the dearth of joy.

The most I could say, the story does have a sentimental touch of whimsy, and is good enough to well up humour-stuffed amusement!

I wonder, how come you could be averse to attaching importance to riches and glamour! What is wrong if a woman does lead you to glamour and riches?" Phillip reacted fretfully.

"She will lead to Hell also!"

"Hel..ll..ll..!" Kumaran shrieked like a chalk on blackboard. Though serious inwardly, yet his voice came across as humorous.

Astonishment flashed across his face. He looked at me with stiff-opened jaw…as if, frozen agape!

"I fail to find a vein of an engineer in you. The thought is out of an engineering skull evidencing clearly that your brain is made of bricks!

There is nothing called Hell or Paradise. These all are intricate illusions to frighten and subjugate the feeble minds. These are nothing but a bunch of pepped up poetic imageries to delude easier sections of people!

Muhammad was a very shrewd union leader who deliberately converted the poetic imagery into reality and presented before the masses. Out of heightened fantasy coupled with peerless imagination, Muhammad championed the concept with unrelenting effort and indomitable spirit to take it to the zenith of importance. The concept of "Hell and Paradise" is actually his impure brainchildren to instil psychological fear into the minds of the people like you. It was all about to plant the seed of fear into human psychology.

To make it happen, he relentlessly disseminated his own "fancied ideologies" to gravitate people in his favour and presented himself as a 'divine guide' sent by God. Furthermore, with great competence and finesse, he authored the so-called "religious Book" and passed it to the masses as though the book was revealed to him by God Himself. He just painted the quaintness of an old-superstition with a new fine brush! The whole rigmarole helped him achieve the patina of respectability from the docile masses of Arab.

Understandably, he was self-conceited, over-blown and overstated mass leader falsely bearing the certificate of divinity. He was innately political and his level of perspicacity was much ahead of the curve. He was an astute player who skilfully maintained a delicate image of a curveball to trick the docile eyes looking earnestly up for divine guidance from him. He bent the minds of the Arabs!

No one can even stand close to his overacting performed on the script of divinity. He is reputed being the brightest actor the earth has ever produced!

I sense in you an internal process of moronic decay that would be imploded sooner or later. I think Richard Dawkins should be invited to teach you a lesson! Wake up sleepy head!" Kumaran thundered. He just roughed up me to his giddy satisfaction.

He hurled himself rudely at Muhammad (pbuh) like a raging inferno having wild steep front. He quickly pumped in and out a lungful of air after having slaked his thirst for criticism. I made an unvoiced salute to his virility in criticism.

"Islam starts with circumcision and ends with circumambulation (around the Kaaba)'!" Phillip cast a lovable aspersion on the thundering.

"Mecca too is mentioned in the Bible pertaining to pilgrimage, unfortunately you are not aware of that. 'Mecca' is mentioned as 'Baca' in the Bible.

"As they pass through the dry valley of Baca, it becomes a place of springs;..." [Psalms: 85:6]

"Why do you get circumcised?" Kumaran expressed curiosity.

"For certain benefits."

"It is primitive, and it attributes to spiritual rigidity.

Do you think people of other faiths have failed miserably to realise the great 'invention' of Islam?" Phillip sniffed. He made the comment with a confident assertion that cannot be deposed easily by the might of a frail logic.

"Beard and foreskin both are natural to human beings. Islam allows the beard to grow even as long as the trunk of a tusker, but shows great apathy for allowing the foreskin to exist naturally!" lampooned Kumaran.

"The resemblance of 'the beard': An artful wind, having expertise in artistic work, collected a tumbleweed found lying detached in a desolate desert, and after a certain degree of preening the wind fixed it to a fanatic face of a Muslim," Phillip lampooned very artfully.

"Do you think the beard of Jesus Christ (pbuh) resembles a tumbleweed?"

"Lunk-head! Comparison should be made between *apple to apple*, not between *apple and pineapple*" Phillip retorted. He attacked me with charging tongue. He cast a half-stern glance at me.

"Fine, what about the beard of Charles Dickens?"

"It's a crop of passion and vision," replied Phillip.

"Beard of Karl Marx?"

"Oh, beard of a great philosopher. It's luxuriantly philosophical!" replied Phillip.

"What about the beard of Abraham Lincoln, the 16th President of the USA?"

"Ah, it's a presidential beard," Phillip replied with a handsome curl in his smile.

"Beard of a Muslim?"

"It's a crop of raw fanaticism! It stinks of maniac! Surely, you can't lump yours into the rest. Be civilized dude!" Phillip launched a scathing lampoon on the beard of Muslims. Then, he curved a smile of pure disdain.

"By the way, what is the stand of the Koran on beard?" Kumaran placed the query immediately almost interjecting me.

Phillip's comment galvanised my feelings into action, but the query of Kumaran stood as an interposer that prevented me from presenting a tackler to the lampoon. Kumaran forestalled me.

I thought it would be better to present the view of the Qur'an on the subject rather than replying to Phillip. I persuaded myself and launched a crackdown on my inner unrest that was provoking me madly to reply to Phillip. I brought the wriggling of my tongue to rest, crushed the unrest into silence and tried to steer the discussion from hitting a bottleneck.

Kumaran's query brought about a ceasefire!

"It is 2KB," Phillip preceded his view before mine. Phillip forwarded it without of my asking. As if, his tongue jostled to say this.

"What is this?" asked Kumaran. His curiosity peaked.

"Keep beard and keep bomb (2KB). I guess, it might have been repeated in every chapter of his Holy Book," Phillip sassed the Qur'an.

Kumaran forwarded his tacit support to Phillip in full concordance. They merged their minds into one for a common purpose.

Phillip's comment did not dissolve into my psyche easily, rather it left a mild psychological cut. The acerbity of the reply compelled me to resort to a mild sadness that swiftly made its way from my heart to face, –it licked my face dominantly. A swift exit from the mood became an imperative as I had already offered them the liberty in asking me any questions or expressing suchlike pent-up feelings having direct or indirect affiliation to Islam. I committed a light dishonour to my pledge.

I evicted the sadness hastily and curved my lips out for a smile to indicate them about my cool disposition.

"Friends, the word 'beard' has made a single naïve appearance in the Holy Qur'an. And, I have not come across any word called '*bomb*' in the Qur'an."

"You know, the havoc caused by a single shot of a nuclear bomb cannot even be matched up with the hundreds of thousand shots of AK47s," Phillip took U-turn and presented a tacky and scurrilous view.

Phillip meant that the word 'beard' might have been mentioned once in the Qur'an, but is steeped in hugely hazardous connotations.

"Do you think the beard of Prophet Aron (pbuh) is hugely hazardous?"

"Why Aron? I think, it's a fun addition," Phillip shot back.

"The moment demands so."

"No, not really," replied Phillip. He cast an unusual glance at me.

"The below verse was revealed against the backdrop of the event when Moses (pbuh), after his return from a divine duty, caught the beard of his brother Aron (pbuh) appointed to look after the affairs of Israelites in his absence. A group of Israelites disobeyed the leadership of Aron (pbuh) and departed wilfully from the Path shown by Moses (pbuh).They, out of fantasy, started idol worshipping. Moses (pbuh) rebuked Aron (pbuh) for his alleged negligence in the assigned duty. The Qur'an says:

"(Aaron) replied: "O son of my mother! Seize (me) not by my beard nor by (the hair of) my head! ..." [Qur'an: Ta Ha 20: 94]

Do you still think that the 'beard' mentioned above does really bear hazardous connotations?"

"Beard or bread?" Phillip fudged the answer and dashed to that query. He just moved away from the pitch of 'beard'.

"What do you mean exactly?"

"Suppose in a given situation, you are required to remove your beard to meet the demand of your professional career, would you?" Phillip pressed me. I find a hidden compulsion launched in his voice to subjugate my choice. He looked at me with lavish attentions.

"It's already shaven off; - it's glistening, it looks glassy."

I forwarded my chin for his closer glance.

"Ah! Not you! I am led to say that the beard has been a signature image of Muslims, and suppose, you are one of those Muslims who dons the tumbleweed-beard boastfully; -my question is, would you *go against the grain*?" Phillip was riding me with impure motive.

"Given the circumstances, it seems a trifle; it's an incidental to main Islam. The soul will not see any decline in its spiritual flowering. Yes I would."

"A rare fundamentalist is dug out from the junk...quite flexible. Am I right?" added Kumaran impishly.

"Clinically or reluctantly detached from *'fundamentalism'*? Lay your elemental instinct bare," Phillip tossed the query.

"The statue of Jesus Christ (pbuh) in Brazil's capital was hit by lightning. Was Christ, the Redeemer in Rio De Jenerio, asked by the lightning on whether he would be stricken first on head or at heart?"

"Very deep reply! A savage attack!" observed Phillip.

He gaped at me with frozen stare. His eyes rained lashings of whips that could force the self-courage of a timid heart to atrophy. His stare was repelling like frowns and loathsome like foul words, and could herald an urge of fear. My reply jostled him to an awakening, perhaps.

"I think, we should elevate you to the next final rank sparsely populated by Muslims: '*the rational fundamentalist*'. You know, Muslims have given way to the pressure mounted by Islam, and eventually been trapped in a sorry state considered as dross by the rest of the world. But, I still belief that not all the promise have been taken away though," Phillip slipped into his usual trade within a slice of time and teased. He generalised Muslims in a pejorative term called '*fundamentalist*'.

"Hobson's choice[1]*?"

"No, not all, -I am not limiting your choices, neither lowering your stature, neither pulling you down. Frankly, and actually, there does not exist better choice though. The '*rational fundamentalist*' is the rarest and the best one. It will raise your stature a few notches; it will glorify you; it will put you *on cloud nine*! It's a special joy for you on being awarded with such serendipity!

These two sects, *the reluctant* and *the rational* fundamentalists, in the domain of Islam are like the two most stable *Lagrangian Points*[2]* L4 and L5 in our nearest space! In that sense, you are quite unique and your blood is worth bottling!" Phillip replied with a very nice astronomical metaphor laced with condescension. His voice trickled in piercing sarcasm that penetrated my bone marrow in no time!

"The polished section of Islam is made of 2RF: '*the rational* and *the reluctant* fundamentalists'. But, if both the sects are searched deeper, one would find the same DNA: the DNA of fundamentalism!

Do you find any qualitative difference between a *crevice* and a *crevasse*? Both actually belong to the family of crack, -the former is found on solid rock, the later on ice," Kumaran derided. His tongue deftly constructed the sarcastically impressive analogies. He pulled himself to a stop giving a supercilious grin that mocked me in silence.

"Why the word 'fundamentalist' is fused with 'rational'? Any reason?"

"The words 'rational' and 'fundamentalist' cannot be merged into only '*rational*' or '*fundamentalist*'. Rather, we have fused the words in '*rational fundamentalist*' so that they retain their 'oneness' and individual 'flavour'.

See, a trail of hints of your elemental character could easily be detected and gathered off the discussion. Though it has given a good handshake to rationality, yet it is not fully off the line of fundamentalism. A whiff of fanaticism still can be smelled, and my extrasensory perception tells me that you are still loyal to fundamentalism.

The course of discussion clearly hints that your soul has pledged an unswerving allegiance to the hands of Islamic fundamentalism," Phillip was forbiddingly quick to reproach me.

"Friends, I am conscious of not being close to tears. I hardly have any qualms in accepting myself decidedly as *rational fundamentalist*. I do accept this with great content, and I would pride myself being an admirer of it.

I would choose handsome career over the beard, and could bury a beard for the prospect of a bread. I could sacrifice beard to shout bread for my famished stomach.

I am not adrift rather it is my calculated decision just to fit myself into the sledgehammer milieu bent to bombard the harmless beard. My attitude may offend some so called '*fundamentalists*' habituated to showing hollow indignation to every trifle. They must delve deep into Islam."

"You are *sailing close to the wind...* a series of reprisals awaiting you...be prepared to bear the brunt of '*fundamentalists*,'" Kumaran put up a caution.

"Suppose, a migratory bird at certain point of time during its flight to cherished destination lost a feather to a brazen wind; my question to the *fundamentalists* is, - should the bird stop and return back to the starting point of its journey?

The answer is 'no'.

It is absolutely recommended that, since the bird is equipped with sufficient amount of 'fat' to survive in the journey, it should not return but reach destination jettisoning the 'trifle' to the care of insensitiveness."

"Here 'fat' means 'job'?" asked Phillip inquiringly.

I nodded.

"Who stops you from being circumcised?"

"Well, to lead off, the view of the Bible is liberal and it is genuinely real.

Circumcision does no longer add any perfection to the pie of our spirituality, and has long been considered as a trifle. Circumcision no longer cheers a spiritual soul, what matters is sincerity and devotion to God. The Bible says:

"For whether or not a man is circumcised means nothing; what matters is to obey God's commandment" [Bible: 1 Corinthians 7:19]

The Bible is wider in giving liberty than obligation," added Phillip boastfully.

"Then, Why the Bible did not allow Prophet Abraham (pbuh) and Jesus Christ (pbuh) to live with liberty? Why were they circumcised?

"*Abraham was ninety-nine years old when he was circumcised*" [Bible: Genesis 17:24]

"A week later, when the time came for the baby to be circumcised, he was named Jesus, …." [Bible: Luke 2:21]

Just look at the verses, -one was ninety-nine years old and other was at his early stage of infancy, but both were circumcised. Seems, the Bible was very hard on them!"

"Jesus Christ (pbuh) obeyed the laws revealed to Moses. But, Paul has clearly instructed us as:

"*Listen! I, Paul, tell you that if you allow yourselves to be circumcised, it means that Christ is of no use to you at all.*" [Bible: Galatians 5:2]

Circumcision excludes you from the grace of Christ," Phillip replied in a tone that was mild like breeze, and authoritative like autocrat.

"Was Paul circumcised?"

"The doubt is superfluous. The verse clearly demonstrates that Paul was not circumcised," Phillip deduced the conclusion putting his faith in the truthfulness of the verse.

"All right friend. Now, just read the following verse,

"Paul wanted to take Timothy along with him, so he circumcised him." [Bible: Acts 16:3]

Why did Paul want Timothy be circumcised, when Paul himself was not? Is not the verse clearly pointing to a perfect dissonance in the Bible? Does any rational conscience approve such mismatch?"

Phillip could not run his tongue. He offered some vague glances instead, -some on the surface of the table, and some on me. He could not anticipate that the Bible too contains such verse.

"Do you follow 'Christianity' or 'Paulanity'?"

"Obviously Christianity," replied Phillip swiftly.

"Then, did Jesus Christ (pbuh) himself, anywhere in the Bible, instruct you not to get circumcised?

Is Paul authorised to interfere in your private affairs? Did Jesus Christ appoint Paul to distort Christianity?"

Phillip was *caught between a rock and a hard place.* He wagged his head in half-disapproving way. The logic forced him to make a face!

"Does a man really require to be circumcised if he maintains celibacy all the way to death?" probed Kumaran.

Phillip wagged his finger towards Kumaran as if he had remembered something. Then he continued:

"Think of Jesus Christ (pbuh), -he maintained celibacy but was circumcised. A sense consists here."

"What sorts of advantages do you reap from circumcision?" Kumaran inquired. He tweaked his nose and looked at me with curiosity.

"I would cite a few advantages here that we reap from circumcision:

-It prevents Paraphimosis (Where foreskin is pulled back and trapped underneath the tip of penis).

-It prevents Balanoposthitis (is an infection of foreskin by bacteria).

-It prevents Urinary Tract infections (UTI). It is caused by bacteria gathered beneath the foreskin.

-It prevents Sexually Transmitted Infections (STI). It helps prevent Syphilis, Chancroid and HIV.

-It helps prevent cancer of penis.

My good man, advantages are multitude, benefits are manifold."

"I have not come across any uncircumcised men in my whole life who has been affected by such symptoms or diseases," added

Kumaran almost dismissing the advantages of circumcision. He snatched a derisive glance at me.

"Please tell me, then how the medical scientists found those diseases in uncircumcised people?"

"I mean, in my friend circle, no one so far has been affected by such diseases," Kumaran quickly tweaked the remark. He appeared quite determined to discredit the benefits of circumcision.

"Well, it's a pocket circle. I am certain, the diameter of your friend circle is minuscule compared to the diameter of the world, and it vehemently denies any comparison."

"Tell me, what scripture does say about the advantage of circumcision?" Kumaran tended to know from the scripture.

"The Bible says:

"Do the Jews then have any advantage over Gentiles? Or is there any value in being circumcised?"

"Much, indeed, in the first place, God trusted His message to the Jews." [Bible: Romans 3: 1-2]

I am quite taken aback by the prodigious loss of memory of the Bible. I am sure, the dodgy concoction of the Bible will haunt Phillip for some years. If circumcision entails religious bigotry, then yes I am a bigot, and certainly Jesus Christ (pbuh) too was a bigot!"

"Who circumcised Adam?" inquired Kumaran.

"He was not born but created, and was '*divinely circumcised.*"

"At what age Muhammad was circumcised?" Kumaran inquired jestingly.

"My good man, Prophet Muhammad (pbuh) was circumcised when he was in his mother's womb. He was born circumcised."

"Why homosexuality is prohibited in Islam?" Kumaran placed the query.

"Do you support homosexuality?"

"Yes I do," Kumaran wagged his head in agreement.

"Then, would you support if every man on the earth turns into a gay?"

"The world will not become gay overnight. How can you disapprove sexual orientation of someone based on narrow religious belief? Where the *milk of your human kindness* has gone to?" Kumaran almost upbraided me. He turned a virtual gun on me.

"This is but a surface thought.

Friends, human beings have unlimited feelings and infinite desires. It is not a wise practice to *throw caution to wind* by ignoring the impacts and the implications of the consequence. To reason, your assessment is based *on the surface* of situation that lacks insights. The beastly desires of human beings could *tip the scales* against humanity!

Anyways, why do you prefer the life of marshy land to marine life? Is it that the life in the marshy land is more natural, thrilling and sophisticated?

Why do you prefer Swaziland to Switzerland for holidaying? Are you more impressed by the scenic splendour of Swaziland? Is it more inviting? The Qur'an says:

"Of all the creatures in the world, will ye approach males? And leave those whom Allah has created for you to be your mates? Nay, ye are a people transgressing all limits!" [Qur'an: Shuaraa 26: 165-166]

The verse is winding a rousing call through despising the act of homosexuality because it transgresses the normal of humankind.

Will you support, if tomorrow, Mr X wants to have sex with an animal?"

"Decency has clearly made itself scarce here! How could you even conjecture that human beings would wish to strike physical relationship with an animal?" fumed Phillip over my remark.

"the bloom does not desert roses even in the darkness, but the humanity does, -it deserts human beings in the pursuit of pleasure and gratification.

Friends, human beings can do the low of the lowest. Human beings could even establish sexual relationship with their own daughters. This is a scary *straw in the wind* announcing loudly about the occurrence of something even worse than this.

Animals too have not been spared from being coerced into sex. The Bible has given an explicit indication of human nature:

"If a man has sexual relations with an animal, he and the animal shall be put to death" [Bible: Leviticus 20:15]

One can see a clear presence of a joke that ridicules the fair conscience of justice. The author has lowered the verse to a farce by sentencing an innocent animal on the preposterous assumption that the animal too does consent for sex! Even, a person of thick faculty will strive hard to find his level of insight into the verse! The verse clearly mismatches the refined morality of a high-class civilisation! The verse is hardly better than a mouldy joke!

Friends, what would you say about the verse which is winding a rousing call?"

"The world has enhanced the faculty of acceptance and welcomed openly both psychological and legal fit of homosexuality honouring the *flesh and blood* feelings of others. Why do only Muslims *swim against the tide*?" teased Kumaran.

"Islam is fettered to a plague of stale dogmas that no prudent legislation in the world values nowadays," Phillip added to the teaser of Kumaran. He cast a scowlful glance at me.

"Phillip is heavily slanted towards personal whims and vagaries. Homosexuality is ignoble, and certainly a disgusting one in the family of least-respected things. The Bible declares a tougher stand on homosexuality.

"If a man has sexual relations with another man, they have done a disgusting thing and both shall be put to death" [Bible: Leviticus 20: 13]

Homosexuality is a potential danger lies dormant in the disguise of 'freedom of choice'. It's formidable, it's lethal and poised to deform the very natural facet of human society beyond recognition. It will prepare own route for the skids…an extinction is waving at."

"Creation will repeat itself. Nothing can bluff it into a permanent stop," opined Kumaran and looked at me with copious attentions.

"What's about the first time creation of life?"

"It is quite evident from the *Theory of Evolution* postulated by Charles Darwin," added Kumaran.

Kumaran believes in Darwin Theory. He argues that human beings are 'filtered animals' evolved from the 'monkey-like species'. Natural selection is the key component of Darwin's theory. Darwin explains that species exhibiting "advantageous variations" can adapt to changing environment better than others, and will be more likely to survive. Through heredity, these advantageous features will be passed on to the next generations. Eventually, the natural selection would help those species adapt to harsh environments to survive and prosper, while species without these advantageous adaptations will lose the battle and gradually slip onto the plane of extinction.

But, nowhere in *The Origin of Species* (1959) does Darwin explicitly mention about the origin of human beings. Darwin's postulation of *'natural selection'* implicitly encompasses mankind.

I decided to grill Kumaran on Darwinism.

"How did the very first living cell evolve on the earth?"

"Frankly I do not possess in-depth knowledge on Darwinism. Many great and rational minds have studied the theory and affirmed its correctness. I have just given my alignment to them. However, it will be a whim, or rather I will say a bizarre turn of mind, if someone asserts that human beings were created by God," stated Kumaran. He looked at me with rapt attentions.

"Darwinism is just a 'theory' –it is not a fact. Neither speculation, nor theory could claim the proven integrity of a fact.

The very fundamental assumption, rather preposterous assumption, of Darwinism is that the very first 'life' on the earth was evolved from a '*life-less*' substance. Arguably, it looks poised to violate the very fundamental of biology that states: "*life begets life*".

Ilya Romanovich Prigogine (Belgian Physical Chemist and Nobel laureate) said:

"*The statistical probability that organic structures and the most precisely harmonised reactions that typify living organisms would be generated by accident is zero.*" [Physics Today 25, pp 23-28]

Explicitly, the statement rebukes Darwinism and discards downright the weird concept of '*by-chance*' generation of '*life*' on the earth."

"The word 'God' is not present in his statement. He never meant that the life on the earth was created by God," argued Kumaran.

"I do agree the word 'God' is a clear absence in his statement. However, the statement is inexplicitly indicating the role of God in creating 'life' on the earth. His statement does also disabuse the correctness of the assumption that says: 'Life was created by the phenomenon called '*by chance*' or '*accidental*'".

"Finally the rigid way of your argument has reduced to flaccidity. I knew that you would finally stop at the gate of God for help! I could see an obvious grimace is running frenziedly on your face and daubing it with the broader brush of helplessness," commented Kumaran.

"I find you as helpless as a flock of shepherd-less sheep.

Life was created '*by chance*', -the statement does require almost nothing, not even the smallest grain of an intelligence. I can see a clear loss of cogency in your being dissolved into the pools of things where dwelling of stupors generally observed. And it happens to people who worship human intellect.

Please apprise me, the very first '*life*' that evolved through the process called '*by chance*' was male or female? If male, then how did the female counterpart evolve in order to advance the generations?

As the 'evolution' went on, the civilised factor called '*humanity*' became imperative to be introduced into the family of things to keep pace with the rules of civility in order to project the human race as the most civilised race in the animal worlds. When, how, and for what reasons, the filtered animals called the 'human beings' introduced the factor called '*humanity*' in social life?

I believe, according to a polished atheist:

'Human Beings= Humanity x Darwinism'.

So, -

When and how did they come to know that incest is morally incorrect?

When and how did they come to know that sex with an animal is a sign of a perverse mentality?

I do have answers to all that. Do you?"

"I know, if God is on your side, you can conquer anything and trample on any principles. God created human beings --is that all that you intend to affirm?" reacted Kumaran. He gave me a sly smile of half-spread lips.

"Yes, God created human beings. Assertively, we have not been evolved from any lower form of animals. It is a confirmation!

"O mankind! We created you from a single (pair) of a male and a female, and made you into nations and tribes, ..." [Qur'an: Al Hujurat 49:13]

God created Adam and Eve (pbut). That was the point of origin of human race. Marriage between siblings of opposite sex was allowed at that point of time for the obvious reason. Adam (pbuh) was a Prophet of God and was instructed accordingly about lawful and unlawful things required to lead life on the earth."

"God created human beings and instructed Islam to call for catastrophe upon non-Muslims," Kumaran observed with an insolent twist of tongue that urged my anger. But I had suppressed it before it licked my face.

"Why Islam is dragged?"

"Terrorism has been a private property of Islam. Islam has been a springboard for fanatics to spill blood," Phillip tailgated his reply very quickly. Kumaran looked at him with thousands of approving eyes and nodding smiles. Seemed, Kumaran expressed his mind through Phillip's tongue.

"Friends, the pitch is set to malign Islam in an every possible way. Seemingly, every unacceptable act of Muslims is quickly linked to Islam. Tomorrow, if a fly gets entangled in the beard of an aged Muslim and killed eventually, the news will figure in a sensational headline as:

'An age-laden septuagenarian Muslim killed mercilessly an innocent and poor fly trapped in his tumbleweed-beard. The fly mistook the beard as bush! The poor fly failed to differentiate between the '*graceless Laden*' and the '*graceful Bush*'!'

Arguably, the news is rigged and has gone rancid! Words like 'Muslim', 'tumble-weed beard', 'merciless killing' and 'Laden' have been rammed randomly and unscrupulously. Such blatant distortions are being pumped into the minds of people on daily basis. The distortion is blatant, and one can clearly find a moral mildew in the heart of the reporter. Hope, you could discern the true aim of the gutter journalism by *reading between the lines*."

"Evasive! How long would you manage to evade from seeing the vile face of Islam? Even a layman knows that Islam is perched into the cosy lap of terrorism!" Phillip roasted Islam with only two terse sentences.

He pushed Islam to that corner where hatred and dislike live like a conjoined twin. I feel beleaguered being pitched into a confronting situation that demanded a fitting response from me.

"I nurse an aversion to entering into such discussion, for I consider it a dross. But, I'm pitched into it; I'm dragged into it.

Anyways, please tell me, for what reason Libya was attacked? Did you ever inquire into the reasons?"

"Do you think Gaddafi was a good man?" asked Phillip. I sensed a wild forcefulness in his reply. He seemed to be a vehement critic of Gaddafi.

"I think you are just trying to be terribly naïve under the pretence of Gaddafi's bad-boy image. If it is so, then why did you destroy the whole country instead of capturing the 'bad boy'?"

"Why did he toppled Idris (1951–1969 CE) and sanctioned widespread anarchy and instigated lawlessness in and around the country?" Phillip retorted in an inquiring mood.

"I do know you know the truth. But now you seem to be appearing pretentiously naive.

Ruler Idris was a good boy because he was Western-backed; - he was the West's blue-eyed boy. Now, I would share the truth.

In 2011, the country faced a 'Military Intervention' carried out by total nine countries equipped with sophisticated mass-destruction weapons. The motive of the 'Military Intervention' was ulterior and deeply vile. It was a three-layered motive all together.

The first motive is to make a '*bill*'.

-Firstly, all the important infrastructures of the 'culprit country' must be '*destroyed*'. Next, the subject country should be '*occupied*' through diplomatic route. Once the country is occupied, and in an opportune moment, prepare the '*bill*' to erect the country from the ruins.

The second motive is to '*occupy*' the mineral wealth of the country.

The third motive is surprising and very dangerous.

-The live performance of the fighter planes on Libya slated to influence the decisions of potential buyers. In all likelihood, it succeeded in opening up a *'shopping window'* meant to market the killer instincts of the fighter planes to the sadistic eyes of the probable buyers. The shopping window rendered thousands of children to limb on crutches, and deprived other thousands of their mother's milk. The country mourned the loss of lives, the wind moaned in the thickets of trees and the sky shed profusely tears of blood at the gory scenes of the one-sided carnage! The roars of the killer fighter jets that sprayed copiously swirling shots of lethal weapons still echoing in the wind subduing blatantly the long due cries of humanity. The attackers *tipped the scales* in favour of a carnage!

Are the killers terrorists or not? Can I call into question the teachings of Christianity?"

"It is all about '*war for peace*'. The main objective was to let the peace prevail in the world," added Phillip.

He appeared stiff to reject downright any persuading to give up the pretence deeply ingrained in him.

"Your actions do not jibe with your speech.

Do you think, the British who occupied India and carried out unspeakable barbarism on Indians and killed thousands of people mercilessly, was for peace?

Do you think the concept of '*apartheid*' applied unscrupulously on '*Black People*' was to put forward peace-theory in the world?

Do you think people who put Nelson Mandela in jail for long twenty seven years, were aspiring for peace?

People of which religion orchestrated the great wars like WWI and WWII and dropped '*two little boys*' on Hiroshima and Nagasaki? Would you please apprise me the figure of deaths?

Think of Hitler, how many Jews did he kill? Does Christianity teach you that?"

"Are you sure that Hitler was a Christian?" Phillip flipped the inquiry that befuddled me.

"Do you differ?"

"Yes I do, -he was not a Christian!" observed Phillip. He cast some uncharacteristic glances upon me.

"Then, who was he?"

"Suppose, he was an atheist," Phillip made an assumption.

"Do you have any evidence?"

"Australian historian Geoffrey Blainey mentioned in his 'A Short History of Christianity, 2012' that: 'Hitler was an atheist,'" added Phillip.

"But Samuel Koehne of Deakin University wrote in 2010: "Was Hitler an atheist? Probably not. But it remains very difficult to ascertain his personal religious beliefs, and the debate rages on."

So how can you say for surety that he was an atheist?"

"So, what do you think who he was?" inquired Phillip.

"He was a Christian."

"Wide guess! What is the proof?" probed Phillip.

"Richard Steigmann-Gall (Associate Professor of History at Kent State University) published 'The Holy Reich, 2003' where he argued that: "In public, Hitler often praised Christian heritage and German Christian culture, though professing a belief in an "Aryan Jesus", one who fought against the Jews. He further argued that the Nazi Party was not anti-Christian as popularly understood.""

"Then, you should read the 'The Response of the German Catholic Church to National Socialism', by Michael Phayer published by Yad Vashem, 1930. The historian Michael Phayer wrote that: "The long term aim of Hitler was to elimination of Catholicism and of the Christian religion".

Do you still think that Hitler was a Christian?" Phillip inquired with an authoritative voice.

"Next what?"

"Can you prove me wrong if I opine that Hitler was a 'Muslim'?" Phillip forwarded a surprise that surpassed the bounds even of my rogue imaginations.

"What?" I shouted.

"According to Speer, Hitler stated in private,

'*The Mohammedan religion too would have been much more compatible to us than Christianity. Why did it have to be Christianity with its meekness and flabbiness?*' Speer too stated that when he was discussing with Hitler, events which might have occurred had Islam absorbed Europe:

'*Hitler said that the conquering Arabs, because of their racial inferiority, would in the long run have been unable to contend with the harsher climate and conditions of the country. They could not have kept down the more vigorous natives, so ultimately not Arabs but Islamised Germans could have stood at the head of this Mohammedan Empire.*'

-Albert Speer (1 April 1997). Inside the Third Reich: memoirs. Simon and Schuster. Pp.96.

Similarly, Hitler was transcribed as saying:

'*Had Charles Martel not been victorious at Poitiers [...] then we should in all probability have been converted to Mohammedanism, that cult which glorifies the heroism and which opens up the seventh Heaven to the bold warrior alone. Then the Germanic race would have conquered the world.*'

-Hitler's Table Talk 1941 -1944, p. 667 translated by N. Cameron.

Now let me summarise:

Was Hitler an atheist?-

You said he was not.

Was Hitler a Christian?-

Some historians said he was not.

Was Hitler a Jew?-

Certainly not.

Was Hitler a Muslim?-

Some evidences are in its favour.

Can you prove me wrong if I say Hitler was more inclined towards Islam?" Phillip stated with conviction.

It sent a shockwave down my spine. I felt cornered as if Phillip had pinioned me against a hard wall. I took an obligatory pause.

"But how it can be?" I questioned myself.

My face rendered a barren expression that muchly resembled a sunburnt arid land.

"Haj Amin al-Husseini (the grand Mufti of Jerusalem) lived in Berlin from 1941 to 1945 as a VIP guest of Hitler. The Muslim Nazi troops of the 'Waffen-SS Handschar Divisions' were regularly reviewed by Haj Amin al-Husseini. Who could deny that he did not present Islam to Hitler?" Phillip placed one more evidence.

It defies description. It froze my venous blood. I could not put up further proof but silently succumbed to his logic. Truly, I could not make out my mind if my mind was bluffed into an uncharacteristic agreement! I found myself resource-less to *call his bluff* to verify.

First few minutes I endured silently the knocks of the fine blend of astonishment and uneasiness, but later I persuaded myself to give in to the 'befuddling discordance.' The moment was unexpectedly weird as I felt a trepidation in acceptance and a vehemence in rejection. I held my conviction painfully at an ambiguous edge that lay somewhere between acceptance and rejection.

"But why did Hitler want to eliminate Christianity?"

"It is very difficult to discern his religious belief. Intriguingly, no one can say with absolute certainty about this. Better we should accept it," added Phillip. He appeared trim and replied in a calmer voice. He snatched a triumphant glance at me!

I find it unpleasant to pull our hearts towards a rank subject like digging out the religion of Hitler, for I believe, such nature of discussion somehow stains the loving face of humanity. Islam too does abhor killing of innocent human beings. The Holy Qur'an says:

"... if any one slew a person - unless it be for murder or for spreading mischief in the land - it would be as if he slew the whole people; and if any one saved a life, it would be as if he saved the life of the whole people. ...". [Qur'an: Maidah 5: 32]

The verse calls forth sublime feelings. My heart goes out to salute the greatness of the Holy Qur'an. The sanctity of human life is placed at the zenith of consideration, and no one, on the face of the earth, could write a better verse that dares to surpass the excellence of the verse rendered by the holy Qur'an. The munificence of the verse does indeed *stick out a mile*, and its magnificence is impossible to be surpassed by the flair of any writer who writes to excel.

It was almost mid-night and we agreed to stop. The sky was serene and jewelled exquisitely with merry crowds of smiling stars that bathed us in dew-soft twinkles. The ethereal exudation filled me with feelings of some mystic dimensions that I hardly had before. The emerging present feelings grew manifold in strength and nullified easily the effects of the 'stress response' accumulated off the discussions. The starry night crushed the 'stress response' and secured an emphatic victory over the predatory force that haunts the manifold of spirit, enthusiasm and peace. The sky evinced romanticism in her appeal accentuated greatly by the presence of her darling moon. The moon was sparkling jocundly like an agate on an elite ring. The sky exuded a crowd of exciting illustrations rich in many melodic content that could easily still a poet's lifelong thirst for some timeless romantic lines.

I felt a mass of moist breeze carrying burbling of a brook was fretting over a rock or winding through a valley. I heard fading fronts of many songs carried along with the breeze from firs, oaks or beeches, or blown from some high song-posts. The low murmurs of dry leaves, jostling in winnowing wind, disclosed multitude of secrets of the night and asked me to retire to the inviting arms of sleep. I sank in sleep like a rock in water.

The next day morning revelation was undelectable...a gory incident badly bruised the golden hands of the promising morning. A speeding overloaded truck, in the dimness of dawn, crushed two pedestrians into death. The crowd swarmed the road and launched a strong agitation. Some political outfit supported their cause and called for a strike until the next day 12 o'clock. The incident attracted crowd giving pretence to many people to *mill around* without a purpose. The fell accident prejudiced the progress of the day. We got the day to be seen as considerably jinxed.

The rising sun started washing the landscapes with her soft aureate rays. My imagination plucked carefully a ray from the stream and tended it with pampering hand. The blade-sharp edges of grasses were dissecting the tender rays into slenderest pieces, perhaps to analyse the presence of different wavelengths. We entered a lawn palisaded sparsely with wooden posts. The lawn was fronting the hotel and adding elegance copiously to its liveliness. At the entrance, some fallen dry leaves crackled under my feet. I enjoyed the fuss of the leaves! While walking, I saw a lonely and determined bittern winging silently northwards in search of a quarry somewhere in a danger-filled marshland. My imagination took wings and flew away with it. The formality '*best of luck*' escaped my lips while I glanced the bittern flying overhead. I sensed a cheapness in the line and tried to drag generosity out of me: '*May the duffer quarry become prolific for you*!'"

The trial was postponed for two days. I intended to resume the discussion from the point we had stopped at.

Chapter 2

"Why God is required for the Universe?" inquired Kumaran. I did not know if he was serious or frivolous.

"Why soul is required?"

"I do not consider soul anymore as a separate entity, –the physical body is the soul itself," viewed Kumaran.

"What does not exist in a stillborn baby?"

"It is simply a death. The baby died while it was inside the womb,"

"What do you think about the sixth sense?"

"The extrasensory perception is gained through mind. This indicates the progress of evolution," stated Kumaran.

"All right friend.

It was arguably expected that from '*an inert*' substance, and through the countless passages of evolution, something like super computers, hypersonic missiles, fighter jets or road excavators sorts of things would have been evolved. But, surprisingly and unfortunately, an exceedingly complex, an extremely sophisticated and an incisively intelligent human being evolved possessing an extraordinary feature called the '*free will*'. You must be knowing that '*free will*' is itself a dreadful idea and needs to be controlled by a Controller. That's why God is required."

"It's a jester's reply.

The contention between the theists and atheists rages wildly when the creation of human beings occupies the centre-stage of discussion table. The perverted belief of the God-fearing people, in some way or other, puts invisible fetters to the free progression of science," reacted Kumaran looking at me directly. He expressed pronounced dissatisfaction at my reply. He crackled at my reply!

"The reply perfectly matches the fit of an atheist.

The sequential development of a 'supercomputer' from an 'inert' substance arguably honours the fit of a linear thinking. This possibility is more logical and pronounced in comparison to the possibility of evolution of a human being from an 'inert' substance."

"Science has stopped expecting anything presentable from the section of people whose outlook has still been struggling hard to come out of the lower orbit of intellect, let alone understanding the finer level of science," retorted Kumaran gawking at me.

"Friend, I do know my views jar on the 'premise' of your belief. I was not expecting this sort of view from an atheist who nurses 'absolutism' in his faith by claiming that the very first 'living' cell on the earth was evolved from a 'life-devoid' substance. My view is just a logical extension of your belief.

Why is there no life on the moon?"

"Everybody knows it…the moon's atmosphere is extremely tenuous and devoid of oxygen," answered Kumaran.

"But elements like argon, radon, neon and helium have been detected in the moon's atmosphere. -

Why no life that inhales argon and exhales radon has been evolved?"

"Madman's arguments! I think your level of intelligence has subsided to a lower level," scoffed Kumaran.

"Trees, unlike human beings, breathe in carbon dioxide to survive. This example shows a variation to your face and reasons that oxygen is not necessarily the only element need to be inhaled for survival!

Question arises, why did no life on the moon that breathes in argon evolve?"

"People who are averse to using intelligence usually appear very quick in assuming the role of God in every things poised to offer tough challenge to their mediocre intelligence," taunted Kumaran.

"Friend, I entreat you to realise your sublime standard being a human being. Angels bowed down before you!

"*... We said to the angels: "Bow down unto Adam". They bowed down...*" [Qur'an: Al-Isra 17: 61]

God had uplifted your standard. Now it is up to you to uphold the bestowed esteem after ascending at the apex of sublimity. You should endeavour to prove the correctness of God's choice. Do not let your sublime intelligence be tricked by some second-rate theories that fail to contest in high-class debate.

Just take an honest look at the verse. Do not demean by calling yourself a 'filtered animal', neither belittle the choice of God Who bestowed generously upon you such incredible grace."

"Who created God?" Kumaran posed the question confidently. His face gleamed and eyes sparkled as he tabled the query. He evinced exceedingly high confidence.

He took off his spectacles and kept on rubbing gently for a little while before pushing it quickly up the bridge of nose onto its snug position. He struck me with his steady but penetrating gaze. The tone of his voice was overbearing and appeared determined to obliterate the faith of those who believe in God.

I presented intentionally a blank expression to him as I was bluffing him that the 'question' was the trickiest and class apart.

My intention was to pull up the standard of his question to the rank of '*dashing and deadliest*', –the '*dashing*' was for him, and the '*deadliest*' was for me. Dalliance in answering the question almost convinced him that the question was truly '*dashing and deadliest*' and could trounce the opponent with great lethality. But he forced me constantly to act sooner.

"Is the Big Bang self-triggered, or Someone did trigger it?"

Kumaran bathed me in the pool of his oblique glance and replied,

"Self-triggered."

"God too is self-created."

His dashing question seemed to have been paled and withered. The reply than which, I think, there is none quicker, shorter and better! Kumaran smouldered inside. The confidence and the enthusiasm that he built basing on the 'question' sooner encountered an abrupt stop. The reply left him nursing the resulting indignation!

"Anyways, I would not stop here rather I would love to convince you in different way. Do you have full cognisance of the '*Personality and Stature*' of God?"

"Nonsensical question?" Kumaran showed his irritation through a harried expression.

He almost disapproved my question and considered it as extraneous for the moment. My probing into the 'Personality *and Stature*' of God teed off him.

"If mine is nonsensical, so is yours."

"Means?" Kumaran reacted inquisitively.

"By the way, why do you want to know the creator of God? What is the reason?" I inquired in a calmer voice.

"Stop *beating around the bush!* Mine is a simple question that seeks straightforward reply," Kumaran appeared demanding with stalwart voice. He triggered his tongue to simmer and gave me a look of distaste.

Kumaran thought that his question was the trickiest one that could definitely floor the opponent. Perhaps he had spent many sleepless nights and squeezed every drop of cerebral fluid to find the answer but finally inked a *psychological agreement* with tenacious failure. The failure in finding the answer compelled him to believe that the very question would definitely push the opponent *into deep water*!

"My good man, to be pertinent, the question does not suit you."

"What do you mean?" Kumaran asked with a thoughtfulness.

"God was not created but evolved. At the beginning, a tiny 'living cell' was evolved from a 'life-less' substance, or through a certain chemical process that occurred '*by chance*'. The process of evolution took hundreds of thousands years to produce the God."

Kumaran draped a thick sheet of silence over him, and his face rued again putting on a rosier hue. His shoulders drooped, his face drained of grace and shrivelled discernibly. He seemed to be looking earnestly for a shell to retreat so that he could *make himself scarce.* He was not of himself. The frustration came much sooner than he expected and could not anticipate that I would apply the *Darwin concept* to tackle his merit-filled question. As a gust of wind ruffles the serene surface of a sea, my reply perturbed the composure of his mind. His cool drained into the pool of distractions. I heard a crackling of his exasperation!

"I can discern your mood. But I want to ask if there is any book that corroborates the theory?" Kumaran broke the silence and placed the inquiry. His voice sank a bit.

"Do you have any model that describes the identity of God?"

"The concept of God is precisely an exciting imagination that I tend to associate it with a dreamy-surrealism. The existence of God is itself a wild and forbidding concept that constantly drains my mental energy into desolation. My human instinct *every now and again* misplaces the concept and urges me constantly that I should crash it against the tough wall of reality. The word 'God' fills my ears with confused murmur; the concept itself is in its twilight existence and has been sent down to a dark silo of obscurity.

Believers are commonly brimming with two harmful concepts: superficial talks and sentimental delusions. The first because it does never try to go to the root of the query; the second because it evades the query entirely.

I crush the concept into pieces and scatter the grains onto a land overrun with barren dreams and fancy-filled surrealism. The concept of God is an illusory force exerted by an uncharacteristic power of enchantment. I trap enchantment in a sorry corner of desolation and keep on pummelling it until the achievement of my total disillusionment. In that way I deal with the concept of God, and for me, -God is an absent data! Since long it has been laid in my cold view," described Kumaran. He gave a nasty pushback to the concept of God. I looked at him with wide eyes.

"That is weird! Anyways, I would present a model of God from the glorious Qur'an, and I hope that that would perhaps convert you to reflect deeply about the concept of God.

"Say: He is Allah, the One and Only;

Allah, the Eternal, Absolute;

He begetteth not, nor is He begotten;

And there is none like unto Him."

[Qur'an: Al-Ikhlas 112:1-4]

Do you still in the dead opinion that God must have a creator?"

"The verses are but representations of sentimental delusions! Better you can present them to Muslims who have severed relation with questing intellect, or have slipped happily onto the plane where knowledge languishes in its twilight existence. But it cannot ruin my questing knack, nor can put me off asking questions," Kumaran retorted and clearly shown his inadvertence to pay a heed to the verses. He is no longer going to *put up with* any such concept whether presented by the Qur'an, or any other religious scriptures perhaps.

"I would definitely answer should you co-operate me in getting it right. It needs a good deal of time and I hope you would not lose your calm." -

"God is created by 'Big God.'"

"Who created the 'Big God'?" Kumaran inquired, though initially he hesitated to step on the infinite path of questioning.

"'Bigger God' created the 'Big God.'"

"Who created the 'Bigger God'?" Kumaran inquired.

"'The Biggest God' created the 'Bigger God.' "

"A bunch of meanders! You are simply fretting time. These are but that trick mind. Stop playing *hide and seek,*" reacted Kumaran exasperatedly.

"Here I am *seeking,* but you are *hiding.*"

"I could clearly detect an awkwardness running frenziedly and daubing a rosier hue on your face," added Kumaran hastily.

"The guess is *wide of the mark*! I think, it is the best possible way to answer your dream question."

"Stop seeking hollow victory over me," grunted Kumaran. He looked at me with cold eyes.

"Never! Neither do I think myself as hands-down favourite, nor do I intend to win a hollow victory over you. Friend, you have *got hold the wrong end of the stick.*

Let me put into logic:

Firstly, you must be cognisant of God, of His personality, of His Stature, then only you can fashion your questions in order to know about the creator of God.

Now please tell me, how would you verify if the 'Big God' is the creator of 'God', or the 'Bigger God' is the creator of the 'Big God'? Certainly, you would not voyage to meet the 'Big God' or the 'Bigger God' physically to verify the veracity of my answers. That means, *at the end of the day*, you have to remain satisfied merely with the 'names' only.

My good man, the question-answer series will never stop, rather will land you in a path that keeps on snaking through a labyrinth. Needless to say, you will eventually be trapped at the very centre of the labyrinth."

"You have cunningly meandered around a cluster of clumsy answers failing miserably to elicit even a single approving response from me. It has left me cold.

I can see a clear gaucheness licking your face while dealing with the question; and the efforts employed so far, nonetheless, have failed to bring in efficacy. These are not logic at all but some mouth's sounds, some persuasive figures of speech," Kumaran put up a blithe denial.

"Friend, the insights into my answers have not been explored correctly. -

If 'God' is created by someone, then most certainly He is no longer a 'God'. Because the creator is deemed higher in sense and bigger in calibre than his creation, -it makes sense. So, in logical conclusion, God does not have any creator. God neither has a 'Beginning' nor an 'End', -this implies that the question '*Who created God?*' stands nonsensical. The Qur'an says:

"Allah. There is no god but He,-the Living, the Self-subsisting, Eternal. …" [Qur'an: Al Baqara 2: 255]

The verse talks a huge sense into human beings. God is self-subsisting and eternal and therefore must be assessed on a different platform altogether. His '*personality and stature*' cannot be assessed on the same platform reserved for animals and human beings.

Every perishable thing has its creator. But surprisingly, you have approximated God to a 'perishable entity' and subsequently have subjected Him to the general rule of logic applicable to *all and sundry*. People on the earth, in general, reflect the knowledge acquired through mundane life.

Here the word '*Eternal*' alone speaks extraordinary profundity about God and invites human intellect to ponder over the deep meaning of the word. It entreats human intellect to come out of the lower orbit of thinking and analyse the word '*eternal*' to its absolute sense. Rationally put, a 'created thing' can never be absolutely independent. So, the 'Entity' which is absolutely independent does never require any creator."

"Believers are always in a great hurry to ascribe many incredible attributes to God in order to give a completeness to their weak and bogus religious ideologies; -ignorant happily fails to recognise shortcomings," Kumaran gave me some sharp stick.

"All right friend, then would you please apprise me who created God?"

"I'm not a believer. I seek answer from blind supporters of God!" reacted Kumaran looking at me obliquely scattering grains of soft disdain upon the field of my belief.

"Does 'North Pole' exist?"

"Yes," nodded Kumaran.

"What is the north of the 'North Pole'?"

Kumaran sneaked a look at me. He perhaps silently reached at the gate of geography for assistance, but returned with a deafening silence. I sensed, failure could not suppress a dig at him.

"Your silence has answered!"

"Why did God create human beings?" Kumaran inquired. Kumaran evaded my question deftly and switched to the subject on creation of human beings.

"Human beings are created just to worship God alone."

"Why does God require worship?" Kumaran wheeled out his natural logic.

"What else should He require from you?-

Can you send your lunch box, or your luxurious limousine to God?

You cannot, and certainly, He is not in that need. His demand is just and exactly justifiable. The Qur'an says:

"I have only created Jinns and men, that they may serve Me." [Qur'an: Al Dhariyat 51: 56]

He demands the 'Service' that ought to be served to Him only."

"What was the reason that triggered God to create human beings?" Kumaran tabled the query.

"The similar question was asked by the Angels too.

"Behold, thy Lord said to the angels: "I will create a vicegerent on earth." They said: "Wilt Thou place therein one who will make mischief therein and shed blood?..." [Qur'an: Al Baqara 2: 30]

The angels put up a slim resistance to the intention of God."

"Then, where did God fail to apprehend the consequence of His decision?" questioned Kumaran.

"Which one would you prefer to touch, 'apple' or 'pineapple'?"

"Apple," answered Kumaran.

"Which one would you prefer to kiss, -'rose' or 'fire'?"

"Rose," answered Kumaran.

"Which track would you prefer to run, -'asphalt' or 'snow'?"

"Asphalt," answered Kumaran.

"If you do have only a single glance in your life, which one would you prefer to see, -'mountain' or 'molehill'?"

"Mountain," answered Kumaran.

"If you are given option to choose between 'reindeer soup' and 'vodka drinks' to survive in the chilled condition of Oymyakon[3*], which one would you prefer?"

"Reindeer soup," Kumaran answered sensibly.

"Being a pilot, just before landing the plane, if you come to know that the landing gear mechanism of the plane is malfunctioning, which option would you opt out before landing the plane, - to exhaust the last of the fuel, or with tank full of fuel?"

"Certainly I would exhaust the last of the fuel to minimise the landing-loss," Kumaran answered wisely.

"If you are given option to choose between 'free will' and 'fixed will', which one will you opt out?"

"Free will," answered Kumaran immediately.

Friend, you have answered to your own question."

I unearthed the preference deeply embedded somewhere in the inmost of Kumaran. The interview gave me a sense of contentment.

"What do you mean exactly," Kumaran asked for elucidation.

"Friend, Adam (pbuh) was bestowed with the '*free will*' which angels were devoid of. God endowed Adam (pbuh) with free will and declared him as His unique creation.

To the question of the angels, God replied, as mentioned in the same verse:

"He said: "I know what ye know not."" [Qur'an: Al Baqara 2:30]

And, in the next verses, God conducted a test between angels and Adam (pbuh), and expectedly Adam (pbuh) came out with a triumphant performance and proved the correctness of God's decision.

"And He taught Adam the names of all things; then He placed them before the angels, and said: "Tell me the nature of these if ye are right." [Qur'an: Al Baqara2:31]

"They said: "Glory to Thee, of knowledge We have none, save what Thou Hast taught us: …." [Qur'an: Al Baqara2:32]

"He said: "O Adam! Tell them their natures." When he had told them, Allah said: "Did I not tell you that I know the secrets of heaven and earth, and I know what ye reveal and what ye conceal?" [Qur'an: Al Baqara2:33]

The creation of angels preceded by the creation of human beings. Angels, though holy and pure, yet emotionally are plastic and endowed neither with '*free will*' nor with '*self-learning*' cognitive faculty. Basically, they are programmed only to celebrate the Glory of God. Everything that surrounds them is 'peaceful and comfortable', and for angels life is *like a walk in the park*. Unlike human beings, adversity, hardship and pain, for examples, are something wherein angels have not been subjected to. In that sense, the creation of angels represents the one side creation of God.

Creation of Adam (pbuh) brings in 'completeness' to the Creation because Adam (pbuh) was endowed with the '*free will*' and the brain which was peerlessly poles apart. Progeny of Adam (pbuh) can apply aptitude called 'self-learning'. A human being, having the experience of frostbite, can impeccably plan, program and equip himself with the essentials to cope with the climatic extremities of Siberia. Unique cognitive faculty enables human beings to study composite data and analyse complex situations in order to maximise the degree of joy and minimise the scale of danger.

Angels put up slim resistance but finally acquiesced in the plan of God. So the creation of human being is not a redundancy, rather it is a unique dimension that gives 'consummation' to the facet of the Creation."

"Even Angels, with linear brains, made a great clairvoyance about the fate of the earth if offered to the creatures endowed with the '*free will*'. How God, being All-Knowing, failed to apprehend the same?

Certainly, mischiefs and bloodsheds are not sorts of soothing scenes to the sight of God, then what did He actually want to prove through His recklessness?" Kumaran inquired thoughtfully.

"None of things will stop you if you want to watch gory scenes of bloodsheds. But remember, at the same time, a blissful sight is waving at you with her loving arms. The choice is yours.

Choice is yours whether you do want to plant a bomb or plant a sapling on the mother planet.

Choice is yours whether you do want to support the weak or supress the weak.

Choice is yours whether you do want to distribute bread or drop bombs.

It depends on you whether you want to be a distributor of love or a trader of hatred. God has offered you both chances poised equally to be used.

Do you think, God shall take offence if human beings start living peacefully on the earth?"

"As evident, the earth was created prior to the creation of Adam meaning God had already drafted the blueprint of His secret plan. Hence God imposed a condition on Adam which God Himself knew that it was no longer possible for Adam to carry out it," Kumaran argued with fragile logic.

"Adam was elevated in stature and placed quite ahead of angels.

This statement alone is sufficient to call for the downfall of your logic. God did neither contrive a secret agenda against Adam (pbuh), nor nursed any personal enmity against him. Such views fade away fast into the clear horizon of falsity. As the Qur'an says:

"And behold, We said to the angels: "Bow down to Adam" and they bowed down." [Qur'an: Al Baqara 2:34]

The obviousness says that Adam (pbuh) was enjoying an elevated status in Paradise. The only condition issued to him 'to follow' was just a piece of instruction, -'do not visit that tree'. That's all. The Qur'an says:

"We said: "O Adam! Dwell thou and thy wife in the Garden;... but approach not this tree, or ye run into harm and transgression."

"Then did Satan make them slip from the (garden), and get them out of the state (of felicity) in which they had been...." [Qur'an: Al Baqara 2:35-36]

Satan turned up in the scene and started crushing disturbing stuff into the minds of the Adams that led them finally commit the 'sin'.

God could see the future and this trait befits God only. God does not revoke His own instructions, neither does He manipulate situations. God's *Stature and Personality* are unblemished and walk side by side without overpowering or undermining each other. God's knowledge is absolute and transcends the narrow boundaries of the 'time and space'. God knew that the Adams (pbut) would commit sin, and that is why He kept ready His 'plan B', -the 'habitable earth'.

God never intend to instigate someone against His own instruction because God does not suffer from logic-dissonance."

"God should rue for His decision, -He committed double mistakes and made us guinea pig for the same. Firstly, He created and sent us on the earth without our consent; secondly, He did not mind to offer us the same opportunity offered to Mr Adam. The discrimination is evident and *below the belt.* The whole event seems born out of a clumsy and unjust system. The Plan of Creation itself bears the sign of a debacle; the presence of human beings on the earth is another fiasco to add to the disappointment; to say the least, the whole scenario is crushed into the sack of failings!

Why should I suffer for the mistake committed by Mr Adam?" Kumaran argued irascibly.

"God is not unjust even in the least sense; neither does He indulge in any sorts of discriminations. Any process must have a beginning and a culmination; and the creation of human beings and their subsequent deportation onto the earth speak profoundly about an impeccable plan executed by God. I have no qualms to declare that God has *the upper hand* over everything. Moreover, He took covenant from you in your previous life (we all were in a state of frozen souls) where you did testify agreeably. And it had happened much before the occurrence of the 'Big Bang'.

"And remember when your Lord brought forth from the loins of the children of Adam their descendants and had them testify regarding themselves. Allah asked, "Am I not your Lord?" they testified, " Yes, You are! We testify." He cautioned, "Now you have no right to say on Judgement Day, 'We were not aware of this." [Qur'an: Al Araf 7:172]

God had sent many revelations throughout the ages only to bring human beings on the right Path. Here is the Qur'an that marks irrevocably the end of revelation. Friend, do not commit the folly by underplaying the sincere urges of the Qur'an, nor downplay the disastrous implications of flouting the divine call. Precisely put, it would be a blunder!"

"That memory is frozen and veiled with dense frosts.

I cannot remember if He did actually take my consent, -it's no longer afresh and no one can remember that distinctly," said Kumaran.

"The Qur'an has been sent to remind you."

"Only 25 percent of population of the world know the Qur'an. The majority does not mind to know it. Simply put, the covenant seems to have slipped into oblivion and no one could remember it. How could I remember what transpired at the meeting with the so called 'Lord' in my so called 'previous life'? It is utterly preposterous; it falls incredibly short of logic!" argued Kumaran. He rolled his eyes in disbelief.

"Had God wished to keep the 'memory' alive, then He would have made you like the creature who does not possess '*free will*'. '*Free will*' and 'the memory' cannot go hand-to-hand because it dilutes the very purpose of the Creation. *Free will* coupled with 'the memory' is redundant according to God's constitution. God again reminds you about the covenant through the revelation of the glorious Qur'an and entreats you to take heed of it.

Admittedly, nobody could remember the covenant for the obvious reason as mentioned, but God, out of His mercy, embedded a natural bent in the minds of Adam's children, who, if not influenced externally or otherwise, will spontaneously take cognisance of the one unseen God Who prevails over everything. It is the 'external influence' that swindles mind, corrupts soul and takes the subject away from the Straight Path, -it invariably kills the very natural tilt of human nature."

"Do you think I am influenced blindly?" Kumaran lurched forward and inquired almost in a half-rage.

"I want to cite the very next verse from the glorious Qur'an which I think is the perfect reply to your query.

"Nor say, 'it was our forefathers who had associated others with Allah in worship, and we, as their descendants, followed in their footsteps. Will you then destroy us for the falsehood they invented." [Qur'an: Al-Araf 7: 173]

The verse presents the scene of the Judgement Day where 'stray children' of Adam (pbuh) would pose the question to their Lord."

"It became a liability for Adam to believe in God because he had seen God, lived in Paradise and was finally transported to the Earth. But we have not seen God, neither the Paradise nor have we received any great communication from God that could eventually make us believe in Him. The events involving Adam seem to be surreal like a fancy dream," Kumaran replied.

"The process of Creation is over, and you cannot go back to the past to steer the situation in your favour.

Friend, ponder over the scenario where everybody is entitled to reside in Paradise as Adam (pbuh) did. Undoubtedly, everybody would have become God fearing like Adam (pbuh). Then where is the test?

If you do think that you have been tricked by God, then the wisest path, without any doubt, is to minimise the loss. If you think human life is some sort of 'loss', then I must say that the 'loss' is a trifle compared to the loss that you might incur in future by not obeying the Creator."

"What would happen if I don't worship Him?" Kumaran inquired in a fit of half-rage.

"'Hell' is the destination!"

"Disgusting! Moth-eaten ideology! I feel awkward being with a gauche!" Kumaran became furious and his furore was curling up to the sky.

He smacked his hand on the surface of the table to release anger. His eyes were simmering with the ferocity of a piercing arrow! He snatched some attacking glances at me. I endured the torture meekly and appeared submissive!

"Your reaction smacks me of a person whose thinking fears to cross the ordinary.

The reaction is not discordant with you, especially people who have placed total faith in the excellence of Darwin Theory. I am not surprised, rather was expecting such piquant reactions from you. Darwin Theory is a psychological captivity that hardly fosters broader outlook, -knowledge hardly thrives in captivity!"

"The peaceful order of the mind sinks into distemper after reading just one Book. The Book replaces all basic human fabric with overstretched fabric sodden with total fanaticism.

The 'Hell' resides in the ignorance of a fool! The concept has attained maturity in certain sect of people deemed as 'head-less' in the modern world: 'O*ut of pace and out of sync* (oops!)'" Kumaran ridiculed me almost to his satisfaction. Indirectly he held up Islam to ridicule. My view on Darwinism fretted him a lot.

"A supporter of 'superstition' can never be an admirer of 'truth'. The clouds could no longer hide the sun! No matter how much you try, you would no longer repress or suppress the truth. I affirm that the concept is a damn reality and rests at the summit of my admiration!"

"Only zealot like you could genuinely be so hyper on such a dull religious philosophy. The Koran has produced fools in millions and has been famous being the breeding ground of hazardous fanatics!" Kumaran stated with an agitating tongue.

His tongue was poised to overtake bigger discourtesy. He painted the Qur'an with a broader brush of detestation. I found his cool being fretted away, and his temper was about to soar to the point of boiling.

"It's all about divine. The Book is the Holy Qur'an, - unparalleled in marvel, tallest in stature and highest in excellence. The Book was authored by none of human beings living or dead, but by the Lord of the worlds.

But which factor has impelled you to become a fervent admirer of Darwinism?"

"Forget about Darwinism for the time being. Now apprise me, what sort of consequence is reserved for an atheist who is righteous and honest?" Kumaran asked probingly.

"Hell is his abode!"

"The concept perfectly matches the fit of a fanatic!" Kumaran blasted me.

His disposition looked roiled, and the fabric of his cool attenuated again almost to the point of breakage. The expression of his face seemed out of the way, and way astonished.

"Friend, I hope light might not be an offence to you.

Your logic is elegant and spirited. But it is not the best. Now, slacken your tense nerve and just ponder over the parameters deemed to be the constant reasons for your existence on the earth. Request you to realise the deep meaning of the Creation with collaborating mind and wide-opened eyes. The denial has clearly disabled you to *see the wood for the trees*.

The Glorious Qur'an says:

"I have only created Jinns and men, that they may serve Me." [Qur'an: Al Dhariyat 51: 56]

The Creator is the sole reason of your existence. He demands that you must worship Him alone. At the beginning of the verse, the word '*created*' precedes the word '*serve*', - the Creator, at the outset of the verse, identified Himself as your Creator and then He transitioned to demand worship.

People expect a lofty respect from a dog upon offering just a crumb. They do expect that the dog must waggle its tail in subservience and servility. If a piece of bread could give you the presumption of being the master of the dog, then just think of your Lord Who created you in the best mould and provided everything for your sustenance and existence. Put pertinently, what else He could expect from you?

"For the worst of beasts in the sight of Allah are those who reject Him: They will not believe." [Qur'an: Al Anfal 8: 55]

In the verse above, God has clearly expressed His dissatisfaction at the primitive ignorance of human beings. Ignorance is, in fact, a very powerful tool that could lower the stature of a human being far below the level of a lower form of animals."

"The Koran is a marvellous springboard! It hurls terrorists into dreadful orbits," Phillip cast the aspersion *like a shot.* Kumaran made an assenting shake of his head in agreement. Both mentally creamed together.

"Have you read the Qur'an?"

"Never urged it my willingness, and in it consists my happiness. It frets my cool whenever I think of reading the Koran. My sensibility urges me constantly not to squander the time of resourcefulness in reading a Book written during the 'period of mess and ignorance'. How the soiled hands and diseased minds could produce a product of world-class standard? It does not make any sense, at least for me!" Phillip disclosed his present feelings about the Qur'an. The sharpness of criticism was prickly.

Pain began to trickle in and was mounting swiftly putting tremendous pressure on me to be distressed. It was delved somewhere deep in my mind as a distressing fragment of memory; It situated itself like a formidable qualm to lacerate any delight that I would receive in the immediate future.

"It's purely an implacable hatred!"

"You can sense easily what could be written in a Book whose output products are: *fundamentalists, fanatics, terrorists, bigots, polygamists, conservatives*. And at the summit- the suicide bombers. If your input is garbage then invariably output will also be garbage, -'*garbage in and garbage out* (GIGO)'!

It's a prolific Book for the people leading lives adrift, and whose sense dismissive of logic, and whose questing intellect is detached.

Simply put, you cannot expect an apple orchard to bloom if the ground is prepared for pineapple bushes. So the urge to read the Book fades away swiftly into apathy!" Phillip vaingloriously expressed zero tolerance for the Qur'an. His assumptions overran the general limit of imaginations; he churned out lacerating derision copiously.

He put up a steep-fronted hatred towards the Qur'an. He looked up the sky with an overpowering attitude giving a powerful thrust to the wings of his self-conceited superiority for a magnificent flight. Seemed, he was swept over by a wave of giddiness welling up in him; he appeared just celestially happy.

"Would you please apprise me what could be written in the Book?"

"It's not difficult to perceive. Well,-

It retrieves the past of the Arab culture;

Details of Muhammad's genealogy;

How he did maintain himself lavishly perfumed and fastidiously clean;

Muhammad's marital life style with his youngest wife Ayesha;

How smartly he did manage his dozen of wives;

Muhammad's career progress as a union leader. His tactics and prowess as an army-general in the battlefield;

The alleged role of Muhammad as negotiator on the Day of the Judgement to save Muslims from the torment of Hell-fire," Phillip assertively guessed.

"None of these are mentioned in the Qur'an."

Phillip appeared half-discouraged because his guesses failed to produce intended results.

Arguably, it is clear that Phillip cannot tolerate the Qur'an for some mysterious reasons. Something *burns him to the ground* and he goes ballistic whenever the names of Prophet Muhammad (pbuh) and the 'Koran' resonate in his ears. May be, he was expecting that the 'Koran' should have been revealed in a grand party hosted by the President of America in the poshest ambience of the 'White House' amid the pompous presence of highly famous celebrities. The party Hall would have been decorated with promiscuous opulence of things of exceptional worth ranging from exquisite chandeliers to ornate table kindled with chiffon-soft appealing light. Then, the party would have immersed itself in gala celebration to monumentalise the moment by shaking legs, exchanging decorous kisses and cheering the moment by holding champagne flute. Then suddenly the rousing-bell would have been wounded by the President himself alerting the party to the herald of revelation. Then the trickling-revelation would have been heralded with a round of long-applause and heart-pounding excitement by the drink-sodden party. Finally, the President would have concluded the occasion with his grace-filled spiritual speech.

Had it been so, then Phillip would have become a herald of the 'Koran'. But to his displeasure, it was revealed to an 'unlettered' Arab living on a meagre sustenance in the awkwardness of an 'uncivilised' world marked by the clear absence of a bare minimum civility. The plan of revealing the Qur'an to an 'unlettered' Arab did not match the fit of a God! This triggers Phillip's rejection of God's choice!

Like Phillip, many during the time of Prophet Muhammad (pbuh) orchestrated countless murky protests concerning the revelation of the Qur'an to Muhammad (pbuh). They massed domineering opinions against Muhammad (pbuh) and relayed the narrative that, "Muhammad (pbuh) was neither *the cream of the crop,* nor his competency *can hold a candle to* the sublime stature of such Project". But, as time went on, the corridor of their murky intentions received many great surprises and disappointment, and finally, the collective efforts of their protests could not scupper the Plan of the Almighty, rather faded away into travesty.

"You have, all the way, praised the Koran to the sky. And If I go by your claim, then one can infer that the Koran is infallible. Is it?" Kumaran forwarded a judicious. He explored a very genuine point. We eyed each other directly and agreeably.

"I appreciate the beauty of your question. Yes, the Qur'an is infallible."

"Infallible?" Kumaran cocked his eyebrows. Phillip smiled fiendishly. I kept on looking at them with a placid face.

"Not infallible, but intolerable!

The question of finding a fallacy in the Koran is itself a misnomer on the same ground as to why people did not find any in the fancied stories narrated during the medieval times. It is as simple as that. The Koran is that Book where a tapestry of imageries, stories and speculations clasp one another and grow thickly in the thick of hearts of Muslims.

After all, some Muslims like Salman Rushdie had already rained due 'respect' to the Koran.

Seems, hysteria of your sympathy towards the Koran could even surpass the public hysteria of antipathy towards the AIDS!" Phillip was simmering. He introduced Salman Rushdie as the trailblazer.

"I feel pity for you!

If I were in your place, I would have presented the Qur'an to Isaac Newton (1643 to 1727 CE), Max Plank (1858 to 1947 CE), Albert Einstein (1879 to 1955 CE), and Alexander Friedmann (1888 to 1925 CE) and asked them to find out 'fallacy' in the Book. Believe me, this would have been absolutely an honourable way to prove the Qur'an wrong. Had they pointed out any in the Qur'an, undoubtedly that would have tripped Muslims facedown! The honour of the Qur'an would have plummeted down steeply. The Prophethood of Muhammad (pbuh) would have crumbled outright. The pride of Muslims would have collapsed instantly. The whole scene would have retreated silently into a shell barren of glory. Unfortunately, you had squandered that great opportunity.

Is not it a shame that you are seeking alliance with Salman Rushdie to pull down the prestigious elevation of the Qur'an? Does it not belittle your intellectual stature? Does the act match the fit of your intelligence?"

"Did anyone stop you from getting the Koran verified by those eminent scientists?" snubbed Phillip.

"We did. We presented the verse *[Qur'an: Al-Alaq 96: 1-2]* to Keith L. Moore (1925 to 2019 CE), a distinguished embryologist (Professor, University of Toronto), who verified the correctness of the verse revealed in the Qur'an.

A verse of the Qur'an changed the life of a Japanese Professor Dr Atsushi Kamal Okuda (Professor of Political Systems at Keio University, Japan).

"*And indeed, We created man from sounding moulded from black mud.*" [Qur'an: Al-Hijr 15:26]

The verse changed his life forever.

Do you still think that person like Salman Rushdie could put up spirited competition to Islam?"

"What do you think of Salman Rushdie -is he ignorant? Evidently he made such remarks against his own religion …will you not consider the remarks with care?" Phillip argued.

"Friends, hardly a day goes by without a satire not targeted against the Qur'an and Islam.

If a 'Muslim' makes some comments against the Qur'an or Islam, it takes hardly a second to get him recognised as progressive, intellect and person of a remarkable stature. The news spreads like the wild fire, and the person instantly gets recognised as the prime of the flock! A certain sect, at the other end, is always waiting impatiently to welcome suchlike and confer them with lot of signal honours. Such mentality represents a society of internal decay.

Dr Maurice Bucaille (French Medical doctor, 1920-1988) wrote a book named "*The Bible, The Qur'an and Science*" in 1976. He stated that the Qur'an is in agreement with scientific facts, but the Bible is not. Dr Bucaille had converted a number of high ranking scholars to agree with him and to subscribe to his view that the Quran is not authored by any human being but actually a Book of Revelations from the Almighty God to His Last Prophet, Muhammed (pbuh).

Roger Garaudy or Ragaa Garaudy (17 July 1913-13 June 2012) was a French philosopher, French resistance fighter and a prominent communist author. He accepted Islam in 1982 and became a prominent Islamic commentator.

Now I am asking you,

Can you show me any Muslim who changed his religion the way Dr Maurice Bucaille, or Roger Garaudy did?

Can you show me a single book written by any person in the whole world wherein he cogently and explicitly explained even a single discrepancy present in the Qur'an?

Friends, Salman Rushdie had easily tricked you all by misappropriating your wealth of prejudice about Islam. You poor lambs paid king's homage to a person who has *feet of clay*. He rose like Pistol star in the galaxy of people who suffered from a threat of psychogenic Islamophobia. Truly, you had misplaced your copious soul and worsened the positive cast of mind!

Taking clue from your logic, I am asking you,

Who do you think more educated and more intelligent- Dr Maurice Buccaille, or Salman Rushdie? Who is more progressive?

Friends, have you ever been informed about Marmaduke William Pickthall?-

He accepted Islam and changed his name to Muhammad Marmaduke Pickthall. He declared his conversion to Islam after delivering a talk on "*Islam and Progress*" in 29 November 1917, to the Muslim Literary Society in Notting Hill, West London. He was a novelist as well as a journalist. He was noted for English translation of the Qur'an. Pickthall was not thrust into highlight because he committed crime by accepting Islam.

Do you know who built the first mosque in England?-

William Henry Quilliam (10 April 1856-23 April 1932) who changed his name to Abdullah Quilliam after reverting to Islam. He established Liverpool Muslim Institute at 8 Brougham Terrace, West Darby Road in 1889. This was England's first Mosque.

It is deeply regrettable that the same people who are crazy about the '*Satanic Verses*', are equally callous about the "*The Bible, The Qur'an and Science*"! The 'Satanic Verses' is made known to the world, but "*The Bible, The Qur'an and Science*" is purportedly kept in the darkness.

The list is long.

The fact is, a cross-section of enlightened people are washing towards Islam."

"The examples do not inspire me. Those are the forgotten events kept in a dilapidated bin placed afar in a wasteland. It is your private cry and it resembles a cry of a soul being emotionally slaughtered in desolation.

Now, please come to the point, is the Koran infallible, or is it just a hollow claim?" Kumaran threw the sober inquiry laced with curiosity and mild ridicule. He eyed me with an uncanny expression.

"I do not talk from the vacancy of intellect. The Qur'an is infallible, and the claim is made by none but the Qur'an itself. It says:

"Do they not consider the Qur'an (with care)? Had it been from other Than Allah, they would surely have found therein much discrepancy". [Qur'an: Nisa 4: 82]

The challenge is open to be challenged by anyone dead or alive.

The Creator does not stop here. To remove even a slightest doubt regarding the origin of The Qur'an, He has relaxed the condition further and permitted human beings to mass helps even from Jinns to produce something like of the Qur'an. He has guaranteed that even their combined effort will result in clear failure.

"Say, "if the whole of mankind and Jinns were to gather together to produce the like of this Qur'an, they could not produce the like thereof …" [Qur'an: Bani Israel: 88]

"And if ye are in doubt as to what We have revealed from time to time to Our servant, then produce a Sura like thereunto;…" [Qur'an: Al Baqara 2:23]

"But if ye cannot- and of a surety ye cannot- then fear the Fire whose fuel is men and stones,-" [Qur'an: Al Baqara 2:24]

The challenge of the Qur'an is humongous, but the attitude of human beings towards the Qur'an is pathetically humorous. From a mere human point of view, we expect many discrepancies in the Qur'an because the Messenger who promulgated it was not a 'lettered' one. Mankind should bear in mind that the true revelation is itself a miracle, and stands on its own merits."

"My intellect refuses to offer any wash of applause to such ordinary claims. Where are the substance that could corroborate the claims of the Koran being a revealed Book?" observed Kumaran. Phillip gave me some haughty glances that I deflected with great ease.

"I beg your patience."

The following verse has thrown some specific challenges to the humankind. It goes as:

"Verily the knowledge of the Hour is with Allah (alone). It is He Who sends down rain, and He Who knows what is in the wombs,..." [Qur'an: Luqman 31:34]

- **No One Can Predict Correctly What Is in the Womb!**

"The knowledge is with Allah (swt) only."

"But child conceived in the womb can be determined whether it is male or female? So, how can it be a challenge?" Kumaran countered.

"My grandmother too can predict whether the resident of the womb is a male or a female. But the Challenge is not as 'cheap' as you think of. The Challenge is not linked to the cheap aspects of mere 'sex' determination, rather it indicates something else deep and profound. The following verse would help you understand the profundity of the challenge. The Qur'an says:

"When she was delivered, she said: "O my Lord! Behold! I am delivered of a female child!"- and Allah knew best what she brought forth-...." [Qur'an: Al Imran 3: 36]

The mother of Mary expected a male child. She was bit 'disappointed' after giving birth to a female child (Mother Mary). But the last part of the verse, *"Allah (swt) knew best what she brought forth"* clearly hints at something which is beyond the cheap affair of sex determination. Little did she know that her newborn baby would become the mother of one of the mightiest Prophets of the Almighty.

But my grandmother could not predict about whether the conceived one would be a Prophet or a pervert, righteous or rogue, pious or impious, champion or chicken-shit. She cannot for sure."

▪ No One Can Find Flaw in the Creation!

"The Qur'an invites excellence of human intellect to find out flaw in the creation of the Heavens. The Qur'an Says:

"He Who created the seven heavens one above another: No want of proportion wilt thou see in the Creation of ((Allah)) Most Gracious...?"

"Again turn thy vision a second time: (thy) vision will come back to thee dull and discomfited, in a state worn out" [Qur'an: Al Mulk 67: 3-4]

With disproportionate audacity, the Almighty has guaranteed perfection in His Creation. Indirectly, the Creator hints that human beings are left only to wonder at the splendours of His Creation.

The Almighty sinks own audacity and offers His Creation to be juried by human beings. Seems it, a group of bi-cycle mechanics has been invited to find out any flaw in the design of a grand space shuttle."

"That does not mean that the design of the space-shuttle is flawless," Kumaran placed his logic. His logic ran counter.

"Do you think, the mechanics are capable enough to find out any patent defect in the space shuttle? Obviously, to the mechanic, the space shuttle is a matter of wonder. How would they find any flaw?"

"Is the challenge confined only to the people whose feet fettered to the earth? How could an observer standing on the earth find flaws that consist in the Universe?" asked Kumaran logically.

"The challenge is extended out to anyone whether he is standing on the earth, or snugged in any Lagrangian point, or trapped in the dumping yard of Kuiper Belt, or standing on the solar system's highest mountain called the Olympus Mons, or catapulted into the Boomerang Nebula, or floating outside the Universe.

The NASA has already collected much of *cosmic background radiation* of deep space by the WMAP probe placed at the Lagrangian point L2. Please check the data if any flaw has been sensed, or found."

"Dust and innumerable asteroids have crowded the points L4 and L5. Is this also the sign of perfection?" inquired Kumaran.

"Let the dirt of the solar system be collected there instead of trickling in onto the earth. You can shift your space colony to the Lagrangian point L3, which still remains unused, if I am not wrong."

"I do know you are habituated *to eat out of God's hand.*

It arouses wonder in me as to why no other planet or satellite in the close vicinity of the earth is made habitable?" Kumaran made a search questingly.

"Superfluous desire!

Friends, the moon is winking at you lovingly. It is just situated at the next-door space. Who does stop you to make it habitable? Why are you searching frenetically elsewhere?"

"So, you do finally agree that there is a 'want' in the Creation?" Kumaran tried to persuade me.

"Please do not *put your words into my mouth.* I find perfection everywhere in the Universe. Nowhere I find any dot of flaw. What I am trying here is to awaken a deep realisation in you about the level of human intelligence.

Just a *stone's throw* away is the moon. Since *the year dot,* the moon has been actually taunting our incapability to make her habitable. It, in turn, actually exposes the level of our intellect. What I find most embarrassing is that human beings, being the supreme creature, cannot even copy 'the technology' used in making the Earth habitable. It calls forth a spell of great shame on us."

"Why axial tilt (angle between rotational axis and orbital axis) of the earth is around 23 degree or so?" Kumaran questioned.

"Just to provide you flavour of different seasons. The duration and intensity of every season appears to be conducive to life and salubrious to health. Don't you like the succession of seasons?"

"Why the axial tilt is decreasing? Is it also the part of the perfect Creation?" explored Kumaran. He hurriedly forwarded the question.

"Perhaps you want to plant a blemish in the Creation!

One day the solar system will inevitably face collapse. This might be the indication of the impending 'Event'."

The order and the beauty of the vast Space and the marvellous bodies that follow regular laws of celestial motions in the Universe are itself exceedingly incredible. The creation of the seven heavens stands itself an insurmountable marvel carved out with the greatest perfection and the finest sophistication. Our eyes return fatigued conceding an emphatic defeat to the majesty of God. It appears simple and drossy to a dull person, but it fills a wise person with its magnificence, wonders and marvels.

I remember the view of planetary scientist of NASA John Aloysius O'Keefe (1916 -2000 CE):

"*We are, by astronomical standards, a pampered, cossetted, cherished group of creatures ...if the Universe has not been made with the most exciting precision we could never have come into existence. It is my view that these circumstances indicate the Universe was created for man to live in*."

Yes, I do compel myself into alignment to the view of the scientist, and would love to add that only Allah (swt) could create such a magnificent Universe with the excitingly finest precision. Seems it, we are left to mourn over the plight of our sight that readily concedes shameful defeat to the majesty of the Universe.

- **The Qur'an Will Remain Unchanged And Unchallenged!**

"This is a miracle in itself. No other religious Books on the earth could boast of such feat; this is the fulfilment of the Promise made by the Almighty.

"Nay, this is a Glorious Qur'an,"

"(Inscribed) in a Tablet Preserved!"

[Qur'an: Al Buruj 85: 21-22]

"Surely We revealed the Message, and We will surely preserve it." [Qur'an: Al Hijr 15: 9]

The verses dispel doubts about the authorship of the Qur'an. Its divine authorship has survived the tests of the times. The Qur'an is preserved not only on the earth, but in the Tablet guarded divinely also. Time cannot blunt it, and corruption fears to touch it."

"'Preserved' means what?" inquired Kumaran.

"The Qur'an can be revived instantly even if all the Qur'ans are thrown into seas. The Book is embedded in the hearts of millions of scholars."

"That means fanaticism has percolated even into the deepest pockets of the heart. Cobwebs of rabid fanaticism have spread its wings across the length and breadth of...," Phillip gave the Qur'an a roasting. He cut the tail of the sentence and left it to an easy guess. He misused the occasion to put down the Qur'an.

"Friends, we have admiringly embedded the Qur'an in our hearts. But, are you aware that the Bible is inscribed on the telescopic sights of 'killing rifles'?"

"What!" Phillip almost shouted at me. His astonishment overshot and he looked at me with mystified eyes though his tongue was imploding internally.

"Calm down friend, I will delve into it after a while."

"How will you revive the Koran if all the scholars are crushed into a sack and transported to the moon?" Kumaran loosed off a bizarre imagination through the sharpness of lampoon.

"I dreamt that a fly was transporting an elephant to the moon. If the feasibility of my imagination could win justification, then surely yours too would reach to fruition."

"But how can you check and confirm that a particular Koran is not tampered with?" probed Kumaran.

"There are many verses in the Qur'an that bear mathematical relation. The following examples, I hope, could bring satisfaction to your queries. The Qur'an says:

"The similitude of Jesus before Allah is as that of Adam; …". [Qur'an: Al Imran 3: 59]

Prophet Adam (pbuh) and Prophet Jesus Christ (pbuh) both are equal in the sight of the Almighty. It implies that the name of both the Prophets have also been mentioned equal number of times in the Qur'an.

Chapter 71 is dedicated to Prophet Noah (pbuh) and it contains total 28 verses, and the simple difference between 71 and 28 is 43. It is interesting that Prophet Noah (pbuh) is mentioned exactly 43 times in total 28 chapters of the holy Qur'an. Furthermore, total numbers of chapters that follow the *Chapter Noah* until the end of the Qur'an is 43 that do not contain the name of Prophet Noah.

The words 'sea' and 'land' are mentioned in the Qur'an 32 and 13 times respectively. The percentage of 'sea' and 'land' on the earth are 71.1 percent and 28.9 percent respectively.

The Book is interspersed with ingenious mathematics that could deter corruption as paint deters rust. Friend, had it not been from the Almighty, surely the brutal passage of time would have blunted it; it would have lost its presence, relevance and essence and most certainly would have found its rightful place in the decrepit memory of human race."

Two of the original manuscripts of the Quran still exist today in the Topkapi Saray Museum in Istanbul, Turkey, and in Tashkent, Russia.

The Qur'an is an immortal masterpiece divinely guarded. Vile trick must not overstep the line, nor any insolent intention should overrun its own limit of insistence to dare to confront with the Qur'an; it's not that Book that can be *trifled with.*

- **Abu Lahab Missed an Excellent Opportunity!**

"Abu Lahab (half-paternal uncle of Prophet Muhammad (pbuh)) was one of the pre-eminently staunch critics of Islam. He sank into an ignoble habit of making the noble Prophet victim of his calumnies. Overcome by a unique sickness, he and his wife both were out for blood of the Prophet and deployed every small turn of their dreadful tongues in churning out derogation against the noble Prophet.

The following verses were revealed during the lifetime of Abu Lahab that say:

"Perish the hands of the Father of Flame! Perish he!

Burnt soon will he be in a Fire of Blazing Flame!" [Qur'an: Al Lahab 111: 1, 3]

Abu Lahab lived almost for ten years even after the revelation of the Surah, and surprisingly he was fully aware of that. The magnificent opportunity was manifestly placed in his way. *Fortune smiled on him* but he just squandered the 'chance' and failed decidedly to deliver justice to his own hatred towards Islam.

Only the Almighty can expose the true encryption of a heart!"

- **Islam Will Prevail Over Every *'-ism'*!**

"Islam attained culmination with the arrival of the last and final Messenger Muhammad (pbuh), and started prevailing over every '-ism' with consummate flair and excellence.

"It is He Who hath sent His Messenger with guidance and the Religion of Truth, to prevail it over all religions, even though the Pagans may detest (it)." [Qur'an: Al Tawbah 9: 33]

The Divine prediction revealed more than fourteen hundreds years ago has now bloomed into a formidable reality."

"Do you remember Genghis Khan (1158 -1227 CE), the great Khan who almost wiped out the name of Islam from the earth,"

Kumaran made stark remark. He reminded me how Mongols reached on the verge of wiping out 'Islam' from the face of the earth.

"'Almost *wiped out*'?"

"The 'ultimate shake' was about to be unleashed by Mongols had the result of the *Ain Jalut* battle (3 September 1260 CE) been different," Phillip remarked through the tongue of Kumaran.

"There is a folly in your thinking. I find a sheer lack of wiseness in your remarks."

"Does my foreseeability not match the fit of prophetic standard?" added Phillip. He failed to find an honest urge in my statement.

"Mongols were forced to retreat after being defeated by Mamluks in the battle of Ain Jalut located just 100 kilometres (aerial distance) away from Jerusalem. Mamluks envisaged a unique battle strategy that took Mongols by surprise. You should owe a great debt of gratitude to Mamluks.

Friend, I could decipher the motive encrypted in your indication. Yes, I do agree that, had the result been different, the holy site of Al-Aqsa would have perhaps found herself weeping in the ruins. But, do you think that the Mongols would have spared the Church of Holy Sepulchre that commemorates alleged 'crucifixion' and 'burial' of 'Lord' Jesus Christ (pbuh)?

Al-Aqsa dazzles in our hearts. It is like an ever-living blossom that smells of smells of ethereality and owns a prized place in the hearts of Muslims. Its desecration or demolition would have created waves of unrelenting pain in the loving hearts of Muslims. We would moan watching Al-Aqsa lying in the ruins.

Even then, Muslims would have not been bereaved of holy sites like Christians. Muslims would still have Mecca and Medina. But, what Christians would have then, had the Church of Holy Sepulchre been demolished?"

"Think about Fatimid Caliph Who demolished the Church of Holy Sepulchre in 1009 CE. We had already received that nasty shock at the hands of a Muslim Caliph. So...what... if it happens more than once?" added Phillip.

"I wish you had analysed the history of Jerusalem with a bit detachment.

History has witnessed how Jerusalem *went through fire and water* with the passage of time and suffered a great deal of terrible uncertainties. But, fate of Jerusalem changed into pleasant destiny since when the Prophet set foot (620 CE) in Jerusalem on his way to the heaven. Since then, no non-Abrahamic faith has ever been able to occupy Jerusalem.

Do you still think that Mongols could have demolished Al-Aqsa?"

"But why did his 'setting of foot' fail to stop Crusaders in 1099 CE? Why did his 'setting of foot' fail to stop the Jews influx?" inquired Kumaran. Phillip looked at Kumaran noddingly.

"Christians ruled Jerusalem barely for 10 percent of the total period spanning between 637 CE to 1967 CE (Israel started ruling in 1967 CE). Muslims ruled for the rest of the given period. Do you find insights here?

Divine ordained that Jews influx must happen. I will discuss on the same in an apposite moment."

"But, how could you deny the fact that the Mongols tripped Islam facedown...?" remarked Kumaran. He cut an unintelligible expression alloyed with an uncharacteristic body gesture. I looked at him in awe.

"*Out of the way* thinking! Perhaps, such thinking is but a distemper!

Mongols decimated Muslims on a large scale and were resolute to clear the earth of Muslims. In the endeavour, they achieved quite a great success well worth the efforts deployed in calling for a fine mix of curse and doom upon Muslims. But the gloom of massacre and the doom of destruction failed miserably to dampen the spirit of Islam, -because Islam is an Idea that cannot be killed by the sharpness of swords. Islam, in general, never felt cut off!

'*The Khan*', who shook badly the existence of Muslims failed to give a fright to Islam. Gradually, they lost the air of invincibility about themselves and surrendered silently to the invincibility of Islam! Islam is immortal like soul but Muslims are mortal like physical bodies."

"Islam will turn to extinction minus Muslims on the earth," Kumaran added his regular logic *off the top of his head.*

"Friends, you should not *shoot from the hip*!

Islam does not follow Muslims, neither does it depend on the existence of Muslims. Islam is an Idea, -the Divine Idea born to outshine all. Idea never gets retarded or killed, though its supporters get.

The world faced massive convulsions in the form of Genghis Khan, -the God-sent curse that descended ruthlessly upon Muslims. His tracks of journey were heavily marked by his deafening growls, fearsome ferocity and unmatched cruelties. The Khans overrun and conquered lands one after another annihilating resistance, exterminating people, enslaving the weaker form of human beings with cruelties unseen and unheard of. The cruelties of the 'Khans' ushered in a new era that overmastered the conquered race with the manifold of fear, fright, trepidation and terror. The tracks trodden by the Mongols were shaken by the tremor of panic, overlaid by blood rivers, overrun by grotesque figures and swathed in mysterious fear. The wind moaned in the mountains and trees. Innumerable examples were set where ferocity and cruelty clasped each other and soared high like naked flames blemishing the blueness of the sky. The repugnance of cruelties got accentuated by the erection of sky-kissing skull-pyramids in the conquered lands. The pages of History of Mongols are full of inexcusable and repugnant incidents that repel me, and perhaps all.

Khans, undeniably, marked the history with many great victories as conquerors. Notwithstanding, the mighty Khans failed miserably to coerce Islam to concede a defeat. The motive of *bring Islam on knees* was ultimately frustrated and retreated to a desolate corner rife with insipid consolations. The Khans certainly won victory over Muslims, but Islam won the real victory, - the victory over *Tengrism*! The history had witnessed in awe, how *Tengrism was knocked sideways* by Islam forever. As battles subsided, *Tengrism* too subsided in strength following the confrontation with Islam, and eventually, with the passage of time, faded away into oblivion pegging a decorous kiss on the enviable face of Islam. The ferocious '*Khans*', who brandished double-edged swords to crush Islam into submission, finally were crashed against Islam and subsequently subsumed in the great fold of the Divine Idea! Muslims gave way, but Islam rose like a bright sun behind the tenebrific shadows of skull pyramids giving an essential awakening to Mongols! Islam overmastered the Mongols with its power of intellect!

An incredible prophecy is embedded deep in the following verse.

"It is He Who hath sent His Messenger with guidance and the Religion of Truth, to prevail it over all religions, ..." [Qur'an: Al Tawbah 9: 33]

The revelation has to be fulfilled, and it will consummate only when Islam transitions into sheer dominance and prevails over every '-ism'. Islam will keep on rising no matter what comes to retard it."

"Islam lags behind Christianity. Christianity tops the list. Do you still think that the claim of the Koran is divine?" Phillip almost rubbished the claim of the Qur'an with his perfunctory ways of reasoning.

"The notion clearly lacks substance and insights. Christianity does not top the list, but the numbers of 'so called prophesised' Christians. Rather clearly, Islam tops the list in the contest and has already prevailed over all. The 'faith' that is practised by maximum numbers of people in the world is Islam. None of the faiths could dare to claim this feat and could stand even close to Islam. The numbers of practising Christians is diminutive and decreasing further with each passing day contrasting greatly with the steady rise of Islam."

"Which religion does get most drubbings in the world? Would you please name that religion? Do you still think that Islam is Divine?" Kumaran took a sharp dig at Islam. He shot a penetrating glance at me.

"Islam gets innumerable drubbings wrongly on daily basis. It has got against its name the most numbers of impure publications and a plague of disgraceful comments. Nonetheless, Islam continues to rise further and further leaving every hate-filled family of things to disgraceful submission. The time has witnessed that how insolent attempts, ulterior motives and vile schemes against Islam have fallen flat, or *gone belly up,* or been buried deep in abyss.

As head tops the assembly line of human body, likewise Islam tops the prestigious vertical of religions. Islam flies with the wings of critics and haters. Islam knows no submission.

Why today Islam is the fastest growing religion in America and Europe?"

"Don't pin happiness on personal whims. The stage is setting up rapidly to show Islam the way it deserves the most. Americans are not heathen like Arabs," Phillip retorted. His tongue appeared piercing like the fine proboscis of a mosquito.

"I have severed relation with whims and assumptions quite long ago. Friends, according to Pew Study by 2050 Muslims will surpass Jews as the largest non-Christian religion in the U.S. More than 10 percent of Europeans will be Muslims, while the number of Christians in Europe will drop by 100 million.

Between the years 1934 to 1984, the statistics (Reader's Digest Almanac, 1986) say that the increase in percentage of world's major religion where Islam tops the chart. In this period of time, Islam and Christianity increased by 235 percent and 47 percent respectively."

"Have you included the number of Christians died in the World War II?" Phillip objected.

"You have forgotten to mention the high birth rate in the third world Muslims countries. Hey, breeding is illegal!" Kumaran commented. I found many abrupt changes in the tone of his voice that resembled the winding of a river through a precipitous gorge.

"I could see easily an unseen disorder and a hidden malice ruffling briskly your mental disposition to the point of messiness. Frankly put, the presence of Islam on the earth perhaps infuriates you to an undisclosed distemper.

Guinness World Records 2003, page 102, say: "In the period of 1990-2000 approximately 12.5 million more people converted to Islam than to Christianity". Birth rate is just a lame excuse. George Bernard Shaw (Irish playwright and writer, the only writer to win an Oscar and The Noble prize in literature) once said:

"*If any religion had the chance of ruling over England, nay Europe within the next hundred years, it could be Islam. No other religion has had such a record of success in uniting, in giving equality of status, of opportunity and of endeavours to so many and so varied races of mankind as Islam did.*" ["The Genuine Islam", Vol.1, No. 8, 1936]

The great mind like George Bernard Shaw did not hesitate in accepting the truth.

By the way, if you think that the curtailed-birth-rate of Muslims could help contain the rise of Islam, then please do it and believe me, I would not resist you, rather would extend my full support to."

"Are you not going against the Koran?" Kumaran made quick but serious inquiry.

"No, not at all. But I do have a request, -please do not kill the life (foeticide, aborticide, etc.) formed in the womb. The Qur'an says:

"Kill not your children for fear of want: ... Verily the killing of them is a great sin." [Qur'an: Al Isra 17: 31]

Killing zygotes or children whether inside the womb or outside of it, is a great sin despised by the Qur'an. But I have not come across any verse in the Qur'an which prohibits the killing of 'despised fluid' called the 'semen'. In fact, the Qur'an says:

"And made his progeny from a quintessence of the nature of a fluid despised:" [Qur'an: Al Sajdah32: 8]

The verse above is self-explanatory."

"Could you dare to deny the fact that Islam was spread with the forcing swords? -

Bloodshed and Islam are the two sides of the same coin. It is like a conjoined twin born in the sand-caked Arabia to call for disaster for humanity. History had witnessed when Islam shed blood in its very first battle, -the battle of *Badr*. Then gradually Syria, Libya, Iraq, Iran and other neighbouring lands were invaded with bigger armies and sharper swords. Progression of Islam was ensured by sheer military actions and oppression which were devoid of human logic and deeper reasons.

Do you still think that Islam was spread by love and peace?" Phillip narrated suppositions holding breath for a longer while, and then slaked a lungful of air for his starved lungs. Kumaran was looking at him with collaborating eyes conjoining his tacit support with Phillip in condemnation of Islam.

"How come Islam, being nascent, could have waged the battle against the non-Muslims? Do you really think that Muslims did *tip the scales* in favour of battle (the battle of *Badr,* 624 CE) against the formidable and overpowering non-Muslims?

Even the fierce critics of Islam have agreed unanimously that the non-Muslims greatly outnumbered Muslims in the battle of Badr. In fact, non-Muslims trebled the number of Muslims. The Qur'an too confirmed the combative strength of Muslims.

"Allah helped you in Badr when you were very weak..." [Qur'an: Al-Imran 3:123]

Though Muslims were weak in strength, yet victory took the side of Muslims forcing unbelievers to retreat with a disgraceful defeat. The battle of *Badr* gave birth to a very crucial watershed that defined the fate of Muslims and the future of the history as well.

Do you know, how many non-Muslims were killed when Muhammad (pbuh) conquered Mecca (after six years (late 629 or early 630 CE) of the battle of Badr)?-

Verily, it was a bloodless conquest achieved on zero loss of life. The chief of Mecca too was awarded with mercy and compassion. Like I said, Islam treats people with mercy and compassion ever found in history.

In the same vein I would like to ask, how many people were killed when Muslims conquered Jerusalem (637 CE) during the time of Caliph Umar (r.a), and how many people were killed when Persia conquered Jerusalem in 614 CE?-

I would tell you, –the city was surrendered to Muslims in a bloodless way. The Caliph himself travelled to Jerusalem to sign the Pact with non-Muslims.

But, Persian attacked the city in 614 CE and massacred thousands of people (some say 90,000 people) and destroyed the Church of Holy Sepulchre. Perhaps, Muslim conquest of Jerusalem was the only conquest in history of Jerusalem when no cry of a bleeding-soul was heard of. No sword was flung upon the neck of non-Muslims either. Rather, swords remained silent in the sheaths with flaccid blades and refused to shed blood for indulgence.

Friends, think about the great Saladin (Salah-Ad-Din Ayyubi, 1137 -1193 CE) when he conquered Jerusalem in 1187 CE defeating the mighty military of the Crusaders. The Crusaders had slaughtered Muslims in a massive scale upon conquering Jerusalem in 1099 CE. They dissipated angers against Muslims through many organised pogroms. But Saladin, inspired by the great endurance of Islam, appeared averse to shedding any blood and offered flowing generosity to the defeated Crusaders and other Christians. He effused mercy towards the Crusaders and to their people in order to show them the tolerance and the greatness of Islam.

The level of mercy, benevolence and magnanimity of Caliph Umar (r.a) and Saladin, two great followers of Prophet Muhammad (pbuh), are enough to disabuse your notion about the noble Prophet. He was merciful *through and through* and always tended to show mercy to all!

Noted historian De Lacy O'Leary in the book "*Islam at the cross road*" (Page 8) clarified the misconception of many people believing that Islam was spread by swords:

"*History makes it clear however, that the legend of fanatical Muslims sweeping through the world and forcing Islam at the point of the sword upon conquered races is one of the most fantastically absurd myth that historians have ever repeated.*"

Friends, you need to think of my motherland India 'ruled' for centuries by Muslims. Till date, more than 85 percent people of India are non-Muslims. Do you still think that Islam was spread by the forcing swords?"

"Spread of Islam entailed bloodshed...Islam and bloodshed are a perfect pair locked in a tight embrace. *Badr* sprang into being as soon as Islam announced its inception. You cannot deny it, no matter what explanation you try to present for vindication," retorted Phillip. He appeared obstinate to run counter.

"I cannot help if one takes root in denial."

"But a mystery that surprises me greatly is that how come Muhammad did not get killed in any of the battles he fought…" Kumaran added. His voice was riding the wave of anguish.

"Hey, Muhammad did never come at the front-line of the battle. He just commanded his army from a well-equipped and fortified tent. So naturally, surprise aside, he would remain unhurt," Phillip added sarcastically.

"Do you think the unbelievers did not try to kill Muhammad (pbuh)? Why did they fail to kill him?"

"Never did he dare to come at the combative front. He camped quite away from the line of action. And searching his tent was *like looking for a needle in a haystack*," Phillip impugned the courage of the Prophet.

"Life was not easy for Prophet Muhammad (pbuh). A plague of threats of assassination was constantly looming large in the wind of Mecca. The whole Mecca appeared to have gone against Muhammad (pbuh) and spread flagrantly secret traps to eliminate him. Plans of assassinating the Prophet were plotted in countless closed-door meetings. The plights of the Muslim community aggravated further into pathetic conditions when social boycott was imposed on them. Muslims then hardly found any dependable rock in the *shifting sands* of their existence.

How non-Muslims failed to kill Muhammad (pbuh) when he was migrating to Medina (622 CE) with a single companion?

Who did stop Umar bin Khattab (before he reverted to Islam) on his way to killing Muhammad (pbuh)?

History knows that Muslims were defeated in the battle of Uhud (625 CE), - why non-Muslims then failed to kill Muhammad (pbuh)? Do you know that Prophet Muhammad (pbuh) was hurt in this battle?"

"He was a fugitive. He secretly migrated to Medina evading the searching eyes of Meccans. And as I said, searching his tent was a daunting task, -and who knows he did not camouflage against the enemy surveillance?" Phillip retorted mockingly.

"Why 'Firroun' failed to kill Moses (pbuh)?"

"How Jews killed Jesus?

Better stop glorifying Muhammad and supporting his surreptitious acts," Phillip countered.

"It seems I cannot make any dent in your stubborn defence. I am giving in.

Anyways, why Muslims are still Muslims in Syria, Iraq, Libya, Iran and Afghanistan?"

"What is the point?" Phillip inquired fretfully.

"Like you said, Muslims conquered Syria, Iraq, Libya, Iran and Afghanistan and subsequently converted people to Islam at the point of sword. Now tell me, why Muslims in Syria, Iraq, Libya, Iran and Afghanistan are still Muslims even after being successively conquered by Mongols and Christians? Why did not they leave Islam and convert to Tengrism, or Christianity? Why Tengrism and Christianity failed badly to make a dent in their faith?

The world knows that the swords of Mongols could easily outsmart the swords of Muslims in sharpness and swiftness. And, Christians are using more lethal weapons nowadays in Syria, Iraq, Libya and Afghanistan. Why did they fail to convert Muslims into Tengrism or Christianity?

Please respond… I am listening to.

Would you please tell me, how Indonesia became a Muslim country? Which mighty sword fell upon them?"

Again, some disrespectful silence greeted me. Though I could not tease from them any response, yet I found answer in the silence.

"The *PEW Study* shows that by 2050 CE, 106 million people are projected to leave Christianity. The *PEW* says by 2100, Islam could surpass Christianity despite the six-century head start of Christianity. Why would they leave Christianity?"

"These are the things of the future. Tell me, what are the miracles that Islam has already achieved to distinguish itself from the others?" Phillip inquired in a serious note.

"I do know these are the things of the future, but you should judge the miracles of Islam by the soundings of the people across the world. After all, the change is *in the wind.*

Miracles have made deep inroads into your hearts and left you enormously obsessed with it.

Prophet Muhammad (pbuh) received first revelation around 610 CE while he was in Mecca. He was forced to migrate to Medina in 622 CE. He fought his first battle in 624 CE in the field of Badr and won. Within next six years (around in 630 CE) he conquered Mecca without shedding a drop of blood. By around 632 CE, whole Arabian Peninsula reverted to Islam. Within the next six years, Islam defeated the super powers like Byzantine and Sassanid empires (in 636 CE) in the decisive battles of Yarmouk and Al-Qadisiyya respectively. And within the next six years (642 CE), Islam claimed dominance over the vast lands stretching from Libya in the west to the Amu Darya in the north.

Let me arrange the events that happened miraculously, -

Islam fought its first battle against an overwhelming army of Quraysh and won.

Within next six years Islam conquered Mecca. The whole Arabian Peninsula reverted to Islam within a span of next two years.

Then, surprisingly within next six years, Islam defeated two super powers like Byzantine and Persia.

Then, within the next six years after defeating Byzantine and Persia, Islam transitioned to dominance spreading wings over the vast lands bounded by the Red Sea in the south, the Mediterranean Sea in the west, the Black sea and the Caspian Sea in the north and the Indus River in the east.

Miracles believed to be the constant companions of Islam. Islam miraculously grew into a formidable power evincing the advent of great changes in human history."

"Those have ceased nowadays to matter as miracles and been blunted badly by the passage of time. Think of *Communism* that ruled the formidable Soviet Union stretching magnificently over 10,000 kilometres from east to west, and more than 7000 kilometres from north to south. It spread remarkably across 11 time zones, if I remember correctly. That was truly a resounding success of Communism to say the least," Kumaran nullified the achievements of Islam. The pace of his tongue was astoundingly fast.

"Did Communism spread during the lifetime of Karl Marx and Friedrich Engels? How many years did it take to turn into a governing ideology since the publications of the *Communist Manifesto (1848 CE)*, or the *Das Kapital (1867 -1883 CE)*?"

"The logic is as null as meaningless!

It does not matter whether it was accepted immediately or later," argued Kumaran.

"Why does it not matter?

Whole Arabian Peninsula reverted to Islam during the lifetime of Prophet Muhammad (pbuh). Does the same happened to Karl Marx?"

"Christianity took three hundred years to transition to dominance after the departure of Jesus Christ. Christianity is now ruling the world especially the whole Europe. The time has no longer succeeded to suppress it further," Phillip added the collaborating views. His confidence nudged up an unbelievably high pitch.

"Friends, the USSR was one-party state and governed by Communist Party from 1922 to 1991 CE. It ruled the USSR only for sixty nine years. The world knows that the USSR was dissolved in 1991 CE burying Communism as its governing ideology."

"Well, then, you should also think of the collapse of the Ottoman Empire. Why did it collapse, and why Islam was rejected?" Kumaran reacted. He reminded me about the disintegration of the Ottoman Caliphate and discharge of Islam from being its governing principle.

"The Ottoman Empire existed almost four hundreds sixty-nine years (1453-1922 CE). The USSR existed a minuscule 15 percent of the ruling-period of the Ottoman Empire. You must be knowing that the USSR was dissolved, but the Ottoman Empire was disintegrated.

Did any state seceded from the Ottoman Empire discard Islam? Do you know any?

But many states seceded from the USSR discarded *Communism.*

Communism undeniably achieved many great feats during its rule. But history says, *Communism* did also many ghastly things during its ruling period. Many forced-labour-camps (*Gulags*) were set up by Lenin and that eventually reached its peak during the reign of dictator Stalin (1927-1953 CE). The camps were no better than the concentration camps set up by Adolf Hitler. With the dissolution of the USSR, communism lost its resounding presence and slipped into the realm of oblivion."

"Turkey became a secular state post Ottoman Empire, -Islam was rejected and became a spent force. Do you know that?" Kumaran added. He almost *swore blind* faith to the superficial knowledge in history, though he appeared way confident.

"Look *far and wide* so that you will get to know the truth. Here, the truth is calling into question the truthfulness of your views.

The Treaty of Luissane (1923 CE) restricted Turkey. Turkey was forced to accept the treaty as to the reason of its defeat in the World War I. In consequence, laws were enforced upon Islam that clipped its political wings.

But, the world has not given so far birth to any power that could eliminate Islam from the hearts of Muslims. Muslims never did reject believing in Allah (swt) nor discard the faith in the final Messenger Muhammad (pbuh). They were, in fact, politically cornered and forced to refrain from implementing the political wings of Islam."

"How could you say blindly that Stalin was dictator? -

He was a great statesman acknowledged by the world. Moreover, during the period of reforms and changes, many fringe and unwanted things might happen as the inevitable parts of the main equation. Great reforms cannot be done by an ice-cream seller. You cannot make everyone happy. Verily Stalin was not a dictator," stated Kumaran.

"Then please apprise me, why did Nikita Khrushchev vehemently started the *de-Stalinisation* process (1956 CE) renouncing the Stalinistic ways?

Stalin intensified oppression by enacting many terrific laws namely *'The Great Purging'*, the *'NKVD Order No. 00447'* and *'Ethnic Cleansing'* to name a few.

You know, the *NKVD Order No. 00447* was issued in July30, 1937. And it was implemented in a lightning pace. Within just fifteen days, by the end of August 15, 1937, close to four lacs Soviet citizens were put to death. The example provides strong basis to discern the brutality and the inhuman nature of the laws enacted. Surely, the laws were not enacted for anything less than a genocide. The period was marked as the period of *'great terror'*. The terror left trails of indelible marks in the hearts of millions. Humanity then crumbled!

Think of Agafiya Lykova who has still been living in absolute isolation deep inside the Taiga near the basin of the river Yerinat. Her parents (*Old Believers* -Eastern Orthodox Christians) fled homes 1936 CE and slipped into the Taiga for a snug. Endured they in the journey the brunt of chilling cold, trekked through many hostile tracks, dodged countless hungry eyes of unfeeling beasts, crossed many fearsome rapids of over-brimmed rivers, braved innumerable curveballs thrown by the nature and then, finally they retreated deep inside the Taiga. They saved themselves from being tortured by the assailing *Stalinist's Purging Wing*. They *went through the mill* and experienced threadbare existence in the thick of the hostile Taiga. They survived on the meagreness of bark-soup and sometimes, filled the stomachs with boiled-leather-shoes that they wore during the journey. Agafiya born in the forest in a hollowed pine washtub, and as time went on, she lost her family to the wilderness of the forest overlaid with unforgiving snows. Tears roll down her wizened face when she recalls the savage rigmaroles of the *Stalinist's Purging Wing* that instilled terror into the hearts of her parents and millions *Old Believers* around."

"Muhammad drove away Jews from Medina. He was unfair and acted *below the belt*. How do you see these autocratic acts of Muhammad?" Kumaran pressed me. His tongue appeared charging and battle-ready.

"The Prophet never drove away Jews or any non-Muslim community from their homes until the agreement signed between them was flouted repeatedly. Prophet expelled *Banu Qaynuqa* from Medina because they had conspired against the noble Prophet. They surreptitiously helped Meccan in the battle of Badr. They flagrantly broke the *Constitution of Medina* signed between them and the Muslim emigrants from Mecca.

Islam is purely a psychological sword having strong affiliation to intellect. It is no longer a surprise that Islam is always targeted, and the propaganda manufactured against Islam, in general, is rogue and *goes through the roof.* Voices against Islam are vile, wild and continuously *raising the roof* for the year dot. Islam, nonetheless, waves at humanity with golden hands, beatific smile and altruistic heart. Islam is famed for being the natural choice of rationality; Islam agrees with intelligence that empowers faculty to attain rectitude of enlightenment nullifying easily the enormity of all sorts of dark propaganda. Islam envisions a better form of humanity by envisaging a way of life deemed to be the most rational. Islam, in its eagerness tries to build humanity of premier class encompassing all fronts of benevolence and shunning all the depressing facets of malevolence. Islam, with the absolutism of truth, reveals the deep secrets of Creation and endeavours to draw the attention of human race towards the deeper meaning of life.

Islam is destined to be the master of all '-ism'. Islam will '*supersede*' them all in a grand way. This is not the personal wish of mine, neither does it depend on your personal displeasure. Friends, it is the Wish of the Owner of the earth Who Wishes that His religion should surpass all."

"The proofs presented so far are insubstantial and arguably do not corroborate the divine origin of the Koran. These are regular and boring figure of speech and do not suggest anything *out of the ordinary* about the Koran. These are nothing but sorts of inane interpretations of some antiquated stories," Kumaran spurned. He looked askance at me with neglecting eyes.

"You need to install a heart as fanatic as his then only you can realise that the Book is from God, else it's impossible," Phillip lampooned.

"I beg your patience. People nurse some exaggerated views about the infallibility of science. I think it is a decent miscalculation. Science is not always the master.

People believed in the astronomical model developed by Nicolaus Copernicus in 1543 CE. The model was famed as "*Copernican Heliocentrism*". It placed the sun near the centre of the solar system depicting motionless, static. The earth and the other planets orbit around it. The model was rejected by science for the obvious reason.

But, the Qur'an, since its revelation, has been saying differently:

"And the sun runs into a resting place, for him: that is the decree of (Him), the exalted in Might, the All Knowing." [Qur'an: Yaasiin 36: 38]

In another verse, the Qur'an says:

"It is He who created the night and the day, the sun and the moon: All swim along, each in its rounded course." [Qur'an: Ambiyaa 21: 33]

The sun has its own motion and is moving towards the destination fixed beforehand."

"Are you sure that Muhammad did not steal such scientific facts?" Kumaran cast doubt easily with limpid voice and unaffected tone.

"What do you mean exactly?"

"See, a great Roman Empire did exist before the coming of Muhammad and had attained unprecedented progress almost in every field. The 'Pax Romanna' (Roman Peace) is the example of stability and prosperity the Empire attained during the times of Caesar Augustus (63 BC-14 CE) and Trajan (98-117 CE). Do you think that they did not work on astronomy?" Kumaran stated. He attempted to highlight the advancement of the Roman Empire achieved during that period.

"Please tell me, what was the need that a union leader like Muhammad (pbuh) would explain astronomy in front of the masses like the Arabs? Does any union leader do suchlike?"

"Evading! My question is simple and plain, -did Muhammad steal or not?" Kumaran insisted. He seemed to be in desperation.

"Muhammad (pbuh) was an *unlettered* Prophet born in Hejaz (present day Saudi Arabia). Hejaz was not the part of the Roman Empire (Eastern Roman Empire (Byzantine)).

How the Prophet could steal the scientific papers kept secretly in a fortified Roman's science laboratory?

If I agree for the sake of argument that the Roman Empire made a huge measure of success in the field of astronomy, my question is why did they not document and publish? Why did they keep the discovery in the depth of secret?"

"The source of such astronomical facts must be different. It was not possible for Muhammad himself to write such facts in the Koran without a stealth," Kumaran showed stiff denial vanquishing brutally the urge of the truth. He appeared *out and out* dismissive of the Qur'an.

"Why did Nicolaus Copernicus fail to steal the fact? Copernicus was born in Poland, and might be that Poland then belonged to the Western Roman Empire. Why did he fail to steal? Do you have any clue?"

Even Albert Einstein too did mistake. In 1917, Albert Einstein applied his theory of *General Relativity* to the Universe and ended up suggesting a model of a homogenous, static, spatially curved Universe known as "Einstein Universe". According to Einstein, the Universe was Static!

In 1929, American astronomer Edwin Hubble observed '*cosmological redshift*' occurred due to the expansion of the Universe and he presented the observation to Einstein. Einstein accepted the discovery and subsequently modified his model of the 'Static Universe'.

The verse of the Qur'an contrasts greatly with the concept of Static Universe as conceptualised by Einstein. The Qur'an says:

"With power and skill did We construct the Firmament: for it is We Who create the vastness of pace." [Qur'an: Al Dhariyat 51: 47]

The word 'pace' indicates the dynamics of the Universe.

- **Evolution of the Universe!**

"*Big Bang Theory* (BBT) is considered to be the most popular theory on the 'evolution' of the Universe. In "*A Brief History of Time*", Stefan Hawkins explained about the '*origin*' (read it history) of the Universe. It says:

"*Early in the Universe, it was extremely compact, hot and expanding rapidly.*"

In other words, at the beginning, the whole Universe was extremely small, extremely dense and extremely hot. After some '*cosmic explosion*', the Universe came into existence and thenceforth the Universe has been expanding. This can be construed as the crude gist of the *Big Bang Theory*."

"Do you think some sort of explosion occurred during the Big Bang?" Kumaran inquired.

"What is your view?"

"No such 'explosion' that a general sense understands," replied Kumaran.

"Can I presume that the Universe was '*infinitely small*'?"

"...fairly said, it was much much smaller," viewed Kumaran.

"How much small is the '*much much smaller*'? Is it infinitely small?"

"Not truly," Kumaran replied after a thoughtful pause. He gave me a glance which is exchanged generally during the meet of a powerful diplomacy.

"How matter interacted with gravitational field at particle level when the Universe was in the state of '*Singularity*'?"

"The laws of physics in Singularity prior to the Big Bang might be quite different than today's physics," added Kumaran. He was way cool!

"Did '*time*' exist before the Big Bang? I mean, what was the value of *time* in 'second/second' (here, '*second*' in numerator is the time of Singularity (before the Big Bang) and the '*second*' in denominator is the present time that we measure on the earth)?"

"The gravitational force was, I would say, extremely high. It is known that, as the gravitational force increases, the 'time' becomes slower. So, presumably, I think, the question of '*existence*' of the 'time' before the Big Bang cannot be treated delectably with much scientific temper,…it was '*non-existent*' to say with decency," stated Kumaran. His tongue moved ponderously like an elephant!

"So, do you think that the '*time*' triggered itself to existence after the Big Bang? Is it a self-triggered phenomenon (dimension)?"

"Ah! Not everything in the Universe follows the '*cause-and-effect*' principle. Causality is not overarching and does not apply everywhere. You can think that way too," Kumaran curated a unique pitch for his reply as if he was settling an intricate case through diplomacy.

"Well. If '*time*' is a self-triggered phenomenon, then why was you looking for the Creator of God? Can't God be self-created? Can't it be without any causality?

Which one, according to you, is more counterintuitive: self-created 'God', or the self-created 'time'?"

"The Universe has a beginning and the 'singularity' is its starting point. Does the God has any defined beginning?" retorted Kumaran.

"Why did the Big Bang occur? What was the need? Which factor triggered the occurrence of the Big Bang?"

"The 'Zero Energy Universe Hypothesis' will help you to understand the Universe. It explains how you can get a Universe from nothing," added Kumaran.

"Were all the four fundamental forces, I mean, the electromagnetic force, the strong and weak nuclear forces, and the gravity force unified at the point of 'Singularity' before the Big Bang?"

"It has to be," replied Kumaran. He gave me a cold stare.

"Then why these four fundamental forces have not yet been united? I have not come across any proven theory that unites these forces."

"The '*Theory of Everything*'. Be in touch with it," said Kumaran brusquely. His voice sank a bit.

"Gravity is described in General Relativity, and the other three forces in Quantum Mechanics. Where is the '*Theory of Everything*'?"

"Science has not yet counted its last breath. In due time, the theory will be published. It is just a matter of time," replied Kumaran looking at me vaguely.

"Based on your arguments, I can infer that the Universe came from nothing (zero energy); the Big Bang triggered itself; the Universe is expanding itself. According to you, the Universe is a self-propelled 'entity' that needs no influencer, nor catalyst nor any intervention.

Can I apply this 'hypothesis' to God?"

"You better call it 'axiom' instead of 'hypotheses'. This is developed by none but science. You can develop your own 'superstition theory' to be applied to God," retorted Kumaran.

"'Axiom' is an unprovable rule and it is not a fact at all. Now let me put the verses of the Qur'an that speak about the 'evolution' of the Universe. The Qur'an says:

"Do not the Unbelievers see that the heavens and the earth were joined together, before we clove them asunder? We made from water every living thing. Will they not then believe?" [Qur'an: Al Anbiya 21: 30]

The 'influencer' is God Himself Who 'triggered' the beginning of the Universe. How can a 'union leader' postulate such a revolutionary theory?"

"A discovery in science has often been proved to be serendipitous for Muslims. Every time, an advancement in science drives Muslims to manipulate the Koranic verses to make it a lookalike of the scientific discovery! It's a culpable habit!" commented Phillip. He maintained a stiff gaze on me.

"Please cite an example to prove your point."

"The world is very much aware of the fact when Muslims instinctively intensified the voice to the level of shrillness to highlight the Koran as the pioneer of the *Big Bang Theory*.

Why did not you raise your voice before the birth of the theory?" Kumaran appeared half-fumed and lost the calm of his tongue partially.

"The *Big Bang* theory does stand nowhere in comparison to the stature of the Qur'anic verses. The *Big Bang Theory* stands diminutive in respect to the marvels present in the glorious Qur'an. Had we changed the meaning of the Arabic words, then most certainly it would have turned identical to the *Big Bang Theory*. However, the case turned up here no way bears any such likeness.

Muslims fear to change even a single jot of the Qur'an, for our souls *shake like a leaf* when the question of changing the verses of the holy Qur'an arises. We loathe the idea of changing the divine verses to avail any narrow service of an uncouth interest. We dare not to fiddle with the divine verses; we are not the people despised; we never intend to lead the mass *down the garden path*!

By the way, do you think, according to the Arabic word as mentioned in the Qur'an, that every living being was actually created from '*alcohol*', but with the advance of science, Muslims clandestinely and out of vile ego, changed the meaning of that Arabic word from '*alcohol*' to '*water*'? Is it?

Do you think Maurice Buccaile too did change the meaning of Arabic words of the Quranic verses prior to authoring his book "*The Bible, The Qur'an and Science*"? Do you think so?

If a verse (in Arabic) in the Qur'an says:

"*At the last leg of 1000 m dash, the sprinter started to flag*".

Do you think that Muslims earlier had interpreted the verse as:

'The sprinter raised his national flag reaching the finishing line'.

Now, they are interpreting the verse as:

'The sprinter became tired after reaching the finishing line.'

Do you think so?

You can think the way it pleases you. But the fact is that the Qur'an remains unchanged, and we welcome you to verify the Arabic version of any verse.

Do you think the *Big Bang Theory* is competent enough to detail the 'evolution' of the Universe?"

"What do you mean," Kumaran just shrieked.

"Is it competent enough to answer my queries?"

"What are your queries exactly?" inquired Kumaran.

"Does the *Big Bang Theory* obey the first and the second laws of thermodynamics?"

"Where is your doubt?" Phillip inquired irascibly. Kumaran was looking at me with wide-opened eyes.

"It is well-agreed that the point of 'Singularity' contained some matter in the form of extremely dense and hot condition. The thermodynamics first law states that, '*Energy can neither be created nor destroyed; energy can only be transferred or changed from one form to another.*'

Now the questions are: where did the matter accumulated at the point of singularity come from? How was that matter created? Does the occurrence of the *Big Bang* obey thermodynamics' first law?

Further, how the disorder of the *'Cosmic Explosion'* was controlled? I mean, how the disorder (Entropy) of a self-triggered '*explosion*' (not literally) was controlled so smoothly and orderly?"

"Time did not exist before the *Big Bang*. 'Time' is a dimension and started with the occurrence of the *Big Bang*. Time is positive and it moves forward only. Therefore, the validation of the thermodynamics laws and the physics start after the *Big Bang*. Your questions now stand absurd," Phillip concluded. He seemed temperate and stated his views with great cool and posh voice.

"Then, I would say that the *Big Bang Theory* actually does not deal with the '*origin*' of the Universe, rather it talks about the '*history*' of the Universe.

Who has given you the scientific prerogative to consider the 'origin' of the 'time' at the point of '*occurrence*' of the *Big Bang*?"

"Does the assumption *fly in the face of* your sense?

You can use whichever *word* that pleases you," Phillip reacted with suspended breath. His voice faltered and trailed off.

"All fine friends. Then, how the 'accumulated matter' in *Singularity* did form? Did it form automatically and out of 'nothingness'?"

"Does the Koran give you any convincing answers?" Phillip inquired jestingly.

"Muhammad (pbuh) did not find any such data in the science laboratory of the Roman Empire."

"Scientists are researching…toiling much on it; you need to be a bit patient," Kumaran replied posh.

"All right. One may ask, if the Universe was concentrated in an '*infinitely*' small and dense point, then, -

why the physical properties of the sun, the earth and the moon differ from one another? Why the earth arguably appears to have been the only habitable planet in the solar system (nay, in the Universe)?

Post '*Cosmic Explosion*', all the celestial bodies were catapulted into their present orbits. Then, how and when the planetary motions did come into existence?

Why the expansion of the earth stopped to the present extent?

Were all the celestial bodies concentrated into that so called '*Singularity*'?"

"The job of asking question is very easy and alluring. In this field, I find no one stands second to you," Kumaran mocked. My first question had already created a discomfiture, and this series of queries forced them to languish in a wound.

"I now remember the famous quote of Noam Chomsky who said once:

"*I was never aware of any other option but to question everything*."

Friends, questioning is a formidable tool with many rewarding results. It removes ignorance, discovers fool, exposes tyrant and exonerate truth from the clutch of allegations. As fire removes dross from gold, questioning eliminates falsity from truth. Analysis spurred by questioning could assay the correctness, the exactness, the precision and the purity of a subject under discussion. Questioning assails the vulnerability of a spurious 'truth'. If I adopt the easier way called 'passivity', I will be ashamed of myself.

The *Big Bang Theory* appears to fumble if pitched against these incisive queries. But, the Genius is genius; the Qur'an says:

"*Say: Is it that ye deny Him Who created the earth in two Days?...*" [Qur'an: Fussilat 41: 9]

"...and bestowed blessings on the earth, and measure therein all things to give them nourishment in due proportion, in four Days,..." [Qur'an: Fussilat 41:10]

The verses state that the earth was made habitable post 'separation'. So, the physical properties of the earth naturally differ from that of the sun, or any other celestial bodies. That makes sense and agrees with rational logic. The Qur'an further says:

"Moreover He comprehended in His design the sky, and it had been (as) smoke: He said to it and to the earth: "Come ye together, willingly or unwillingly." They said: "We do come (together), in willing obedience." [Qur'an: Fussilat 41: 11]

The verse clearly tells us that the sky was replete with smoke prior to the existence of the celestial bodies. The verse informs further that the planetary motions were induced into the bodies at a certain point of 'time'. Certainly, the 'motions' were not induced '*by chance*'.

The Qur'an further says:

"So He completed them as seven firmaments in two Days, ... And We adorned the lower heaven with lights, ..." [Qur'an: Fussilat 41: 12]

It is quite clear that all the celestial bodies were not at all concentrated in the extremely small point (Singularity) as 'implicitly' said in the *Big Bang Theory*. It can be inferred from the verse that the celestial bodies were created after the creation of the habitable earth.

"And the earth-We have spread it out." [Qur'an: Qaaff 50: 7]

The verse confirms that the earth was smaller at the time of 'separation', and later on, it was expanded to the limit of the present expanse.

The discussed verses provide astoundingly crucial scientific data about the 'evolution' of the Universe. I know, my declaration *flies in the face of* your obdurate belief. Undoubtedly, the Qur'an can easily overshadow the stature of the *Big Bang Theory*.

I would like to place a few more queries:

Is the General Relativity theory applicable for '*Singularity*'?

Is it true that the *Big Bang* occurred in a picosecond or so?

I seek confident assertion. I hope you would not resort to speculation."

"You need to think of the *Large Hadron Collider* which is simulating the conditions existed during that picosecond moment. You would definitely get answers.

By the way, how could you dare to say that the earth is the only habitable planet in the Universe?" inquired Kumaran.

He had flipped quickly through the statements made earlier by me. He fixed his eyes on me inquisitively, though his mind was wandering in the wilderness of imaginations. Seemed, we both were contradistinctively separated afar, and he was not ready to tolerate me further as his discomfiture were fast beading into something worse.

"The existence of another habitable 'place' is some sort of an immature imagination of scientists; the scientists are immured within childhood fantasy!"

"You have *gone off the deep end*!

Nothing sort of such extreme nonsense was expected, *least of all* you! Yours is an insane thought borrowed from… ." reacted Phillip. He rolled his eyes in exasperation!

He cut off the last word from the sentence and left it to my easy guess. The guess does not require even a lower form of merit; - even a careless guess could easily put forth an efficacy.

"Friends, I have not inferred this *in vacuity.*"

"Tame your inner rebel and quash the riot of senses," Kumaran simmered. He snatched a rude glance at me.

"Please do not rubbish my view. Let the maverick sense out of the silo,"

"Perhaps your irreverence for scientist has come out of the cage.

Do you think the quests of searching habitable planets need an urgent review?" stated Kumaran irately. He offered me a scowlful glance much in the same way as Phillip looked at me. I fenced off myself.

"Scientists, no doubt, deserve recognition and reverence. But a certain unseen sense prevents me from feeling envy towards the feats achieved so far by scientists concerning the Universe. I feel, they have just *scratched the surface* of the Universe notwithstanding the deployment of their brightest efforts.

Candidly, I persist to wonder at the profundity of the Qur'anic verses that talk at length about the 'evolution' of the Universe. Avowedly, I have no qualms about recommending the superiority of the Qur'an to *one and all.* The fact is that the world has failed envyingly to find any better match that can match the level of superiority of the Qur'an."

"A mole-hill, frenetically and surely out of sheer ignorance, has sumptuously highballed its own altitude while comparing with a mountain," Kumaran thrashed me. The kick of his boneless tongue broke virtually the strongest bone of my body. The metaphor was laced with causticity that could dislodge the calm and contentment of a settled mind.

"Friends, brilliant hits a target that a few can do.

Talent hits a target that no one can do.

Genius hits a target that no one can see.

But, the Qur'an hits a target that no one can even imagine.

Scientists have already collected a presentable measure of data concerning the Universe. It has been quite a long time and the outcome of the endeavours is known to *one and all.* Evidently, science has not been able so far to put up any optimism that vows for the existence of a habitable place. It is an *out and out* failure of the scientists.

Contrarily, if you ask me to quantify the '*probability*' of the existence of any habitable place in the Universe, affirmatively it is 0 percent"!"

"Is your inference infallible? Can it be wrong?" Kumaran pressed me for reply.

"Yes infallible!"

"Should '*space exploration*' be stopped?" Phillip inquired like a shot.

"If the purpose is to find a 'habitable place for human beings', then the answer is 'yes', –it should be stopped."

"Hail to you! Certainly, an opaque curtain of fanaticism is drawn fully upon you cutting out completely the light of knowledge forever. Seems rationality has stopped talking sense into you long ago.

I am forced to pull my tongue to utter that, -a slum-dog is trying hard to overshadow the brilliance of the scientists! A slum-dog, with a pocketful of knowledge, wants to give a nasty drubbing to the eminent scientists of the world," Kumaran thrashed me to his satisfaction. He threw razor-sharp criticism and assailed my views inconsiderately.

"Do you want to be awarded with the Noble Prize?" Phillip could not resist a nasty dig at me. I knew my 'stand' on space exploration would attract censure, but I endured it without irritation.

"Understanding the 'Evolution of the Universe' is not *a walk in the park*. Much criticism has already been heaped up on me, and I feel, it is reckless and *out and out* directionless.

Please tell me, why Stefan Hawking is not awarded with Nobel Prize?"

"The world knows it…Stefan Hawking has not been able to prove his 'discoveries' experimentally," Kumaran replied looking at me with sharp directness of his charging eyes.

"Now you are talking sense!

That means his discoveries happened to have based on '*scientific philosophy*' and cannot be proved experimentally. Philosophy had played an important role in postulating the kernel of the *Big Bang Theory*.

As I said, this is an inference drawn from the verses of the holy Qur'an. Let me put my view logically:

The Almighty took total 'Six Days' to complete the whole Creation.

He took first two Days to separate the earth from the heavens. Then, He took another two Days to make the earth liveable. And in the last two Days, He completed the creation and the decoration of the seven heavens. I want to emphasise that the Almighty took two Days to make the earth habitable, I repeat, it required two Days to make the earth habitable alone. How in the last two Days, He could have made another planet habitable in addition to the creation and the decoration of the seven heavens? It does not agree with any rational sense.

Further, the below verse states that the Almighty established Himself on the Throne after the accomplishment of the Creation. His activities of Creation '*ceased*' after six Days. He did not 'create' anything further. The Qur'an says:

"It is Allah Who has created the heavens and the earth, and all between them, in Six Days,…?" [Qur'an: Al Sajdah 32: 4]

I am still looking for an affirmation, or at least a cogent assurance from scientists about the existence of any habitable place, let alone the question of quantifying the probability of the same. The limpid truth is that science has not yet dared to announce something that could lessen doubts and kindle a fair hope. The fumbling of science has reduced my hope to despair. Perhaps, I have to wait till the Hour of the Doomsday which certainly overruns the allotted time of my life on the earth."

"I think there is a flaw in your logic!" Kumaran stated after a little cerebration.

"What is this?"

"The inference drawn is nothing but a by-product of the Koran, and I think it goes well arguably with the repute of an assumption. Though you have put forward your brightest cerebration in deducing it, yet it cannot be put side-by-side with the 'certainty'. It is not easy to unbox the riddle of the massive Universe.

As mentioned, making an 'earth-size' planet habitable requires two Days. I would argue that there remains a valid possibility of making another habitable planet quite smaller than the size of the earth in the last two Days. It may happen to be any celestial body -a smaller planet, or a satellite, or an asteroid, or even a small hyperbolic asteroid like '*Oumuamua*'.

The outright rejection of the presence of a habitable place does not cease to surprise us; it is really very hard on the ears!" Kumaran argued and placed his views logically.

"I have severed relation with both assumption and speculation. It is a rational deduction from the truth.

The *Oumuamua* is a homeless fast-moving interstellar rock and has been travelling continuously in the space like a tramp. It drew nearer to the sun at perihelion and headed fast away from it outgassing. Insane tumble and brazen rotation are the predominant motions of the *Oumuamua*. Its high axis ratio, slender chest, pointed nose and the faint glow do not make it eligible to be a member of an asteroid family. It is just a homeless rock born of self-disintegration of its parent, or out of a nasty knock unleashed by a rogue star. Once you land on the *Oumuamua*, you will be thrown violently off its surface!

Anyways, how did you assume that a fraction of the last '*two Days*' was surplus to the requirements of creating and decorating the seven heavens?"

"Did God divulge anywhere in the Koran that He took the whole of the last two Days to complete the creation and the decoration of the heavens? The verse stated above does not say so," replied Kumaran. Kumaran brought up the point *on the table*.

"What do you think, how much percentage of the '*two Days*' was surplus to the requirements of completing the creation of the seven heavens?"

"Let's say 25 percent of the last Day were surplus to the requirements", Kumaran made an optimistic assumption looking at me with a rapt glance.

"Do you think that the Almighty does not understand the 'vulgar fraction' and He casually rounded off 1.75 Days to 2.0 Days?

Anyways, if I go by your assumption, I can say 0.25 Day were in surplus that means 1/8th of 'the two Days' remained unproductive. It implies that the Creator still had time to make a habitable planet that measures 1/8th of the earth. If I place the draft copy of calculation at the gate of astronomy, it would suggest of a celestial body that is ½ of the moon, or 1/8th of the earth.

Do you know any celestial body that measures 1/8th of the earth?"

"May be certain satellites or even asteroids …!" Kumaran ideated ponderably.

"Do you think *Phobos* and *Deimos*, -the satellites of the *Mars*, might be suitable for human living?"

"Yes, might be," Kumaran nodded in optimism.

"But the reality does not stoke any optimism up to your idea. Both the satellites are not suitable for human living because they are devoid of atmosphere conducive for living. Moreover, the surface of Phobos (captured asteroid) has been pounded into powder by eons of meteoroid impacts. Furthermore, the Phobos is nearing to the Mars, and in the near future, it will either crash into the Mars, or break up into pieces.

You should look for other celestial bodies."

"Space exploration is not a one day job. It takes time and demands intelligence," added Kumaran.

"I am not insisting that science must immediately confirm the precise distance between the positive and negative charges of an electron. Science is conceptually clear about the existence of the electron's dipole moment, and with the enhancement of technical capability, if not today then tomorrow, science will be able to measure such excitingly precise data. That's all fine.

But the effort employed in space exploration is about six decades old, or so. How long will you toil in the barrenness of hope? The presence of a habitable place is just a fragile idea alloyed with clumsy anticipation and lame speculation; the concept itself is hazy and maladjustive to the temper of scientific discussion. It is like a siege of a long illness!

Even till date, I have failed to find any confident assertion from science about the existence of a habitable place?"

"Even Stephen Hawking mentioned the possibility of existence of aliens. He said:

"*If aliens visit us, the outcome would be much as when Columbus landed in America, which didn't turn out well for the Native Americans*".

Do you think this is a hollow statement?" Kumaran tried to persuade me.

"I think we can quash the 'rumour' right now. Phillip is the right person to confirm on the existence of 'aliens'."

"Why Phillip?" probed Kumaran.

"Jesus Christ (pbuh) is 'God', and he came on the earth and had countless interactions with acquaintances. He must had informed them about the whereabouts of the 'aliens'."

"Don't give any dysfunctional twist to the discussion," Phillip reacted.

"Does the question sound absurd?"

"Not absurd… it's preposterous," reacted Phillip irately.

"I think, the Father in heaven had perhaps sent his another 'begotten' son to be crucified in the lands of the aliens. Phillip must be knowing it."

"Your appearance matches the standard of a gentleman, but your conduct's decorum has been shaken off! You need to learn to refine your tongue. Do not try to dilute the spirit of discussion," Phillip reacted starkly.

"Anyways, my good man, the statement of Hawking does not interest me much as it lacks insights. The statement might have conquered you easily, but it has failed to prod me into agreement. It is hazy, vapid and does not seem enriching.

Hawking said that the aliens are superior to human beings. -

Is it an assumption, or a confirmation? Further to that, where do they come from?

I think these are loose assumptions made by Stephen Hawking. Whatsoever, I want to clear my stand that the word '*alien*' itself is a misnomer and does not go well with the stature of my rationality.

Surprisingly, I have observed countless people getting suddenly enamoured of the word '*alien*' as if a thousand of splendid dreams have mesmerised them. To my strong conviction, it is a powerful fiction to arrest the infantile imaginations of children, and its acceptance, at the most, remains valid in the messiness of clumsy assumptions and inside the premises of the fancy-filled film industries. The furore over the presence of 'aliens' is a bit melodramatic, and the speculation regarding the same could be anything but science.

But I have found insights in the below statement made by Stephen Hawking. He said:

"*Look up at the stars and not down at your feet. Try to make sense of what you see, and wonder about what makes the universe exist. Be curious.*"

Do you know, why and when do human beings become curious?-

Certainly, when the level of intelligence ceases to apprehend the intricacies and the complexities of something cogently, clearly and convincingly, then only appears the question of curiosity. We all, including Mr Stephen Hawking, are very much curious.

Friends, I detest the way you get infatuated with human brains. I never worship human brains the way you do. I worship the 'Brains' that produces the 'brains' of human beings."

"I wonder, and surprisingly, not a single Muslim country ever landed on the moon, even though, it has been a crazy vogue in landing moon on their national flags. Don't they sense any disgrace in their unattempted failures?" Phillip jibed. He expressed criticism disparagingly.

I lurched forward a bit as the remark *took me by surprise*!

"It's not quite apropos of the nature of the discussion. The question hardly bear any relevance to Islam; I shall not be drawn on such queries."

"I am not pitching you into discomfiture. Just keep your nationality aside for the time being, and frankly present your views from Islamic perspective," Kumaran insisted offering me the much-needed looseness.

"Well, my good man, I looked at both of them with my cool and composure, and narrated:

'The Moon does not support life. So, any exploratory attempt to find life on the moon is itself a superfluous attempt.'"

"Where did you find such unbelievable confidence?" Phillip inquired in a pejorative sense.

"Prophet Muhammad (pbuh) split the moon to still the brazen insistence of the unbelievers. Had there been any life on the moon, he would not have split it for sure. The Qur'an says:

"The hour has drawn near and the moon has been cleft asunder. …." [Quran: Al-Qamar 54: 1-2]

The verse is profound.

Gentlemen, it will be a different debate altogether if you are striving to establish an orbital-tourism around the moon."

"Is there any evidence to this miracle?" Phillip pressed me.

"Is there any evidence that Jesus Christ (pbuh) raised Lazarus from death?

"Lazarus come out!" "He came out,…" [Bible: John 11: 43-44]"

The evidence is still present at Bethany (West Bank). You can flit around the world to make yourself richer by an experience," Phillip replied fittingly.

"This is merely a view and in clear contradistinction to reason. After all, this is not an evidence, but a speculation.

The world witnessed the splitting of the moon. Moreover, the world has not dared so far to question the purity and the authenticity of the Qur'an.

By the way, do you have any evidence that refutes the claim?"

"The one who is claiming should prove," said Phillip.

"Was the moon split half and distanced apart?" probed Kumaran.

"So you said."

"Had it truly occurred, the chance is, the split parts would have becomes satellites of the sun, or the sun would have gulped them down," added Kumaran arguably.

"But it did not happen so.

Please tell me why the moon does not revolve around the sun, though the sun attracts the moon with the force which is more than double the force of the earth on the moon?"

"The gravitational acceleration of the earth on the moon is much higher than that of the sun on the moon. The earth dominates the moon," stated Kumaran.

"The extension of *Hill Sphere* of the earth is about 1471000 kilometres, and the distance between the earth and the moon is about 384400 kilometres. The moon is placed comfortably well in the gravitational sphere of influence of the earth.

Even if the moon is split apart, it will be well within the *Hill Sphere*. So, the question of moon being snacked by the sun does not fit the sense of astronomy."

"When split, what happened to her motion?" asked Kumaran questingly.

"It was a miracle done by the Almighty through the Prophet."

"This is the difference between you and me,…the line *'you and me'* ideologically is oxymoron. The *'you'* believes in miracle whereas the *'me'* believes in science. *'You'* heralds miracle, and 'me' hails science.

'Miracle' is that event where intelligence *makes itself scarce* and gets locked with superstition in a tight embrace," criticised Kumaran.

"Motion dynamics of the moon during the event remained unaffected, else, by logic, any perturbation in her motion would have certainly affected the whole motion dynamics of the solar system at least."

"The flow of your logic is manifestly smooth *like a knife through butter* trampling down the stringent conditions required to satisfy the cogent asking of science. Does it require any thought, experiment or any great evidence to prove the veracity of the 'miracle?" retorted Kumaran.

"Science experiences setbacks when asked to explain phenomenon like 'miracle'. Miracle is not a superstition but a phenomenon that demands excitingly higher level of intelligence, ingenuity and a well-coordinated plan of execution. Science falters here.

The moon has already been visited by some mighty countries. The endeavourers must have collected lots of scientific data that could be utilised to envisage a proof to refute the claim of the Qur'an. Please ask them if they do really have any counter-evidence …I am really burning to know it."

"Is your claim sacrosanct?" Phillip pressed me.

"Of course yes."

"Obstinacy does know no medicine that could negate its soaring effect except the passage of time," commented Kumaran.

▪ **The Moon Cannot Be Made Habitable!**

"The moon is just a *stone throw* from the earth. It is lovely, enchanting but plastic. It has been entreating human beings, fashioning entreat as a challenge, to make her habitable.

Scientist have *cudgelled their brains* failingly to find any presentable response to the challenge."

"Tunnel vision!" reacted Kumaran strongly.

"You have already made several touchdowns on the moon and taken many remarkable strides towards the exploration of the moon's surface. Henceforth, an obviousness is looking forward to hear from you about the findings. -

Can the moon be made habitable?"

"Exploration is an ongoing process. Science is not an overnight success...it requires time," responded Phillip.

"Is it an attempted failure?"

"Unattempted failure is disgraceful," retorted Phillip.

"The Qur'an declares that the moon is made for time-reference for the inhabitants of the earth.

"...He makes the night for rest and the sun and moon for the reckoning of time: ..." [Qur'an: Al-Anam 6: 96]

Needless to say, if the moon is made habitable, certainly, the inhabitants of the moon will no longer refer the moon itself to calculate the time. The integrity of the verse will fall down and the Qur'an will cease to be true!"

"Science is an offence to you...that much I could say," reacted Phillip.

"I know your view about the moon is hung painfully somewhere at an ambiguous edge that swings between speculation and confirmation.

Friends, you should *wipe the slate clean* and start looking at the moon with fresh vision. You should *take up the cudgels* for your own defence as your genius are constantly hit by the Qur'an!"

- **The Doomsday!**

"Friends, can you tell me the exact time when the Doomsday will occur? Can scientists predict it correctly?"

"One day the Universe will come to a stop. This is known to all," replied Kumaran.

"Your view perfectly matches with the Qur'an, and we all know that. The Qur'an says:

"The hour will certainly come; there is no doubt; yet most men believe not." [Qur'an: Mumin 40: 59]

But, my question is, when will it occur?"

"Why are you so eager to know the date? What is great in it? Is there something seriously critical to marvel about?" inquired Kumaran.

"Please ask the scientists to predict the date. I am eager to know if they are capable to challenge the Qur'an."

"Suppose no one can. Then, how is it going to benefit you?" Kumaran questioned.

"The benefits are rewarding and manifold. The most important one is that the Qur'an will remain unchallenged in the contest. And, no one can panic Muslims by spreading false predictions. Nowadays every Tom, Dik and Harry, taking full responsibility, starts predicting the date of the Doomsday. It spreads panic and terror into the hearts of common people. But it fails to inject any tremor in the hearts of Muslims, -Muslims remain the least affected of all. The Qur'an says:

"They ask thee about the Hour, ..Say: "The knowledge thereof is with my Lord alone. None but He can reveal as to when it will occur. ..." [Qur'an: Al Araaf 7: 187]

The audacity of the verse has certainly overshadowed the excellence of the scientists. Scientists will never be able to confirm the date of the Hour.

But, the Qur'an, in many verses, has clearly given the hint of occurrence of the Hour, and it will occur very soon."

"Very soon?" wondered Kumaran.

"Yes...very soon.

The following verses were revealed fourteen hundred years ago.

"The Hour has drawn near and the moon was split in two." [Qur'an: Al Qamarb54:1]

"...then they will shake their heads towards you and ask, "When will that be?" Say, "Perhaps it is soon."'"..." [Qur'an: Al Isra 17: 51]

The verses hint clearly the nearness of the Hour.

Do you find this revelation astonishing?"

"How can it be astonishing until you confirm the Date?" snubbed Kumaran.

"What, according to you, might be the life of the earth before the Hour? Could you predict?"

"Perhaps you have got an excitingly precise prediction...!" mocked Kumaran

"Yes... and, perhaps, it does not go beyond one thousand years."

"It will thrust an astonishment into the calibre of science," mocked Kumaran.

"What's your view?"

"One thing looks to be sure that by the time the Hour overwhelms the earth, human beings would lose existence due to the cumulative effects of multiple events. Global warming is one of them. The threat is menacing and its effects will snowball rapidly rendering the earth inhospitable. The next in the league is, that has made scientists legitimately worried, the hitting of a giant asteroid…it could wipe out the human race," added Kumaran.

"Not really! The earth would not be devoid of human beings, rather it would be teeming with them. The Qur'an says:

"The Trumpet will be blown and …all those on the earth will fall dead;…" [Qur'an: Az Zumar 39: 68]

The Hour would take human beings by a nasty surprise!"

"Let the verse be yours and the science be mine," observed Kumaran.

"Could you tell me, how is it going to occur?"

"Cosmologists have postulated many theories on the ultimate fate of the Universe. One such theory concerning the future of the Universe is known as the "*Big Crunch.*" It says:

"*The universe will one day stop expanding. Then, as gravity pulls on the matter, the universe will begin to contract, falling inward until it has collapsed back into a super-hot, super-dense singularity,*" stated Kumaran.

"The expansion of the Universe is accelerating or decelerating?"

"Obviously accelerating," replied Kumaran with a blazing confidence.

"Then, how the expansion will slow down and reverse? Which factor will trigger the Universe to *get through* the deceleration to meet its ultimate fate in the form of the *Big Crunch*?

Do you think that the reversal of the 'Big Bang' theory will occur? Do you think that the whole Universe will shrink back to the so called 'Singularity'?"

"Gravity will overcome the expansion; the Universe will shrink into a Singularity," replied Kumaran.

"Do you think that 'time' will still be positive? As Phillip said earlier, 'time' is a dimension and positive only, and it is associated with the expanding Universe.

Do you think that the 'time' will still remain positive with the contracting Universe?

By the way, how a continuously inflating ball will suddenly start shrinking? Will someone suddenly start extracting energy already pumped in?"

"The theory says that the *density of matter* in the Universe is quite high and that might trigger gravity to overcome the expansion of the Universe," reflected Kumaran.

"Scientists say that the Universe started expanding about 10^{-32} of a second after the *Big Bang*. Scientists further state that the rate of expansion of the Universe at present is comparatively faster than the rate observed after the *Big Bang,* and it is so because of the presence of *dark energy*. According to LAMBDA-CDM model, the rate of expansion will transition into dominance in future.

So, how the expansion process will suddenly reverse?"

"May be, once the critical density of all matter is reached, the *Big Crunch* will occur," replied Kumaran. His tongue sputtered to a stop.

"To reach critical density, do you need extra energy from outside the Universe? If so, who would provide it, and what would happen to the validity of thermodynamics first law?

Friends, '*Big Crunch*' is hypothetical and not a guarantee. Other camps of the scientists are not in perfect agreement with the theory."

"One can clearly see your receding to the central nature of Muslims. As expected, now you would pull up the Koran to the heralded-elevation of the 'Big Freeze' theory in an effort to present the Koran as the trailblazer. It's a bizarre adventurousness indeed!" Phillip added with a curt voice.

"The Qur'an is dwelling in ultimate elevation…the Qur'an has worked its way up the summit. Please state the *Big Freeze* theory, and then I shall present the verses of the Qur'an."

"The '*Big Freeze*' theory states:

"*The expansion of the Universe will continue forever. If so, the Universe will cool as it expands, eventually becoming too cold to sustain life. This theory requires the Universe to be either flat or negatively curved. It maintains that the universe will expand forever, getting colder and colder.*

As existing stars run out of fuel and cease to shine, the universe will slowly and inexorably grow darker. Eventually black holes will dominate the universe, which themselves will disappear over time as they emit Hawking Radiation. The 'Big Freeze' is a scenario under which continued expansion results in a Universe that asymptotically approaches absolute zero temperature."

Now, let me summarise:

1. The Universe will expand continuously;
2. The Universe will expand forever getting colder and colder;
3. Stars will run out of fuel and cease to shine;
4. Universe will eventually grow darker giving birth to black holes which eventually disappear over time as they emit *Hawking Radiation;*
5. The Universe will reach absolute temperature and cease to hold life.

Now, the turn goes to you," stated Phillip. He cast a sanguine glance at me.

"The series of events that would immediately precede the 'Doomsday' have been hinted clearly in a quintessence form in the Qur'an.

"It will be no more than a single Blast." [Qur'an: Yaasiin 36: 53]

"At length, when there comes the Deafening Noise," [Qur'an: Abasa 80: 33]

"When the Sky is cleft asunder;"

"When the Stars are scattered;"

"When the Oceans are suffered to burst forth;" [Qur'an: Al Infitar 82: 1-3]

The verses hint that the initiation of 'The Process' will start with a 'blast' or a 'deafening noise' and that will be the forerunner of the Doomsday.

The verses assert that the Universe will face a massive convulsion depicting whirlpools of frenzied violence.

Will the Universe keep on expanding at that moment? - I am not sure.

So, the verses do not explicitly go against the point no. 1) and 2) of the *Big Freeze theory* that supports the concept of continuous expansion of the Universe.

The Blast will then be followed by a series of catastrophic convulsions. The Qur'an delineates beautifully:

"He questions: "When is the Day of Resurrection?"

"At length, when the sight is dazed,"

"And the moon is buried in darkness."

"And the sun and moon are joined together," [Qur'an: Al Qiyamah 75: 6-9]

"When the sun is folded up;"

"When the stars fall, losing their lustre;"

"When the mountains vanish;" [Qur'an: Al Takwir 81: 1-3]

Darkness will dominate the very moment as stars will lose lustre. The sun will die; the moon will plunge into darkness and eventually be subsumed in the 'powerful field' of the dead sun.

The verses go *hand in hand* with the point no. 3) and appear agreeable to point no. 4).

Further, inference can be drawn from the verses about the thermal condition of the Universe. As darkness prevails, the temperature of the Universe eventually may slip into an abyss.

Here, the Qur'an gives a tacit agreement to point no. 5) of the Big Freeze theory.

Do you still think Muslims tuned in the Qur'an to the tune of the Big Freeze theory?

Why does the Qur'an not explicitly agree with point no.1) and 2)?"

"That does not mean that the Koran is right and the Big Freeze is wrong. How could you be so sanguine about the ultimate fate of the Universe that would end in the occurrence of the Big Blast?" queried Kumaran.

"The famous scientist Alexander Friedmann (Russian Mathematician and Physicist) developed the matter dominated dynamic equation of the expanding Universe (1920 CE) where he postulated three possibilities about the future of the universe. In his equation, the 'Density Parameter' ($\Omega=0$ (*flat Universe*, may expand forever), $\Omega>0$ (*closed Universe*, universe will stop expanding), $\Omega<0$ (*open Universe*, will expand forever)) represents the future of the universe.

The Friedmann equation indicates that the global (spatial) geometry and the fate of the universe can be either of the above three cases. The 'density parameter' (ratio of observed density and the critical density of the universe) determines the overall geometry of the universe.

The objective to present Friedmann here is to evidence that the scientists too are not much sure on how the Universe would end. It has almost been a perpetual habit of science to come up frequently with new theories only to dump them later in landfills. Nowadays, the least of rational minds talks about the *Big Crunch!*"

"It is evident that the sources of light will be lost and the earth will be engulfed by darkness. How then your God conduct the affairs of the Day of Judgement?" Kumaran inquired with polished lampoons.

"The earth will be illuminated with the light of the God. The Qur'an says:

"*And the earth will shine with the light of its Lord:....*"

[Qur'an: Zumar 39: 69]"

- **Resurrection!**

"Resurrection is a fact or fiction?"

"Do you have any empirical evidence for that?" demanded Kumaran.

"Why do you think that the empirical evidence is the only evidence that can be considered as cornerstone to judge something?"

"The truth depends on it, and I do accept it as it touches upon the reality," replied Kumaran.

"Have you done the DNA test to verify whether your father is actually your biological father or not?"

"I believe my mother, -she is beyond doubt. But, the reality is that I can also verify that through DNA test," Kumaran stated in affirmative tone. He asserted his point.

"Friend, think of the thousands of past generations when the DNA test did not exist at all. They just believed in the sanctity of their mothers' words."

"You mean that you believe in Resurrection because the Koran asks you to believe in? If this is your logic, then I find myself happy being susceptible to unbelief," Kumaran stated expressing dissatisfaction.

"Do you believe in *Big Bang Theory*?"

"Yes I do," affirmed Kumaran.

"Did you witness its occurrence?"

"It is publicly heralded and scientifically proved," replied Kumaran.

"How can you believe that without watching the occurrence of the *Big Bang*? Don't you think it is a mismatch to your conviction?

Your reply drives me to infer that, *at the end of the day*, you have to have believed someone to believe something.

As you do believe the scientists, so I do the Qur'an. Many a time, scientists make mistakes, but *there is no mistaking* the Qur'an is infallible. It does not make mistake."

"He is unnecessarily heralding the vapid verses of the Koran. I have a solid proof; -Jesus was killed on the Cross and later he came back to life," Phillip placed his point almost interjecting me. He tried to *take the wind out of my sails*.

"Does the Bible say so?"

"Yes," replied Phillip haughtily.

"Friend, I would definitely discuss on this after a while.

Unbelievers' usual cry is, 'when we are reduced to bones and dust, how can we be brought to life?' The Qur'an reports the verbatim questions of the unbelievers:

"They say: "what! When we die and become dust and bones, could we really be raised up again?" [Qur'an: Muminuun 23: 82]

In response, the Qur'an replies:

"But does not man call to mind that We created him before out of nothing" [Qur'an: Maryam19: 67]

"Does man think that We cannot assemble his bones?"

"Nay, We are able to put together in perfect order the very tips of his fingers." [Qur'an: Al Qiyamah 75:3-4]

In the verses above, the Creator has put the adamant attitude of unbelievers on the 'frying pan'. But in the following verse, the same has been taken from the 'frying pan' and put directly on the 'fire'.

"Assuredly the creation of the heavens and the earth is a greater (matter) than the creation of men;...." [Qur'an: Mumin 40: 57]

The unsentimental directness and rational incisiveness of the verse could directly hit the human intellect. The job of creating a human being can be accomplished playfully…it is very easy for Him."

"How the fingertips of Canadian born gangster Alvin Karpis will be arranged perfectly? He had removed his fingertips in a surgery," Kumaran perhaps mocked. His voice linearly trailed off.

"His DNA profiling is stored and already known to God. He can arrange his fingertips perfectly to that finest pattern he was born with. If human beings can record fingertips without any physical contact (Scanning Kelvin Probe-SKP), then just think of the calibre of God who created human beings.

It is a sign of ignorance if the designer of a space shuttle is asked whether he is capable to re-design a bi-cycle, which he has already designed and developed.

Many simple yet radical ideas shake the very foundation of reality-centric-knowledge. For most humans of the 15th century, the notion of Earth as ball of rock was something of nonsense. The book '*Biocentrism*' by Dr Robert Lanza (best known for his ground breaking work on stem cells), shatters the humans' ideas of life, time and space and even death. It releases us from the dull worldview that life is merely the activity of an admixture of carbon and a few other elements. The theory releases many dogmatically Darwin minded human beings from the notion of '*by chance creation of life*'. The Biocentrism suggests the exhilarating possibility that life is fundamentally immortal. The author has placed life at the apex of universal existence instead of considering it as an accidental by-product. 'Biocentrism' shakes the fossilised beliefs and views of readers about the reality. The theory would provide the readers many shocking new perspectives that the reader will never see the reality the same way again.

Life is an adventure that transcends our ordinary linear way of thinking. When we die, we do so not in the random billiard-ball-matrix but in the inescapable-life-matrix. Life has a non-linear dimensionality, – it's like a perennial flower that returns to bloom in the multiverse. '*Theory of Biocentrism*' (Quantum Physics) says that the death is merely a change of form of state.

So, death is not 'the end'!

Many mistakes have happened to science, but mistake itself has become a 'misnomer' when it comes to happen to the Qur'an, -the Qur'an is infallible. The Qur'an says:

"That this is indeed a Qur'an most honourable,"

"A Revelation from the Lord of the Worlds."

[Qur'an: Al Waqiah 56: 77, 80]

Now, please apprise me, how all these 'scientific data' could have been mentioned in the Qur'an more than fourteen hundreds years ago?"

"I find a keen sense urging you incessantly to uphold the Koran as the pioneer of science, and at the same time, an insolent eagerness constantly instigating you to disavow the feats of science achieved so far in magnificent level. A dreary habit that misuses one's intellectual resources looks poised to provoke you to oversell the Koran, no matter what if it has to belittle the eminence of the science, or to exploit the adventurous efforts of scientists employed so far.

Since the absolute absence of God rules my mind, the science alone determines the course of my outlook and the tilt of majority of population determines my disposition, so obviously a 'Book' produced by an unlettered Arab, in the times of ignorance, cannot coax me into giving in to its insensate demands," assailed Kumaran.

"A tree is known by its fruit," Phillip made a sharp.

"What do you mean?"

"It's all about the 'originality' of the Book. Had the Koran been original, then most certainly its scientific temper would have been reflected amongst Muslims. Plagiarism does not lustre, neither does it appeal, nor does it drive. It may offer you stingily a pocketful of sunshine, but not the generosity of the sun. Muslims are *barking up the wrong tree*," criticised Phillip.

"Who is Avempace?"

"He was a scientist born in Spain…that much I do know," answered Phillip.

"Being the possessor of '*…that much I do know*', how come you could say that the Qur'an failed to unleash its scientific temper amongst Muslims?"

"Do you think he is Muslim?" inquired Phillip loudly. It was suggestive of a shriek.

"Yes. 'Avempace' is the latinised name of 'Abu Bakkar ibn Muhammad ibn Yahya ibn as-Saigh at-Tujibi ibn Bajja' (1085 -1138 CE). He is known for his works in astronomy, physics, botany and medicine. His works in astronomy influenced Galileo Galilei. He introduced the idea that talks about the sex of plant.

Now, think about Averroes. Ibn Rushd (1126 -1198 CE) is latinised as 'Averroes'. He was the author of more than 100 books and treatises. He wrote about many subjects including medicine, astronomy, physics, philosophy and mathematics. He wrote a medical encyclopaedia called '*Kulliyat*'. The West renamed it as '*Colliget*'.

You should think about the father of modern medicine 'Avicenna' (980 -1037 CE).

Regrettably, the real names of those great scientists have been buried under the deep cover of obscurity. A very few could identify them as Muslims.

I can give you examples of many great scientists inspired by the Qur'an. Where you were, when Muslims scientists, inspired by the Qur'an, were reigning over science?"

"What about now –Newton, Plank, ..? Where are you now?" retorted Phillip.

"Newton, Plank, …have not been inspired by the Bible. They perhaps distanced themselves from the Bible. I think their choices are right."

"'Distanced *themselves*'…means? Are not you belittling the Bible?" Phillip made rapid inquiry.

"Please park this inquiry for a while. I would discuss on this a bit later."

"Do you still doubt the originality of the Qur'an?"

"Where are you now?" Phillip pestered me again evading my question.

"First, lift up the sanctions imposed unfairly, -you cannot expect a tree to bloom if deprived of water."

"Do you still doubt the originality of the Qur'an?"

"I am not in denial. The question itself turns up as irrelevant for me," responded Kumaran looking at me with vague eyes.

The reply inflicted a cruel befuddlement on me, offering little or almost no clarity, in a sense, to understand his inner stand. I was assailed by the ambiguity of the reply, and I failed to find any clear-pointed direction in his heading. His denial was quite sharp and clear, but his inner alignment looked steeped in deep vagueness. His reply was steeped in ambiguity, his expression was clouded with enigma and he himself was enshrouded with cryptic hints. I failed to find out the right one and ended up drawing more than one interpretations about him. The burden of the confusion made my sense half-extinguished!

"Seems it, a person is stuck miserably in a comet which is a light year away from the earth. The ice of the comet is sublimating fast to vapour rendering the comet eventually in a state of disintegration. The desolate figure is left in a pitiless condition and crying aloud for help… asking for a magic spaceship that would transport him safely to the earth. Your condition resembles that…," added Phillip fretfully.

He gave me a way cool stare ...copious by amount, blazing by appearance, obstinate by direction...seemed it a brazen mountain-spring rolling down with an indecent mood.

"Insensate remark, -it is widely out of the way!

Neither did I urge you to bring in a sudden change in your notion, nor did I beg a favour for the Qur'an. Yes, I requested you to prove the Qur'an wrong ...and well, that is the highest ceiling of my expectation.

Friends, I invite you both to come out of the dull shell of denial and deploy your best intelligence to counter the Qur'an. The opportunity is poised favourably in your way to test the sublimity of your intelligence, incisiveness of your arguments and above all, the authenticity of your assumed superiority. Do not fumble the opportunity, and if still think that the 'Koran' is a bluff, then you must *call Koran's bluff* to the challenge! You are called upon to showcase the flair of your genius!

If your ego has not fettered you to denial, and if the denial has not blinded you to facts, then you would certainly find that the Qur'an is truly *out of the ordinary*."

"You should not hastily ink an agreement with the divine authorship of the Koran, because the time is very powerful and capable enough to conduct a tough test. May be, one day, as the rains wash away colony of loose soils resting on a stone, the time will see the Koran receding into oblivion withered and graceless. I believe, in the future, Muslims would hear many dreadful news when their boastful ways of religious thinking get rejected one after another conceding total disenchantment to their enamoured hearts. On that day, Muslims would make a face! They would murmur in isolation realising how foolishly had they misplaced their intellectual resources in the illusory radiance of the Koran," Kumaran pinned his hope on the lap of future and boastfully tried to retain the aura of his arrogance. Then he gave me simmering glance copiously.

He appeared giddy with a welling of self-satisfaction. I found a sparkle in his eyes and a fiendish smile on his lips. Both lightened his heart to a great extent.

"In the Qur'an, the Lord is literally entreating you to *call to mind* the very fact of your creation from just a drop of a quintessence fluid. Then, He reminding you further, how He formed you with great care in stages in the layers of darkness in your mother's womb. How can you ignore Him? Allah (swt) says:

"Was he not a drop of fluid emitted?" [Qur'an: Al Qiyamah 75:37]

"He makes you in the wombs of your mothers in stages, one after another, in three veils of darkness. That is Allah –your Lord! ….How can you then turn away?"

[Qur'an: Az-Zumar 39:6]

He created Adam (pbuh) from a simple mix of soil and water. Then He created Eve (pbuh) from the body of Adam (pbuh). He created Jesus Christ (pbuh) with His 'words'. Then He transformed His technique of creation completely into a new one where a quintessence drop of fluid is enough to create a human being in the womb.

Do you doubt that He would not be able to create you again? Do you think His techniques of creation have reached exhaustion? Would He not be able to create you again from the lump of bones of your body burnt (or buried)?

Here in the verse, the Lord has set his tone in a unique normal and almost getting tearful. It has been in my constant conviction that it is much easier eliminating the plight of poverty than removing the obstinacy of arrogance; I have again realised it correctly."

"I would like to quote here H. G. Wells (English writer, 1866-1946), who says:

"*Then for four years more until his death in 632, Muhammad spread his power over the rest of Arabia. He married a number of wives in his declining years, and his life on the whole was by modern standard unedifying. He seems to have been a man compounded of very considerable vanity, greed, cunning, self-deception and quite sincere religious passion. He dictated a book of injunctions and expositions, the Koran, which he declared was communicated to him from God. Regarded as literature or philosophy the*

Koran is certainly unworthy of its alleged Divine authorship." (A Short History of the World: XLIII. Muhammad and Islam, 1922)

The last sentence spans the true aspects of the Koran. Hope you can fathom the rest," stated Phillip haughtily.

"What does the sentence '…*and his life on the whole was by modern standard unedifying*' mean?"

"Just look at the preceding part of the sentence, '*he married a number of wives in his declining years*', -it speaks about deviated principle and detestable morality of Muhammad," Phillip iterated exploring the disparagement encrypted in the excerpt.

"Friend, I wonder how a person who led debauched lifestyle could judge a person who led an austere lifestyle full of challenges and missions. It does not call forth sensibility. How could he judge a person who always carried the best pattern of conduct and borne always an unblemished character never found in others ever born on the earth**?** It is no longer hidden, rather the world knows that H G Wells had affairs with a significant number of women. He seems to have been a man of heightened debauchery.

In the last sentence of the excerpt, he denied the Divine origin of the Qur'an. Would you please apprise me what sort of conviction led him to conclude that?"

"What do you want to know exactly?" Phillip inquired making eye contact.

"My good man, forget the Qur'an for the time being, now please tell me, is there any Divine Book that Mr Wells read?"

"The Bible is the Divine Book," Phillip jostled to show the divine authorship of the Bible. Then, he appeared frozen and his tongue seemed reluctant to utter anything further …his tongue just sputtered to a halt.

"Please, cite some verses that support its Divine authorship."

"There are many verses in the Bible in fact.

"God stretched out the northern sky and hung the earth in the empty space." [Bible: Job 26:7]

The verse displays a profound knowledge that hints the presence of the gravitational force.

"...and the fish of the sea that pass through the paths of the seas." [Bible: Psalm 8:8]

The verse hints explicitly the existence of ocean currents that help fish identify the path they travel through," added Phillip.

"I too have quoted numerous verses from the glorious Qur'an that speak about astounding scientific facts. Don't they convince you about the Divine origin of the Qur'an?"

"The time gap between the Bible and the Koran is almost six hundred years. The Koran, in all fair assertions, poised be a product of plagiarism. We have had already enough of time on the topic," Phillip replied with a collected cool. He murmured out copious disapprovals.

The unsentimental directness of allegation, the haughty exertion of tongue clearly showed that Phillip permitted his belief to remain frozen in this stupor forever.

"Well. Now, I am announcing that the whole Qur'an is from God, -every word of the Qur'an is the word of God.

Could you announce the same for the Bible? Is the whole Bible from God?"

"What do you want to prove?" asked Phillip.

"Do you think that the following verse is also from God?

"When he threatens the pillars that hold up the sky, they shake and tremble with fear." [Bible: Job 26:11]

Is the sky supported by 'pillars'?"

"You cannot understand the Bible with suspended sense. You should not scramble to snatch an honour for the Koran. I wish some sense should jostle you to a realisation!

Do not scratch the surface of the verse, –you need to penetrate it to reward yourself with the insights deep-delved here. On the surface, it seems a laughable stuff.

Now tell me, when do you require 'pillars'?" probed Phillip.

"To prop up an object against the gravity."

"Pillars are required to resist 'pull force'. Here, the verse, through allegorical use of the words 'pillars', has implicitly indicated the existence of the 'gravitational force'. The verse is simply great and insightful," stated Phillip. He gave me an uncharacteristic smile.

I looked at him in awe! I was searching for faithful rationality present in his 'axiom of wisdom'. My astonishment murmured in disapproval on thinking that 'how cunningly he converted an antiquated verse into an antique piece of science!'

"The verse of the Qur'an is an antipode to the Biblical verse.

"God is He Who raised the heavens without pillars." [Qur'an: Ar-Rad 13:2]

What do you think about the verse of the Qur'an? Does the use of the words '*without pillars*' reject the existence of the 'gravitational force'?"

"It shows clearly that Muhammad plagiarised the Biblical verse and tweaked it," alleged Phillip. His lips pulsated a bit. His eyes rolled.

"Does the tweaking impair the logic of science?"

"Perhaps, Muhammad had observed a pillar-less balloon clung to a suitable hover above his head. I believe that he tried to bend the incoming honour of the Bible towards the Koran. That's why he added the word '*without*' in his crookedness to get the Biblical verse tweaked," lampooned Phillip with a sass.

Phillip clung obstinately to his views like limpets cling morbidly to a loose rock against the ferocity of rapids. In his brashness, he submerged wisdom by obstinacy and promised aid to the fumbling verse. Surprisingly, he maintained a cool disposition even after flouting the sense of rationality with blatancy; no sign of guilt intruded into him at all.

"Friend, 'pillar' resists the '*pull force*' which is predominantly one-way. '*Pillars supporting a roof*' –means that the earth attracts the roof towards its centre and the force of the earth's attraction is predominantly higher than the force of the roof exerted on the earth. But '*a pillar-less roof hanging above the earth*' means that the pull forces exerted on each other get balanced, meaning the force exerted by the roof on the earth is equal to the force exerted by the earth on the roof.

Just think about the 'gravitational interactions' between the earth and the moon. The moon does not fall on the earth like an apple.

Do you think Mr Wells read the Qur'an before drawing the conclusion, '*regarded as literature or philosophy the Koran is certainly unworthy of its alleged Divine authorship*' as mentioned in his excerpt?

This is the glorious Qur'an –intrepid, independent, ingenuous and incomparable! Truly the correctness of Mr Wells' choice suits the mood of pulp fiction.

Now, I am asking you both, which verse fulfils the bizarreness of fiction, and which verse complies with the temper of science?

Which Book would you offer to your children to foster scientific knack –the Bible or the Qur'an?"

"If you want to breed distemper in the minds of your children, then offer them the Koran!

It does not surprise me any more when Islam claims that it alone has a monopoly on the truth. Such kind of thought embraces bilge," responded Phillip. I saw a palpable irritation running on Phillip's face.

"Yes, certainly! There is an honest substance in the claim. The absolutism of truth is steeped in Islam, because it inherits a divine vein! Now, *the ball is in the court* of intellectuals, masters and geniuses who are athirst for challenges.

Mr Wells had proved himself deft in writing fictional science though failed miserably to apprehend the real world and the affairs pertaining to this office. I too laud his ingenious skills and deftness in creation of fictions, but could not resist myself taking a dig at his bleak performance in understanding the real phenomena of science. He subconsciously invited attrition to his own ingenuity that eventually blunted his scientific temper. He allowed his faculty to rust!

Prophet Muhammad (pbuh) never dealt with fictions. He was born to deal with the affairs purely pertaining to reality. In fact, fiction attracts infantile mind and in that sense, neither the character nor the temper of fictions ever interested the Prophet. In his capacity as the last and final Messenger of God, he confronted with the prevailing ignorance and the intolerance of his immediate tribes and the tribes around. He put his conscience in the right place to pull up the decaying conscience of the superstitious society sunk into the quagmire of abominable practice of burying alive the female children! He felt the stings of women degradation, debauchery, drunkenness, lawlessness, bloody skirmishes, tribalism and many countless savage cultures that plagued the society before the advent of Islam. Hardships and adversaries followed him like shadows and put up numerous determined obstacles to thwart and intimidate him. But he *turned the corner* from despair to optimism in both fronts, -in liberating the society from the clutch *of ignorance,* and in executing the Divine Project assigned to him.

With all fairness, I can say, Mr Wells is a well fit to comment on affairs that concur with fiction because it encourages things like bizarre imaginations, irrationalities and infantile infatuations that cater elegantly for childish amazement. Dealing with reality is not his *cup of tea*!

The last sentence *'regarded as literature or philosophy the Koran is certainly unworthy of its alleged Divine authorship'* has clearly exposed his indolence in effort, inadvertence in attention and indisposition in sincerity to explore the marvels of the glorious Qur'an. It happens when a floating cyst in eye blemishes the vision.

The following verses were presented to Keith L. Moore, a distinguished embryologist and author of several medical books (Professor, University of Toronto), who verified the correctness of the verse revealed in the Qur'an fourteen hundred years ago.

"Read in the name of your Lord Who created;

Created human being from a clinging clot" [Qur'an: Al-Alaq 96: 1-2].

Did H G Wells understood the verses the way Professor Keith Moore understood?

I cannot stop my wonder as it does know no end when I think of the sense of Mr Wells in giving divine certificate to the Bible and denying the same to the glorious Qur'an. I am left to remember the single word about Mr Wells that has done this great mischief in him is 'egoistic'! An obstinate ego has intruded mischievously into him!"

Chapter 3

"Creation, Destruction and Resurrection -in this reversible cycle, God has outrageously displayed an autocratic attitude towards the humankind. It seems, as if, Hitler too contributed his clairvoyance to the drafting of the Plan.

My astonishment stops nowhere whenever I try to search the purpose of the Creation. The trilogy of '*Creation, Destruction* and *Resurrection*' does not mesh well with my sensibility and repeatedly fails to convince me the correctness of the Creation. The purpose of creation quickly goes *way over my head* proving itself as formidable riddle that I, time and again, fail to crack. And, *in the end*, my questing efforts *all the way* go *up in smoke.*

My wonder does know no end and wanders in the labyrinth of twisting roads to find any smallest sign of presence of the Creator. My eyes droop in a faint and my soul retreats wearily into self-isolation in failing to find Him. In my search, I always encounter the deafening silence and the absolute absence of God. His indifference towards His own Creation has been a theological conundrum that always outsmarts and tricks even the best of my ingenuity. It appals and preys upon me constantly.

He demands worship for Him alone and that, I think, has earned Him the reputation of a jealous. The life is a drag to live and to live in this world is itself a melodramatically a big thing. The life here on the earth, at least, is not a cinch. The world has degraded to a ball of mess and is pitched miserably against a hard border where disorder, distress and hardship set in to transition to the next punishing level. Just look around with incisive eyes and adroit mind, you would certainly find a sea of bad things and an island of good things. The grievances are unending, the list is quite long," Kumaran stated. He heaved a sigh of relief.

"Put your grievances into words. Why don't you communicate to God?" I began in a provoking manner, "Surely you would be enriched by an experience."

"Please communicate on my behalf to your beloved God," Kumaran replied jestingly casting a niggardly glance at me.

"Sure, I will," I began, "Please dictate me in writing."

To Mr God,

I seek Your attention.

You seem to have slipped into the deeper state of slumber after the great event called the Creation. Your 'believers' (one hard-core fanatic is present with us) praise You to the sky. He has bored me with his indefatigable efforts in glorifying You as the Most Merciful, the Most Gracious, the Most Caring, All Wise, All Knowing, and all that. But, the reality speaks something different and portrays You as an maladroit Lord who has failed to execute the human affairs the way it should have been executed. Our hopes have been dashed, expectations have been frustrated, asking have been denied, and now the Creation is crying in the wilderness of hopelessness, chaos, and disorder. The stage is set in to hit the skids.

If I go by the words of Your admirer present with me, then, -

1. Why weak and innocent are being suppressed and oppressed by the mightier?
2. Why the poor starve to death?

3. Why children are born stunted, mentally challenged and physically handicapped?
4. Why does not your punishments come instantly on the wrong doers?
5. Why suicide bombs, atomic bombs and many lethal and devastating weapons are coming into existence?
6. Why natural calamities like earthquake, cyclone, tornedo, famine, flood etc. come down heavily on the earth?
7. Why does 'Islam' sound terrifying? Why has your intended religion badly degenerated to detestation?

Kumaran,

An unbeliever

Dear Children of Adam,

I received yours. To lead off, My 'beginning' had never begun and My 'end' shall never end, –My existence is 'Absolute' and not fettered to the feeble coordinates of the 'time-and-space'. I am the 'Absolute'… yes your read is right,… and the factors like laziness, fatigue and slumber never dare to intrude into Me. They have been introduced to the earth given with the charge of wearing you out linearly to the brink of old age. They all retire after achieving the summit of their assailing interplay that gives way to death. I did reveal in the Qur'an:

"Allah. There is no god but He,-the Living, the Self-subsisting, Eternal. No slumber can seize Him nor sleep ..." [Qur'an: Al Baqara 2: 255]

I created the earth and the heavens and everything between them in the best mould providing all necessities in exactly due proportions. I endowed human beings with many sublime features and elevated them as unique race amongst My creations. I am the reason for your existence. Had I gone into slumber then certainly you all would have been reduced to heaps of scraps.

Now let Me clear your grievances.

1. Why weak and innocent are being suppressed and oppressed by the mightier?-

I am asking you,

Who sold the innocent black people of Africa to America, or to any European countries for slavery? -

Certainly their own fellow human beings.

Who bought the black fellows for slavery? -

Some human beings who boast of superiority and flaunt fairer skins! I revealed in My last revelation that:

"O mankind! We created you from a single (pair) of a male and a female, and made you into nations and tribes, that ye may know each other. ..." [Qur'an: Al Hujurat 49: 13]

The verse is great and profound like the sky. As the vastness of the sky does not know the east and the west, as its unblemished blueness does not loathe the presence of the dark clouds, so is the verse of the Qur'an that transcends all the petty forms of colours, caste, tribes and nationalities. It rises above all human manufactured discriminations and treats all equally with grace and love. I revealed the verse aiming to instil love, kinship and bond into you so that you may refrain from the smallness of dislike, pettiness of pride and meagreness of self-centric attitude. Revealed in the verse and many places elsewhere in the Qur'an that I grow likeness for the righteous because I love righteousness.

Unfortunately, human beings have trekked the wrong path rejecting the entreatment of the verse. Importance of righteousness is buried deep in the dark corner of a barren landscape and none cares to heed its soulful cry. Life is adrift here, righteousness is receding, ambient is inclement, conscience is placed at the hands of crookedness, depravity has topped the list, -I am seeing humanity bursting from inside and crying of anguish. Even the colour of skin has made a good inroad into the sphere of human intolerance, -people *look down upon* people and people enslave people! Passage of numerous civilisations have failed miserably to offer the essential correction to oppressions, injustice and indiscrimination. The past civilisations had been *a crying shame* for you because they did nothing much to eradicate the ignoble practices from the psyche of the societies. Rather they retreated silently from the obligatory duties of touching up the defects of human societies.

Just think, why Abraham Lincoln (16th President of America) was assassinated? -

I too issued the '*Emancipation Proclamation*' as mentioned in the verse below to abolish slavery.

"*... Give a slave his freedom. ...*" [Qur'an: Al Maidah 5: 89]

Efforts flopped in finding My whereabouts and they retracted the murderous tentacles spread out in My search. But Lincoln was on the earth and tasted the outcome for advocating the '*equal rights theory*'.

History is inhabited with many such incidents. Search deeper and you would find notorieties welling up inside them. They are set in like '*sleeping cell*' lurking behind to transition into cruelties anytime putting on the uniforms of militancy to eliminate the dangers that challenge their *status quo*.

Why Nelson Mandela was made 'jail-slave' for long 27 years? -

I know you do know the answer. Do you think apartheid is less than a plague?

Hitler purified the Germans by killing mentally and physically challenged people. The tradition is still alive but wrapped in a euphemistic word called 'Euthanasia'. Physically retarded and less privileged are considered nuisance to the society and have been subjected to dark glance and harsh voice. Indeed evil has acquired a place adjacent to your conscience.

Would you kill Stephan Hawking suffering from Cerebral Palsy?

Why are you so averse to sharing this planet with handicaps or people differently-abled? Where has gone the *milk of human kindness*? Have your cup of compassion and camaraderie been exhausted? If it is so, then better you create another planet for your 'private living' and I promise, I shall give you a space in My Dominion free of cost. Or else, if you do have scientists of My Calibre, let them make the Moon habitable, -the moon too will be offered *on a platter*. But mind that, I have not given you any authority to enslave or kill any innocent and physically less privileged human being. Earth is My Property, and I am the Absolute Owner of the earth.

The oppressors have been allotted a certain period of peaceful respite. One day, torment will surely befall them and no one in the entire Universe would be of any help. I have clearly mentioned in the glorious Qur'an:

"Let not the Unbelievers think that our respite to them is good for themselves: We grant them respite that they may grow in their iniquity: But they will have a shameful punishment." [Qur'an: Al Imran 3: 178]

I have just allotted them a little respite, -let them be sunk deeper into sins, let the cup of their iniquities be full. Surely, they will be *brought to their knees* in humiliation.

2. *Why the poor starve to death?-*

Your way of classifying people is little short of insulting that clearly lacks sagacity. The prevailing definition of 'poor' is peculiar and falls victim of skewness. I sometimes wonder at your thoughts employed in differentiating people like -rich or poor, highborn or lowborn, highlander or lowlander, king or slave, opulent or indigent, ingenious or ignorant and so on and so forth.

Whereas I categorise people like —'believers' and 'unbelievers'. That's all. Financially laggards are called poor by you, but laggards in 'Faith' are called 'poor' by Me. An 'unbelieving' Nobel Laureate is immensely respected by you, but an 'illiterate, righteous who worships Me only' is far nobler to Me.

I will respond honouring the angle of your complaint.

The earth is provided with a great measure of necessary resources. I have mentioned in The Last Revelation:

"… bestowed blessings on the earth, and measure therein all things to give them nourishment in due proportion…" [Qur'an: Fussilat 41:10]

My Public Distribution System (PDS) is well thought of, structured, equitably poised to provide service and benevolence to all. I revealed in the Holy Qur'an:

"Those who … spend (in Charity) out of what We have provided for them, secretly and openly, hope for a commerce that will never fail:" [Qur'an: Fatir 35: 29]

The verse has found its numerous repetitions in the Holy Qur'an as to draw your attention to the importance of charity. If every 'rich' spends 2.5 percent of savings, then the poverty will make a quick egress from the earth. Plight of poverty will think twice to return.

I have solicited the rich (on behalf of the poor) to spend in charity deemed to be a splendid loan to Me. A few have honoured my solicitation, but most of them behave like purported transgressors overcome by the nasty power of avarice. They find better attraction to the glitters of this world. I revealed:

"The (material) things which ye are given are but the conveniences of this life and the glitter thereof; but that which is with Allah is better and more enduring:…" [Qur'an: Al Baqara 2: 245]

The real prosperity does exist in giving not in amassing. Charity does not deplete the coffer rather fills it further in many ways… some real and some surreal. Wealth is ephemeral and multiplies itself in the malpractice of profiteering that gives a delusionary self-satisfaction to its depositors. Avarice is a curse in the disguise of indulgence that knows no bound and stops nowhere, -it plays with the mind like a delusion and preys the mind like a hunter. It is an unseen double-edged vile sword. Wealth is enticing like exotic dish, alluring like glamour, but is actually a tangle that ensnares the animal of avarice! Regrettably, human beings have failed to understand the wile of the wealth!

The poor must not envy of the wealth and grandeur enjoyed by the rich. The 'believing poor' should bear in mind that the 'Gift' of their Creator is grander and far more superior to the worldly glitters and grandeur. I revealed in the Qur'an:

"Strain not thine eyes. (Wistfully) at what We have bestowed on some of them, nor grieve over them: but lower thy wing (in gentleness) to the believers." [Qur'an: Al Qasas 28: 59]

The 'believing poor' should be patient and steadfast in remembrance of their Lord. For sure, the Promise of their Lord will never fail, but surely be fulfilled.

Your economy policy is partial and heavily slanted towards the rich. It facilitates to flatten up the coffer of the rich by draining the purse of the poor. The rich rise to opulence by amassing interests accrued on the deposit, and the poor fall to destitution paying the interests incurred on the loan. With guaranteed safety and security, the sum, with each passing day, keeps on growing proffering a golden hand to the rich to opulence. The system puts the rich on the wheel rolling in wealth leaving the poor flagrantly *out in the cold*!

You can easily sense the 'wrong' in your system by looking at the shrinking stomachs of the poor shrieking loudly for your attention clung fondly to the bulging bellies of the rich! Despair in their eyes, enfeeblement in their voices, flaccidity in their muscles, paleness in their faces all these speak lots about your system! The system offers a cold indifference to the poor.

I would cite some examples of your skewed economy policy:

About 0.13 percent of the world's population controlled 25 percent of the world's financial assets (Global Issues 2004).

The poorest 40 percent of the world's population account for 5 percent of global income. The richest 20 percent account for 75 percent of world income (Global Issues 2013).

About 51percent of the world's 100 wealthiest bodies are corporations (Global Issues 2006).

The world's billionaire just 497 people (approximately 0.000008 percent of the world's population) were worth $3.5 trillion (over 7 percent of world GDP) (Global Issues 2006).

The existing system has two outcomes: one is 'bright' and the other is 'blight'. The 'bright' goes to the rich, and the 'blight' goes to the poor. 'Bright' becomes 'brilliant' and the 'blight' becomes 'bleak'.

If you still do think that the existing banking system is sacrosanct, then you need to shift your focus on the statement made by Jean Tirole (Nobel Laureate, Economics 2014), who said,

"*Banking is a very hard thing to regulate and we economists, academics, have to do more work on this.*"

His statement converts to believe that the current policy needs correction.

The world's wealth balance is remarkably lopsided. Even in the twentieth century, almost half of the world's children live on the poverty line or below it. According to Global Issues 2013:

Number of children in the world was 2.2 billion and out of which 1 billion children were on the brink of poverty. Means every second child was in poverty. If every rich spends in charity then the demon called 'poverty' will make a quick egress from the earth. I revealed in the Holy Qur'an:

"O ye who believe! Devour not usury, doubled and multiplied; but fear Allah..." [Qur'an: Al Imran 3: 130]

"If ye do it not, take notice of war from Allah and His Messenger. ..." [Qur'an: Baqara 2: 279]

I am not going to drop atomic bomb from the heaven, but will inject 'psychological weapons' into you. There is no one above and beneath the earth to stop Me in executing My Action. If I intend, I can seize your hippocampus and can inflict diseases like *Alzheimer's*, *hypoxia*, *medial temporal lobe epilepsy*. No 'hi-tech' available in the whole Universe that could revive your dead neurons, because it is I Who has developed this machine and it is I Who knows how to make it defunct beyond repair. Who is there to stop Me if I intend to subject you to *cerebral haemorrhage*? I informed you:

"By no means shall ye attain righteousness unless ye give (freely) of that which ye love;" [Qur'an: Al Imran 3: 92]

I provide wealth to whom I wish as to test who amongst you are righteous and who are rapacious. My solicitation bears the resemblance to– 'a master requesting his mightier pet to share food with its siblings. But no amount of request of its master could dodge the dogged determination of the domineering dog until and unless it is whacked on the head'.

Hunger is the biggest killer on the earth. Your irresistible lust for wealth pushes your fellow human beings to the edge of abysmal poverty. Every day more than 22000 children die of hunger. Only 20 percent of the rich use 76.6 percent of products for their private consumptions, and 20 percent of the poor use only 1.5 percent of products for their private consumptions! This is the outcome of your economy policy! You have *taken the rise of* the poor!

Just think, why have you failed to curb '*economy recession*' in spite of having hundreds of Nobel Laureates in economics?

Actually, it's a clear '*economy swindle*' designed and developed by the rich! The system can never minister to the poor!

3. *Why children are born stunted, mentally challenged and physically handicapped?-*

Have you created any '*Sputnik Moment*'[4*] being healthy and able-bodied?

Which better feat have you achieved being good-sighted than the blind Greek bard Homer?

I understand the angle of your complaint. -

Do you not often find beautiful newborns in dirty dump yards?

Do you not often hear the news of newborns flushed out in toilets?

Are you not aware of the numbers of foeticide and aborticide done by human beings?

Are you not the same human beings who kill mercilessly unborn babies in the wombs, but shed crocodile tears seeing the scene of a fawn being killed by a pack of foxes? Are you not those hypocrites?

My repeat warnings on illegal sex have faded away into deaf ears and faced a tough defence of cold indifference. Debauchery and 'free sex' have been glorified weirdly and welcomed grandly as the new normal of your social life. I informed in the glorious Qur'an:

"*Lost are those who slay their children, ….*" [Qur'an: Al Anam 6: 140]

Had I guaranteed you that no child would be born as differently abled, then surely the human beings would have done full mis-utilisation of My promise. They would have kicked the 'womb' to verify the truthfulness of My promise! The womb of an expecting mother and the punching-pad would have become *one and the same!*

Why have you forgotten to mention the havoc created by human beings? What about Hiroshima-Nagasaki? -

That fearsome 'Little Boy' (name of the atomic bomb dropped on Hiroshima) that killed 70000 people instantly and another 70000 people after five years still raging beastly in the track of remembrance. The 'Little Boy' did cost you $2b and gifted you 140000 skulls in return! Do you think the 'Little Boy' did not kill or mutilate any little children? It took the lives of thousands of innocent little children and created indelible scars into the psyche of human race! Do you think I dropped those atomic bombs?

Do you remember Chernobyl Disaster?-

Around 6.9 million people were exposed to radiation. Thousands of children were afflicted with thyroid cancer due to high dose inhalation of Caesium-137 and Iodine-131 radioisotopes. Do you think I caused the disaster?

The list is long!

Had I made the moon habitable, surely you would have already made a hat-trick in dropping atom bomb after Hiroshima and Nagasaki!

1. Why does not your punishments come instantly on the wrong doers? -

This is a fatuous complaint and barren of insights. I suggest you must give a serious thought to it. Anyways, if I approve your grievance, then the scene on the earth would dwarf the scene of Hiroshima and Nagasaki! Doom will engulf the whole earth so much so that not a single human being will be left behind to stand by your coffin to mourn over your sudden demise. I revealed:

"If Allah were to punish men for their wrong-doing, He would not leave, on the (earth), a single living creature: ..." [Qur'an: Al Nahl 16: 61]

But I have just granted a little respite. Every act will be justly compensated.

2. Why suicide bombers, atomic bomb and many lethal and devastating weapons are coming into existence?-

I did not send Adam with atomic bombs, neither with any Intercontinental Ballistic Missiles (IBM), nor with the Fractional Orbital Bombardment System (FOBS). Nor did he land on the earth with a stealth fighter aircraft.

Moses too was not equipped with any nuclear deterrent submarine.

Neither was Muhammad sent with the $E=mc^2$ foreshadowing the development of nuclear bombs.

All My innocent Messengers were sent on the earth to disseminate the Divine Message. They were sent to guide the human beings on the right Path, -the Path that I have chosen for you all. I revealed in the glorious Qur'an:

"Do no mischief on the earth, after it hath been set in order, ..." [Qur'an: Al Araf 7:56]

The earth is thumping on its orbit fearing constantly mischiefs on your part. Menacing examples are being set every day in disguise of '*war for peace*' through the cowardly display of live performance of sophisticated weapons on innocent civilians of weak countries. Libya is a burning example. Indeed your lust for power and avarice for money have thrown the essence of humanity into an abysmal disgrace.

World War I, II, Crusades, attack on Vietnam, Iraq, Afghanistan, Libya have shown your slant for war and highlighted your abnormal affinity for destruction. To My dismay, and it really pains Me, when I see My sublime creation has failed repeatedly in finding peaceful options than waging war against each other. Seems, the base instinct of a wilder beast has intruded rudely into human beings. 'Shame on you' when you do boastfully place the option of war *on the table.*

You have happily forgotten to mention the most devastating weapon that has been killing 8000 people every day. ARA (AIDS Research Alliance), NIH (national Institute of Health, America) and many dedicated organisations have been toiling to find the cure of this lethal weapon. Billions of dollars have been sunk. I instructed you to treat 'sex affairs' in the most modest way possible but you replied it with *free-sex*-therapy covered with glossy insignia of modernity. Your carnal-festivity has turned into a cancer in society.

Do you think Adam carried the lethal virus of AIDS from the heaven? Just think, what could have happened had Adam carried the virus?

Have you heard about Swaziland (a sub-Saharan country)? -

In 2004, the country suffered an AIDS crisis with 38.8 percent of tested pregnant women infected with HIV. The residents of Swaziland have the lowest documented life expectancy in the world and it is just 31.88 years. In 2006, the prevalence of HIV/AIDS in Botswana was estimated at 24 percent for adults.

A virtual 'hell' is created here on the earth. Do you feel any remorse for creating such 'lethal crop' on the earth?

Do you think I helped someone create these?

3. Why natural calamities like earth quake, cyclone, tornedo, famine, flood etc come heavily on the face of earth?-

What else should I send from the Heaven? -

Should I send ambrosia for your majestic lunch, or nymphets along with antique champagne bottles for your high-octane nightclub jamboree laced with spine-tingling music and soaked with light-kindled liquor?

No nation is left where I did not send My Messengers to invite people to the Straight Path. Regrettably, they were ignored and *given cold shoulders,* and many were treated beastly, and many were slain for no reason at all. I sent My mercy again and again and lastly, I sent My greatest mercy in the form of Muhammad.

Muhammad is an 'Idea', -yes, he is a 'divine-idea' sent for the mankind. The 'idea' unquestionably is the most prized creation of your Lord. The 'idea' is sublime by conduct, supreme in power, premier by position, pre-eminent by reputation, tender by character, compassionate by nature, altruistic by outlook, sweetest by tongue, golden by heart, respectful by eyes, humble by demeanour, gentle by touch, celestial by talk,….and many more. He is the way, he is the light, he guides you on the Path that leads unto Me,…and he is My beloved. Deprived is he who has distanced himself from the 'idea', -loss is yours, and the loss is core. Human race without Islam is like a fruit without pulp and with the seed cursed at the core!

Travel the earth and you will find numerous evidence of My revenge, -the evidence are galore with many piquant stories. I did not spare them who annoyed and humiliated My Messengers. They vilified My Messengers, I vanquished their pride *for donkey's year;* they slain my Prophets, I slaughtered their existence from the earth. They were left but humbly succumbed to the rigour of My revenge. I am severe in punishment. I revealed in the Qur'an:

"As to those who deny the Signs of Allah and in defiance of right, slay the prophets, and slay those who teach just dealing with mankind, announce to them a grievous penalty."

[Qur'an: Al Imran 3: 21]

Do I sound Fascist? Actually, I do have the rights to be a Fascist. It befits Me only!

The other way around, it is My plan to test you through many hardships. I revealed:

"Every soul shall have a taste of death: and We test you by evil and by good by way of trial. To Us must ye return." [Qur'an: Al Anbiya 21: 35]

Paradise is not an easy availability. I test believers through many ways as I wish.

4. Why does 'Islam' sound terrifying? Why has your intended religion badly degenerated to detestation?-

You too have coined many words that are but terrifying by nature. It can make one to *shake like a leaf* in anticipation of fear! The words sound fascinatingly fearsome, and the way they sound simply prevaricate the actual meanings.

'*Angle of attack*': Generates aerodynamic lift.

'*Black box*': Flight recorder.

'*Dirty dozen*': Inventors of the first IBM PC.

The singular style of coining words amazes Me, and at the same time presses Me to ponder over the nature of your skewed way of thinking.

I too coined the word 'Islam' for My Intended religion and it sounds soothing, agreeable and invites serenity. It is simple and straightforward. As there is a fine pencil-line between 'simple' and 'simplistic', so is between Islam and peace.

Yes, I can understand the angle of your complaint.

Dog can even rough up Nelson Mandela if caught with bomb dropped in his pocket surreptitiously by a rogue. Dog possesses programmed-only, one-dimensional intelligence linearised simplistically to fit the brain-curve exclusively suitable for a dog. Such is the brain dog is given with. You must also be aware that a dog can even be faithful to Hitler.

But I have bestowed human beings with brains peerless and poles apart. The purpose is, -you must put it to analyse problems complex and complicated. It kindles in Me an emotion that erupts in utter disgust when I find human beings stumble blindfolded into the clutch of vile propaganda conceding swiftly whole soul and total intelligence in allegiance to the blatant propaganda that targets Islam. They love to live in the constricted corridor of outlook and find instinctive aversion to applying the sublime brains bestowed with. It fires Me with wrath.

Yours is a sophisticated one and finely blended with excellent grains of intelligence to enable you to investigate complex cases suchlike. That is why your brain is placed qualitatively and functionally poles apart. For sure, it cannot be displayed in exhibition *side-by-side* with the brain of a dog.

If the Pacific Ocean is found to be carrying corpses, would you slander the Ocean?-

Certainly, this is not the fault of the ocean; the ocean is innocent.

Islam was strange to the people even at the time of Muhammad. Many resorted to animosity and designed countless schemes to kill Islam at its nascence. But failure consoled them as they always failed to scuttle the ship.

They planned, I too planned and undoubtedly I am the best of planners. I revealed:

"And the unbelievers plotted and planned, and Allah too planned, and the best of planners is Allah." [Qur'an: Al Imran 3:54]

Resistance, propaganda and hatred have been constant companions of Islam. They never leave Islam alone but follow like shadows and wing frequently fusillade of their characteristic shots at Islam. But, with the passage of time, as shadows get killed by light, the anti-Islam family of things too get vanquished by the intellectual light of Islam. Islam gives them a terrible letdown in a loving manner.

Do you find anything terrifying in the Qur'an? Does the below verse commingle with brutality?-

"We ordained therein for them: "Life for life, eye for eye, nose or nose, ear for ear, tooth for tooth, and wounds equal for equal." But if any one remits the retaliation by way of charity, it is an act of atonement for himself. And if any fail to judge by (the light of) what Allah hath revealed, they are (No better than) wrongdoers." [Qur'an: Al Maidah 5:45]

Yes it is but at the first glance. It is horrific; it befits uncivilised societies. The verse is antithetical to humanity and fosters a thought that encourages counter-enlightenment. It suits the societies where civilisation has never descended upon. Such sorts of innumerable thoughts might be jerking your mind, - right?

But, call to mind, it is the same civilised human society that supported the attack on the whole country for a crime of an individual! At that time, the ghost of humanity intruded very rudely into them. Is not it freaky?

The mercy encrypted in the verse has not been deciphered properly. If you delve deep into it, you would find that I have placed immense mercy in it. My Intention is not to fill the earth with injured, wounded and physically incomplete human beings. The verse itself acts as a powerful deterrent and is capable enough to preserve the law of the land.

Think of the atomic bomb –it creates fear and acts as deterrent. It retards the wild flame of a dispute from culminating into a war.

Likewise, the above verse is just a psychological weapon!

Do you have any complaint about the verse below? Do you think the verse supports incitement to violence? Does it frighten the peace away from your mind?-

"Remember thy Lord inspired the angels (with the message): "I am with you: give firmness to the Believers: I will instil terror into the hearts of the Unbelievers: smite ye above their necks and smite all their finger-tips off them." [Qur'an: Al Anfal 8: 12]

Well, the verse was revealed against the backdrop of a battlefield targeting the unbelievers who had taken deep plunge in insolence, inequities and betrayal against the fledgling Muslim community. Horrors of unspeakable oppressions carried out against Muslims. Believers were buried neck-deep in scorching desert and forced to profane Islam. Many were left to the mercy of pitiless desert with hands tied with legs until they withered away to a frail piece of dry wood. Rather than be praised by the untidy tongues of unbelievers, they preferred to be killed. This is a small example that could make you aware of the nature of brutality inflicted on the believers. The verse is all about to stand against oppressions and tyrannies.

Look at the verse below. I revealed the verse concerning the life of an innocent human being. Nowhere will you find the likes of this.

"--- if any one slew a person - unless it be for murder or for spreading mischief in the land - it would be as if he slew the whole people: and if any one saved a life, it would be as if he saved the life of the whole people". [Qur'an: Maidah 5: 32]

Here in the verse, I speak on a note of great compassion that I nurse for the mankind. The verse speaks aloud about the intensity of My love for you. It placates mind with safety, it soothes soul with tenderness, it tends heart with love and it elevates human beings to attain the highest peak of humanity.

Nothing is enough to do enough justice to My favours bestowed upon you, even the seas as ink would exhaust to write all the high praise for Me. In short, nothing is enough to write enough about Me.

The answers to the following questions could actually develop a formidable dose of antidote to your sickness of conceiving Islam as terrifying.

Why Islam is racing ahead in the contest? Why Islam is the most accepted way of life in the world?

If truthfulness is the elemental grain of your character, if fairness is the undercoat of your instinct, then surely the questions will activate you to think if really something has gone wrong in your thought process. I have bestowed you with an independent brain, -preserve its liberty and do not let it be enslaved to the service of others.

I like to remind you again that I am the 'Absolute Owner' of the earth. It is My Property. There is no one, in the whole Universe, even in the Universe that you could imagine in bizarre dreams, to have any iota of share with My affairs. I am your Lord, your God and the God of the all worlds. It is I alone Who decides the affairs of the worlds, and you do not have any say in this regard. I revealed in the Qur'an:

"O ye who believe! Fear Allah as He should be feared, and die not except in a state of Islam." [Qur'an: Al Imran 3: 102]

The world has never had better principle in guiding human beings rightly than selfishness. As food is laced with sleeping pills, as drink is spiked with alcohol, so are the people in this world who have been tricked by the glitters and deceived by the artificiality. As insects get instinctively attracted to light, they too get happily dragged and trapped at the very centre of a glamorous labyrinth full of attractive delusions that produce nothing but a morbid tenacity in pursuing lofty boast and false pride. They are blown aimlessly like critters in the wind.

Possessor of feeble minds, holders of tenuous resolve and the men of lesser understanding are singing the parody of this world with full-throated ease.

Here death roams freely and preys at will and does spare none. The stint on the earth is just the testing phase of the life, - the final return is to Me, -surely, you will return to Me. Surprise aside, this is not the fable taken from the Arabian Nights, nor is it plucked from a deep obscurity, rather the 'Fact' was reborn as 'Islam' in the Arabian Peninsula. So, I entreat you to trek My way before leaving the earth ... it is the best for you if you really keen to understand. And, never sink into disbelief about the following verse, neither dare to *trifle with* it.

"*Do you think that We had created you without any purpose, and that would never be returned to Us*?" [Qur'an :Al Muminun 23:115]

Certainly, the mission of the verse will come into action once your breath counts its last. It is not a null warning!

The Creator

Allah

Chapter 4

Kumaran appeared self-composed and still like a submissive shell. His appearance was out of the ordinary and hardly guessable. The change, if any, did not lick his placid face; I made varied guesses to detect his inmost upheaval but failed.

I heard the sound of silence that whispered into my ears and slipped a few suggestions to me to guess at Kumaran.-

Was he close to erase the name of super star Darwin from his enamoured heart?

Was he pushed at the crossroads to welcome the rejection of Darwinism?

Barely had I completed my guesses, Kumaran suddenly bounced and interjected:

"The reply could not still the hunger of my questing mind.

It is entirely fanciful...it nearly *jumps out of my skin* and preys upon me like nightmare whenever I conjecture the scene of the *Day of Judgement* where God Would preside over the Chair, the gruesome hell, the glamorous paradise, the Hereafter and all that rigmaroles. It nauseates me even to think of such tenebrous affairs reserved for us.

It appears perfectly fine and appropriate if those are crushed into the works of fairy tales that defy logic and usher high-class fancy for children. The tale is fantastic and has all the necessary ingredients for audience engagement. The actors namely the God, Muhammad and the Koran who inhabit the tale are outstanding!

Wonder ruffles rudely the calm of my mind whenever I think of these amazing brain-children of the Koran!"

He cast a niggardly glance on me in a half-contemptuous manner. Kumaran woke up putting on his natural pattern of conduct displayed all the way in the discussion. By the way, he appeared *as right as rain*.

"Has the science denied the existence of Hell and Paradise?"

"Do you know precisely where do they exist in the Universe?" Kumaran imposed the question on me by tweaking slightly.

"Do you know the exact address of the earth?"

"Everyone knows the address:

Name: The Earth

Designation: The world,

Tribe: Planet,

Nearest identification landmark: The moon

Extended Family: Solar System,

Orbit location: Third Planet of the solar system

Galaxy: Milky way

Lane: Orion Arm,

Cluster: Virgo Supercluster," Kumaran stated.

"Friend, the Virgo supercluster is a local supercluster and it is no more than an elongated patch in the map of the Universe. The earth inside the supercluster, if exaggerated, seems like a tiny blue dot, or something even smaller than that. It is, no way, easy to find the Hell and Paradise in the Universe that contains more than 200 billion galaxies."

"Do not belittle the progress of science; -it has made a huge leap forward in the field of astronomy. Do you expect that the scientists should start searching Hell and Paradise believing blindly the idea of Muhammad?" Kumaran reacted temperately.

"I love science and never intend to belittle it. Unlike you, I do believe that science too has its limits.

The deep-space images from Hubble show that the observable Universe contains ten times more galaxies than thought previously. And imagine, how many galaxy do exist beyond the observable Universe?

The earth is just a tiny blue dot in the Universe. The biggest known star of the Universe is *UY Scuti* whose diameter is 2, 37,600 crore kilometres and can gulp down 4 billion suns at a time. It is 5219 light years away from us. Even with a magic spaceship that travels even faster than the speed of light, you will never be able to reach the UY Scuti, let alone the Hell and Paradise."

"Then, you must announce the sites of Hell and Paradise as prior information to scientists," insisted Kumaran.

"The Paradise is located at the seventh heaven. The holy Qur'an says:

"*Indeed he saw him (angel) another time by Sidrat-ul-Muntaha (at the Lote Tree of the most extreme limit in the seventh heaven) near which there is Jannat-ul-Mawa (the Paradise of Abode),....*" [Qur'an: An Najm 53: 13-15]

We are not meant to travel there. Not even a splendidly magical spaceship could ever do that wonder. In fact, even a 'capable spaceship' would not succeed to enter the premises of the heaven...it is well-guarded by a mighty defence! The Qur'an says:

"*And We have adorned the lowest heaven with lamps and made them as missiles for devils...*" [Qur'an: Al Mulk 67: 5]

The verses cited above, if analysed, clearly hint that the divine endowment of visiting the heaven goes to the Prophet Muhammad (pbuh) only."

"I find in you an obdurate insolence that looks down upon the excellence of science. Science will commit suicide at the announcement that Muhammad visited the heaven!" taunted Kumaran with his usual derogation. Perhaps science has given him final authority to derogate from the glory of the noble Prophet.

"Science commits suicide when an atheist 'affirms' that human beings are merely 'filtered animals'!

Prophet's journey to the heaven comprises two different stages as described in two different chapters of the Qur'an namely

Al-Isra, and An-Najm. The former speaks about his journey on the earth (Mecca to Jerusalem), and the later speaks about his journey to the heaven. And that happened in a single night.

"*Glory be to One Who took His servant by night from the Sacred Mosque to the farthest Mosque,*" [Qur'an: Al Isra 17: 1]

"*And he certainly saw that 'angel descend' a second time at the Lote Tree of the most extreme limit in the 'seventh heaven'*," [Qur'an: An Najm 53: 13-15]

Do you think, in the verses consist science's unhappiness?"

"Muhammad truly did a super-wonder. Firstly, he travelled '*through time*' (speed<<light speed) on the earth, and then he travelled '*through space*' (speed>>light speed) to reach to the seventh heaven. Understandably, Muhammad broke the barrier remains so far frozen in the list of 'unbreakable phenomenon'.

I am ashamed of the failure of the science in finding the site of Hell and Paradise, while an unlettered Arab travelled to the seventh heaven and returned in a single night! The failure of science instigates my wonder to disappear into frustration! The 'speed of light' will lose all its glory and retreat into a primitive shell!

To apprise you, the nearest galaxy Andromeda is 2.537 million light years away from us. This little information will knock you to a nasty realisation and herald a renewed thought in you.

In the verses consist science's suicide note!" mocked Kumaran.

"Can anything overstep the limit of the 'light speed'?"

"Nothing!" asserted Kumaran. He snatched a confident glance at me.

"Why the 'light speed' is the ultimate limit for speed? Has someone fixed the limit of speed?"

"No one has fixed the limit of 'speed'…it achieved the zenith on its own.

Nothing is known or discovered yet that could overstep the speed of light," observed Kumaran.

"Big Bang occurred of its own accord; all celestial bodies came into existence of their own accord; the Universe has been expanding fast of its own accord; the size of the earth stopped at the present expanse of its own accord; the force of gravitation came into existence of its own accord; the moon is inhabitable of its own accord; the earth is habitable of its own accord; the excitingly precise rotation, revolution and translation of the satellites and planets in our solar system came into existence of their own accord; and what not…

If everything in the Universe is happening of its own accord, then why the 'speed' alone limits itself to the 'speed of light'? Why does it not overstep the limit?"

"The theory of 'time dilation' says, 'time' slows to a stop when the 'relative velocity' approaches the speed of light. The meaning of 'time' ceases to matter when something travels at the speed of light. So, in that sense, light travels 'through space'. If the limit of speed exceeds the 'light speed', then, may be that the concept of the 'space' would perish," stated Kumaran.

"Even if you travel at the speed of light, it is said that more than 95 percent (some say 100 percent) of the Universe galaxies will be out of our reach, as many are 18 billion light years away from us.

So, even if you travel faster than the speed of light, the 'space' will not fall short of distance! Then, why the 'speed of light' is the limit?"

"As I said, '*time dilation*' is the reason that restricts the speed of light," asserted Kumaran.

"Is this sort of 'time dilation' the ultimate form of 'time dilation'?"

"Please disclose to the world if you do know something else," tweeted Kumaran half-jestingly.

"I am citing some verses from the holy Qur'an that indicate to two different forms of '*time dilation*'. The Qur'an says:

"*Verily a Day in the sight of thy Lord is like a thousand years of your reckoning*." [Qur'an: Al-Hajj 22:47]

The verse clearly indicates two different 'time frames' that can be correlated with a 'dilation factor'.

"*The angels and the spirits ascend unto Him in a Day the measure whereof is as fifty thousand years.*" [Qur'an: Al-Maarij 70:4]

Here in the verse, though the speed of the angles and the distance to destination are not mentioned, yet the verse indicates a sort of 'time dilation' that requires an excitingly precise or ethereal sense to apprehend it.

We know, as the speed approaches the speed of light, the distance ahead gets compacted, and the rate of compaction increases with the increase of the speed. So, it is the speed that decides whether you can reach the seventh heaven or not. Speed of the light might be a 'proven barrier' to human beings, but no longer remains it a barrier to the Creator.

Do you think, the speed of the angels, as mentioned in the verse, cannot overstep the speed of light surpassing the established limit of 'time dilation' that we measure with respect to earth's frame?"

"I have heard of massless Photon that travels with the speed of light in vacuum. But, science has not yet confirmed any elementary particle called 'angel' which seems to be more 'massless' than Photon. I do not know if the 'angel' on its way to the heaven, created any medium that produced better *permittivity* and *permeability* for electric and magnetic fields (waves) 'unification' that helps the speed move faster than light.

You can do it by trampling on the laws of science," Kumaran placed argument rationally. It could compel those overcome totally by the excellence of science.

"I am not trampling on science, rather I am overrunning the stretch of the runway set so far by science. No way it is going to dishonour science.

Science that we have discovered so far is pathetically restricted to a very small corner of our galaxy.

Friend, we have just made a little progress in paying a visit to lunar gateway, or at most the Mars, let alone galactic or intergalactic 'time frames'. We must be aware of our limits being earthily 'animals'. The Power of the Almighty transcends all, let alone the flimsy barrier of 'space-time'. The verse clearly says that the Almighty took His servant Muhammad (pbuh) to show him the splendours of His Creation.

"*Glory be to One Who took His servant by night…*" [Qur'an: Al Isra 17: 1]

You must know that the 'vacuum speed of light' is not actually a speed but a constant having the unit of 'speed'. Speed of light is constant in vacuum that implies that *permittivity* and *permeability* too are constant. With the change of medium, the values of the said constants could be changed resulting in a subsequent change in 'speed'. Cannot the medium be changed by the One who created it?

And, I would like to inform you that due to the expansion of the Universe, the distant galaxies are moving from us with speed faster than the speed of light. You must be aware of the fact that the expansion of the space is no longer governed by the Theory of Relativity. So, arguably, something faster than light already exists!

Would like to inform you that the phase velocity of light in 'charged plasma' medium can be faster than the speed of light. I would like to cite an important verse from the Qur'an that consists of insights and profundity.

"*O company of Jinn and mankind, if you are able to pass beyond the regions of the heavens and the earth, then pass. You will not pass except by authority.*" [Qur'an: Ar-Rahman 55: 33]

The word 'authority' is applicable to the class of servants like Jinn and humankind. You can develop your own 'authority' by developing a magic spaceship that requires an infinite measure of energy to match the speed of light (v=0.9c). Else, look towards the King. The King Himself is an 'authority' and issues space-pass whomsoever He wishes. The 'pass' was once issued to the noble Prophet Muhammad (pbuh).

Friends, even angels were made to bow down before you. The obviousness entreats that you should behave the way that matches the fit of a human being. Regrettably, your intellect is not as lustrous as it seems.

"*... We said to the angels: "Bow down unto Adam". They bowed down...*" [Qur'an: Al-Isra 17: 61]

Come out from the obstinate orbit of linear thinking and give wings to the flair of your intelligence. Let it lustre.

By the way, would you please bend this question towards Phillip?"

"Which question?" Kumaran inquired though he knew what I meant.

"Please wheel this question to Phillip, '*Is it possible to journey to the heaven*?' And believe me his answer will sledgehammer you."

Kumaran looked at Phillip and asked, "What's your view?"

"Jesus is Lord. No Physics could prevent him from journeying to the heaven. Association of Muhammad with the 'heavenly journey' stands clearly as the most preposterous notion," Phillip forwarded his view that jarred on Kumaran.

Kumaran looked at Phillip half-agape. He dislodged his glance from Phillip painfully and swung it towards me and began,

"He not only has frustrated me but you also."

"He has been in the habit of snubbing Prophet Muhammad (pbuh).

Jesus Christ (pbuh) was raised alive to the heaven. It is no longer a big deal for the Almighty to nullify the influence of the 'space-time'. Its execution is easy for Him.

Suppose after 500 years, surely by that time we both would not be on the earth, science discovers the existence of Hell and Paradise. Now tell me,

How would you benefit from your belief and how would I from mine?-

Surely, you would be a loser.

And, suppose after 500 years, science proves that the Qur'an is wrong and there is nothing sort of Hell or Paradise.

How would you benefit from your belief and how would I from mine?-

The answer is, -neither you nor me. And definitely, I would not be a loser!

On collective sense, the weightage of 'intellectual probability' is still on my side. It *tips the scales* in my favour. Now tell me, who possess more 'rational' knack -you or I? Does your logic agree with the theory of probability?

Friend, scientists will never be able to visit Hell and Paradise."

"No one will stop you if you want to shout at the top of your voice. The fact is that there is no scientific proof so far about the existence of Hell and Paradise. The concept of Hell and Paradise is extraordinarily a surreal thing that partners with cherished imageries," observed Kumaran. My frequent mentioning of Hell and Paradise frosted him quite.

"Science has already taken its due measure of time in its endeavour. I am really astonished that how the failure of the science could be an impressive piece of 'fact' to you?

What do you think Stephen Hawking is a scientist or a philosopher?"

Kumaran looked at Phillip with begging eyes. Phillip reciprocated the same. Both sank in obligatory silence.

"I fail to remember if I had ever asked you to do the Qur'an a favour.

Rather I have always instigated your intellect to prove the Quran wrong, and this has always been the pitch of my arguments. Now, you must be clear about the fact that the Qur'an has a permanent appetite for challenge.

Philosophy has established arguably a fair relation with science and allied to work together to provide solution to many great conundrums that the science alone is not capable to provide.

Surely, the job of finding the sites of Hell and Paradise is not as easy as it sounds, and science knows that very well."

"I have found you off on the subject of Hell and Paradise. What's the matter?" Kumaran questingly forwarded the query to Phillip.

"I'm a theist and I believe in the existence of Hell and Paradise," Phillip replied gliding his fingers across the downy head.

Kumaran looked at him with astonished eyes pounding streams of mysterious glances that Phillip minded not to value. Kumaran, first time indeed, made a gesture towards Phillip which was quite out of the way.

"Who would fly faster to Paradise -you or Phillip?" Kumaran peppered his inquiry with a jest. He instigated me with a sharp-witted query.

"What do you think who would?"

"How could I know who would," Kumaran reacted without wasting a slice of time.

"Then how did you anticipate that we both would reach Paradise?"

"This is my axiom because you both are theists and God fearing. Paradise is awaiting impatiently you," Kumaran said half-jestingly.

"There is a single way to Paradise."

"Do you mean 'grave worship' is the only way that leads to Paradise?" Phillip threw the jibe.

"Where did I say grave worship leads to Paradise?"

"Then why do Muslims visit *Mazhars* and worship tombs?" Kumaran evidenced a specific '*religious habit*' of some Muslims.

"They do worship '*tombs*', -it's a dreary version of idol worship," Phillip added quickly. He cast a shaking glance that I absorbed without a jolt.

"I do agree many Muslims visit *Mazhars.* Some offer prayers standing by the side of the *tombs,* and some pray to the *tombs*.

Islam permits to offer prayer to the tombs of pious personalities by reciting the very first chapter (Surah Al-Fatiha) of the

Qur'an. In this act, the person is inclined to invoke the blessing of Allah (swt) on the 'dead' person. Islam permits it.

However, Islam does not permit to pray to any dead person conceiving him as a link between the people and Allah (swt). Praying to a tomb of any dead person, conceiving him as the facilitator between the people and Allah (swt), is absolutely forbidden in Islam. Islam does not permit that.

I too have seen many crooked human nature. -

The '*special worship zone*' is thought to be the representations of multi-religions. My wonder stops nowhere when I see that the '*special worship zone*' consists of a Mazhar (having tomb inside) for Muslims instead of having a Mosque. The concerned authority knowingly or unknowingly or out of some impure motives indirectly belittles the very principle of Islam. It desecrates the purity of Islam and scars the unblemished image of Islam.

Islam is extremely intolerant to any kind of image that could blemish its purity. Mosque is devoid of any tombs, sculptures, pictures or something that impure the essence of Islam. Mosque is the true '*local*' place of worship for Muslims.

If sense prevails and sensibility accompanies, Muslims will never go against the following verse of the first chapter of the Qur'an. Muslims will never dare to transgress the essence of the verse:

"Thee do we worship, and Thine aid we seek." [Qur'an: Al Fatiha 1: 5]

Here in the verse consists the beauty of Islam! It offers an umbilical connection to Islam and courses like blood in the vein of a true Muslim. Its severance from the tenets of Islam will ruin the very foundation of Islam. I hope that it clears the air once and for all!

During the beginning of every prayer, it is obligatory to recite the surah. It reminds us that there is none worthy of worship except Allah (swt), and there is none other than Allah (swt) able to help us. So the Absolute Helper is Allah (swt) alone and help can be sought directly from Him. The instructions are clearer than crystal."

"But Muslims who pray to tomb are men of lesser understanding? Don't they understand Islam?" inquired Kumaran authoritatively.

"Friends, had Islam permitted '*grave worship*' then certainly the grave of Muhammad (pbuh), the most valuable creation of the Almighty, would have fronted the tenets of Islam. The fact is that the Prophet's grave is kept secluded from the masses. The Qur'an clears the air:

"Muhammad is no more than a messenger: ..." [Qur'an: Al Imran 3: 144]

Allah (swt) warns that people should not feel inclined to pay more than '*human honour*' to someone who was the truest, the purest and the greatest of men. But Allah (swt) is eternal and only He deserves the absolute devotion."

"Who is God, – Allah or Jesus Christ?" probed Kumaran rapidly.

He did not utter anything further as the name of Jesus Christ figured in the question. Kumaran just stopped right there fettering tightly the advancement of his tongue. No doubt, he brought up an intricate matter into discussion.

"Allah (swt) is the God of the worlds," I continued being inconsiderate of reactions from Phillip, "And Jesus Christ (pbuh) is His Messenger; Jesus Christ (pbuh) is not God."

Phillip gave me a dreadful outrage whose lethality could be placed adjacent to the firepower of a notorious gun. He oozed spectrum of sharp rays that could easily fret the figure of 'anger' on the surface of a wooden table.

"That means that Phillip is denied Paradise! Do you mean that the Christian world has mistaken Jesus Christ as God?

You should prime your mind before making such blatant remark, because Christianity is the leading faith on the earth," Kumaran cautioned me.

Kumaran's views added an indignation to the accumulation of outrage. Phillip narrowed his eyes in anger and outpoured indignation upon me for a long while.

"The 'so-called' Christianity leads by a slender majority against Islam. Majority is not entitled to decide which is *right* or *wrong,* but rationality is.

By the way, and by way of reasoning, then do you think that you are unconsciously associated with a wrong faith which trails behind Christianity and Islam?"

"Come out of the dark cell of narrowness and do consider my view with a broader sense. What I am trying to say is that you should be careful in revoking any notion deeply established in the minds of people," Kumaran stated the same but with glossy coating.

"Friends, my logic has been deprived of due cerebration, –it's almost *blown in the wind*! Majority is not always right, and prerogative should not be awarded to majority to take decision. If this is the way of reasoning, then I would request you to call to mind when majority of people in the ancient times incorrectly believed that the earth was flat. Friends, I am striving to infuse rationality into you. It is just an essential correction to your linear thought process.

By way of reasoning, do you think that the whole Muslim world has mistaken Jesus Christ as Messenger of God?"

"Both cannot be right. Who are ignorant –Muslims or Christians?" Kumaran posted caustic queries seemingly *going overboard.*

"Christianity is racing ahead in the league with a huge margin. Christianity has displayed its brilliance in Europe, whereas Islam has performed like a duffer in 'Islamic countries'," Phillip made sharp remarks perhaps in retaliation. He sublimated his anger into these sentences.

"What was the belief of the Roman emperor Constantine the Great, –did he consider Jesus Christ (pbuh) God or a Messenger of God?"

"How come the name of the Roman Emperor appear all of a sudden?" reacted Phillip. He reacted at the suddenness of the appearance of Roman Emperor's name.

"It seems unexpected but apropos. You should be aware of the history of Christianity, and how did it spread in Europe.

He was the reason behind the dominance of Christianity in Europe. With the happening of the conversion of the Roman emperor Constantine the Great (306-337 CE) to Christianity, the whole Roman Empire began to transition from Paganism to Christianity, and eventually Christianity became the dominant religion in Europe. It was the power and the influence of the king that led the whole Empire converted to Christianity.

I would like to remind you that though the numbers of prophesying Christians top the list, yet the numbers of practising Christians lag far behind the numbers of practising Muslims. Islam tops the list in acceptance.

In PEW study, 2012, 23 percent of Americans who affiliated with a religion were not religious and 6 percent were atheists or agnostics.

Now please tell me,

Why those high thinking Americans distancing themselves off Christianity and washing towards atheism?

Why did they grow dislike for the Bible?

Why did the Bible repel them?"

"This is the greatness of Christianity. It offers liberty to individual, -it liberates depressed soul, pulls up the mind from narrowness and provides magnificent wings to its followers. It does not make its followers denizens of darkness like Islam. The Bible is not a siege of illness," replied Phillip adding much emphasis on liberty.

"Please tell me, those 23 percent non-religious and 6 percent agnostics Americans who chose their own way of thinking, did they read the Bible or not?"

"Suppose they did it after reading the Bible, then what do you want to prove?" Phillip placed the trial statement.

"That means the Bible is not convincing."

"Suppose they did it without reading the Bible, then what do you want to say?" Phillip stated the second possibility in a more aggressive way.

"That means the Bible is not attractive."

"The Bible brings liberty. The Bible offers royal dimensions to the way of life. It endeavours continuously to elevate the form of human life and adds splendours to its every dull facet languishing in the sorry corner of gloominess. The Bible heralds delight.

Studies show that the Koran is the antipode to the Bible. It truncates the liberty of soul, subjugates the freedom of mind, gags the dissenting voices and creates the circumstances of reduced freedom. Islam is like a constricted conduit that throttles free flow of liberty and acts as a retard on civilisation. The Koran sends down tremors of trepidation across the joyous hearts of the people who love to enjoy the lives under the tenderness of free sunshine. Manifestly, the Koran does not find a way with the world," Phillip retaliated.

"Eating flesh of swine may be a figure of freedom, but to me it's a sign of ignorance. I prefer intelligence to ignorance. Friends, it is not a question of freedom but of intellect.

Now please tell me, does the competence of the Bible fail to match the intellect level of those polished 23 percent and 6 percent Americans? Why did they distance themselves from the Bible?"

"Do you think they are washing towards the Islam? Are they hugging the Koran," added Phillip irately.

"'They were not Muslims by birth', I began, 'by the way, Dr Maurice Bucaille had hugged the Qur'an'."

"Salman Rushdie had rejected the Koran," Phillip replied with an unmistakable assertion in his voice.

"But Salman Rushdie did not hug the Bible either. Friend, think of Richard Dawkins, -have you asked him why does he not believe in the Bible?"

"Do you think he is advocating for the Koran?" Phillip made a swift retort. Then he cast a glance that exuded a dew of certain retaliation.

"Perhaps, he skipped to reading the Qur'an. But Dr Maurice Bucaille read the Qur'an and was much convinced to convert himself to accept the divine origin of the Qur'an.

Richard Dawkins, perhaps, had read the first chapter of the Bible."

"What's wrong with the first chapter of the Bible?" Phillip inquired in a vehemence and looked at me obliquely. He snatched a rude glance at me.

"It can make a rational mind to loathe himself for reading the Book. It will instantly shake one's admiration for rationality. The following bulk of four verses are potentially frivolous enough to morph a Christian into a staunch atheist.

"So God made the two larger lights, the sun to rule over the day and the moon to rule over the night; ..." [Bible: Genesis 1:16]

Do you think the moon too generates light?

And, in the following verses, either Eve is telling a lie, or the author of the chapter. The first verse tells us that –if they eat '*the fruit*' they will die, but the next verse says when they ate '*the fruit*' they found themselves stripped naked. The verse clearly says that they were overwhelmed by the shame of nakedness.

"God told us not to eat the fruit of that tree or even touch it; if we do we will die." [Bible: Genesis 2: 2]

"As soon as they had eaten it, they were given understanding and realised that they were naked;.." [Bible: Genesis 2: 7]

The anomaly is clear.

In the following verse, Lord was busy in evening walk in the garden. He failed to see Adam and Eve, and started shouting about their whereabouts.

"That evening they heard the Lord God walking in the garden. … .But the Lord God called out to the man, "Where are you?" [Bible: Genesis 2: 8-9]

God was walking in the garden! God did not know the whereabouts of Adam and Eve! The verses talk about a 'God' of reduced divine power.

Now, I beg your attention on the following verse that says:

"When he threatens the pillars that hold up the sky, they shake and tremble with fear." [Bible: Job 26:11]

Do you think the sky is propped by pillars?

The Bible turns up high as the most influential springboard to launch people into the orbit of atheism. These sorts of verses irritate genuine intelligence and make one develop detestation towards religion. The verse breeds disinclination for rational people.

The pool of Christianity is shrinking!"

"Are you not *jumping in at the deep end* without much consideration? Are you not offending Christians?" Kumaran tabled the query taking reference of my statement made earlier. I looked at him in disbelief.

"You need to restrain the blatancy of your tongue.

It is the *dead hand* of raw fanaticism of the Koran that instigates Muslims to manufacture such desecrating statements. Clearly they used to infer many critical conclusions being fully inconsiderate of the overall context and the background," Phillip sharpened his voice and threw the piece in the form of a mild tantrum.

"Friends, I am no way in the habit of collecting information from TV talk shows, nor from any discussion-table surrounded by people who brag shallow knowledge and glorify imperfection in information.

I am here not to provoke someone, nor to create an unnecessary sensation, nor to override the established belief by my obsession, personal wishes, private feelings or undue considerations. I am here to represent the truth.

Jesus Christ (pbuh) is a Messenger of God and that can be proved from the Bible itself.

I wonder, why Jesus Christ (pbuh) did not state categorically the simplest statement in the Bible that "*I am God*"."

"The sentence "*I am God*" has suffered a long familiarity and become almost trite.

If the president of America is visiting India tomorrow, he would not announce that, "I am the president of America"; because he is already known to all!" Phillip stated with an authority.

"Agreed. Suppose, after 500 years, if Mr X wants to know who the president of America was during a particular period of times, then how he would confirm?"

"Certainly he should check the list of names of American presidents kept in the White House." Phillip replied.

"In the same way, if I want to know whether Jesus Christ (pbuh) was God, certainly I should check the scriptures dealing with the divine affairs of Jesus Christ (pbuh). In the whole Bible, the statement "*I am God*" is a clear absence.

Moreover, why God should come on the face of the earth to be killed?"

"He was not killed but sacrificed. You need to understand the sentiment of the sacrifice in the way deemed to be encompassing and global. His sacrifice was to redeem the sins of human kind.

He is the Redeemer, those who believe in him will be saved," Phillip replied maintaining his cool and composure. He appeared much mellowed.

"How your faith in Jesus' sacrificial death could save you from the Hell fire?"

"People by nature are inclined to commit sins and used to live in it. Once you are baptized in the name of Jesus Christ, you are actually baptized all the way into the union with his death. In that way and so, you seem to have become an integral part of his sacrificial death. As he was raised from death, so you are. It is well known that, accountability for sins ceases after death and that invariably offers you a new avenue to lead a celestially sinless life. The Bible says:

"For surely you know that when we were baptized into union with Christ Jesus, we were baptized into union with his death. By our baptism, then, we were buried with him and shared his death, in order that, just Christ was raised from death by the glorious power of the Father, so also we might live a new life. For since we have become one with him in dying as he did, in the same way we shall be one with him by being raised to life as he was. …" *[Bible: Romans 6: 3-11]*

The death of Jesus Christ and the union with him through baptism offer you a sin-free life. The death of Jesus Christ has already paid for your sins. Bible further says:

"For sin pays its wage---death; but God's free gift is eternal life in union with Christ Jesus our Lord" [Bible: Romans 6: 23]

"…and we will also possess with Christ what God has kept for him; for if we share Christ's suffering, we will also share his glory" [Bible: Romans 8: 17]

The Spirit of God resides in your mortal body, and the union, as accorded through his death, will give you the eternal life. Being in the union with Jesus Christ, and being a stakeholder of his suffering,…it entails that you too deserve his glory," Phillip explained.

"I want to hear from you,

How powerful was 'Lord' Jesus Christ? Was he as powerful as his Father?

How much The Father Loves His Son?"

"The begotten Son of God can invariably be a God only. So, Jesus Christ was as powerful as his Father. In fact, Jesus Christ was very dear to His Father. The Bible says:

"…And a voice came from heaven, "You are my own dear Son. I am pleased with you."" [Bible: Mark1:10-11]

The verse confirms that the Father was very pleased with Jesus Christ. He was the Lord sent in human form by his Father," Phillip replied in an affirmative tone. He seemed to have assumed that his views were irrevocable.

"Begotten Son?" I continued in a wonder, "Do you mean the Father is the biological Father of Jesus Christ (pbuh)?"

"God begot Jesus Christ and sacrificed Him to redeem our sins.

"Mary said to the angel, I am a virgin. How, then, can this be?

The angel answered, the holy Spirit will come on you, and God's power will rest upon you. For this reason the holy child will be called the Son of God." [Bible: Luke1:34-35]

The verses do need no explanations," Phillip stated.

"Do you mean that God's reproductive process resembles the reproductive process of a human being?"

"Nowhere does it say that God's reproductive process resembles that of a human being. The reproductive process of God transcends our general concept. The statement "*the holy Spirit will come on you"* speak profoundly about the reproductive process of God," Phillip narrated as if he was speaking before the Church-congregation.

"Then, why did you use the word *'begotten son'*?"

"It's just to establish a divine relation between the Father and the Son. It speaks about the profound closeness between them," replied Phillip tentatively.

"If this is the logic, then you have to agree with me that, John (pbuh), son of Elizabeth (wife of Prophet *Zechariah (pbuh)*) was too the '*so-called begotten Son*' of God, -because his mother too was filled with the presence of Holy Spirit. The Bible says:

"When Elizabeth heard Mary's greetings, the baby moved within her. Elizabeth was filled with the Holy Spirit" [Bible: Luke1:41]

Do you think Prophet John (pbuh) too was a '*begotten Son*' of the Father?"

"John had a father but Jesus Christ didn't. You can mine out the deep connotations of this statement," observed Phillip.

"I fail to understand why did Jesus Christ (pbuh) call himself '*the son of man*'? The Bible says:

"Jesus answered him,…from this time on you will see the Son of Man sitting on the right of the Almighty,…" [Bible: Mathew 27: 64]

Did he not insult his own 'Biological Father' by claiming himself the 'Son of Man'?

Who is right: you or Jesus Christ (pbuh)?"

"Mother Marry gave birth to Jesus, in that sense he was the son of man. With narrow outlook and shallow understanding, you would never be able to understand the Bible. The Bible is deep and profound. To find the gem you need to mine deep," replied Phillip though he struggled much to make the reply.

"How God created Adam (pbuh)?"

"God created Adam from soil," replied Phillip.

"How did God create you?"

"You too do know it. He created me and all other human beings, except Jesus Christ, from a single drop of sperm," Phillip stated with confident assertion.

"How do you make a pen?"

"Why does this question turn up?" Phillip shrieked. He seemed to have been hit by a freak shot of a verbal attack.

"Please state the process."

"It comprises of several engineering processes of component formations and moulding," Phillip outlined the process tersely.

"All right friend. Now you are quite aware of the know-how of manufacturing a pen. Now, can you produce a pen through a completely different process by just injecting a drop of special fluid into a secured mould?"

"What do you want to derive from it?" Phillip inquired contacting eyes with me. He sensed in me something *out of the ordinary*.

"I have not got the answer. Can you produce a pen by just injecting a drop of liquid into the mould?"

"No," Phillip made a curt reply averting eyes from me.

"Now I would like to invite your intellect to ponder over the capability of God on the matter of creation. -

He first created Adam (pbuh) from soil, and produced Eve from the left rib of Adam (pbuh). Just look at God's deftness at creation. Is not it wonderful?

Then, He ordained the creation of human beings from a drop of sperm. Look at the astounding capability of God in altering the process of creation.

Now, I am asking you, why God, being God, would establish 'sexual relationship' to produce Jesus Christ (pbuh)?"

"Adam is not Lord, and we human beings are not like Jesus Christ.

So, to produce a Lord, to produce someone who resembles God, God had to have performed that very '*act*' that ensured the 'transmission' of all the Godly qualities into Jesus Christ," stated Phillip.

"What was the need that Lord Jesus Christ should take birth from a womb of a human being? Why did the Father intend like this?

Why was he not directly sent to the earth like Adam and Eve?"

"Just to show his miraculous birth, and the wonder that he did in infancy by speaking to people. It was more impactful," Phillip stated dismissing the impact of the event where someone is descending directly from the heaven amongst the masses.

"Which is more impactful: someone descending from the heaven amongst the people, or someone taking birth in human form?"

"Think of Adam and Eve, they barely created any impact though they both descended from the heaven," Phillip replied without thinking much about the rebuttal from me. He resorted to a lame logic.

"None was there on the earth to watch them descending on the earth. Your logic does not make any sense."

"It may suit your logic, but not mine," Phillip retorted sensing the preposterousness of his logic.

"Friend, you did claim that Jesus Christ (pbuh) was bestowed with the *divine glory* equal to that of his Father. But the Bible says:

"...I will not let anyone share the glory that should be mine and mine alone" [Bible: Isaiah 48:11].

Who is right: you or the Bible?"

"The question itself is improper. God is One in three: the Father, the Son and the Holy Ghost, and all three are equipoised and bestowed with equal divine power...Unicity of God is found in this Unity!" Phillip narrated with great deftness.

"This is not Unicity of God. This is an aberration and a fine mix of fabricated ideas!

In the following verse, by way of reasoning, Jesus Christ (pbuh) himself admits that he can do nothing on his own. He does what he sees his Father doing. The Bible says:

"I am telling you the truth: the son can do nothing on his own; he does only what he sees his Father doing. ...". [Bible: John4: 19]

And in the following verse the Father says that the coming of the Hour is known to him only. He alone knows when the Hour will come about. The Bible says:

"No one knows, however, when that day and hour will come—neither the angels in heaven nor the Son; the Father alone knows." [Bible: Mathew 24: 36]

The verse confirms that Jesus Christ (pbuh) was not bestowed with any divine power. Do you still believe that Jesus Christ (pbuh) did claim divinity?"

"The Father and Jesus are actually One. The obviousness can be found from the following verses.

"Whoever has seen me has seen the Father. Why, then you say show us the Father?... I am in father and father in me." [Bible: John 14: 9-10]

The verses clearly corroborate the divinity of Jesus Christ!" replied Phillip in an adoring way.

"Friend, this is nothing but an epitome of linguistic trap, - a ruse laid to trap naïve souls.

The verse indicates the 'objectives' of both God and Jesus Christ (pbuh), -in that sense both are '*One*'. That does not mean that physically they are '*One*'!"

"*I am in Father and Father in me*", -does it not mean that both are '*One*'?" Phillip tried to defend his claim. He put up a strong defiance.

"I do agree for the sake of argument. Let's analyse the following verse.

"When that day comes, you will know that I am in my Father and that you are in me, just as I am in you." [Bible: John 14: 20]

The verse clearly says that the disciples are in Jesus Christ (pbuh) and Jesus Christ (pbuh) is in the Father. Logically put, that means all disciples are in the Father.

Do you think disciples too are '*Gods*'?

To clarify further, I would cite the law of chemical equilibrium. It says:

'*It states that if an entity A is in equilibrium with an entity B, and if B is in equilibrium with an entity C, then by the law of chemical equilibrium you can say that entity A is in equilibrium with entity C. That means A, B and C all are in equilibrium state and possesses similar chemical properties.*'

If I deduce from the law, the disciples too are 'Gods'! Is it?"

"Nowhere in the Bible are the disciples called 'Gods'. But, Jesus Christ is called Lord in numerous verses of the Bible. The Bible says:

"May God our Father and the Lord Jesus Christ give you grace and peace." [Bible: 1Corinthians 1:3]

So, you cannot equate disciples with Jesus Christ," replied Phillip.

"Then how can you equate Jesus Christ with the Father?"

"*Jesus is in Father* and he is also the Lord, -so logically you can equate him with the Father," confirmed Phillip. His voice was flowing and assertive.

"Many places in the Bible Jesus Christ (pbuh) has called his Father 'God'," I began, "Is there any verse in the complete Bible where the Father has called Jesus Christ (pbuh) '*My Lord*'?"

"No," replied Phillip.

He looked at me with thousand thoughtful eyes. Perhaps, the query hit him down to a new line of realisation.

"If they are 'One' and possess equal glory and divine power, and the verse "*I am in Father and Father in me,*" stands by your logic, then what is wrong if the Father calls Jesus Christ (pbuh) '*My Lord*'?

Is there any verse in the complete Bible where the Father calls Jesus Christ (pbuh) '*My Lord*'?"

"It's not obligatory that the Father should call his *begotten son* 'My Lord'" Phillip replied tersely. He appeared half-evasive.

"All right friend, is there any verse in the complete Bible where mother Mary calls Jesus Christ (pbuh) '*my Lord*'?"

"I think some of your stupid senses is scuffling with you! What is your question exactly?" Phillip inquired impatiently. His temper climbed to a point where irritation beads into exasperation.

"How mother Mary would achieve salvation if she does not call Jesus Christ (pbuh) 'my Lord'?"

"She believed that by heart," replied Phillip.

"Is it mentioned in the Bible?"

"No," Phillip replied. His tone of voice lacked refinement.

"Do you think that those, who were involved in the crucifixion of Jesus Christ (pbuh), should be awarded with the eternal life?"

"How could you even say like this?" Phillip reacted vehemently. The question seemingly upset him, but he *put a brave face on it.*

"I think you have not come across such question before.

You should be grateful to Judas Iscariot and his secret cabal who accomplished the alleged 'crucifixion' immaculately. After all, their efforts produced the much-coveted thing called the '*salvation*' for you.

Please tell me, if Judas and his team should be awarded salvation or not?"

"Suppose they don't deserve 'salvation', then what do you want to prove?" Phillip inquired in a haste.

"That means that they committed crime. They killed Jesus Christ (pbuh) against the Will of the Father.

Peculiar indeed! I have found a person in you who loves to eat meat but hates the slaughterer!

Is it agreeable that you should reap 'salvation' on sinner's head?"

"It was the Divine Plan of the Father. Through the sacrifice of His Son, the Father set the criteria for salvation," observed Phillip.

"The logic bears semblance of a farce!

Friend, you need to understand the difference between a 'divine plan' and a 'devilish scheme'.

Jesus Christ (pbuh) underwent through a series of humiliations on his way to the Cross. The Bible says:

"Then they spat in his face and beat him; and those who slapped him said, Prophesy for us, Messiah! Guess who hit you!" [Bible: Mathew 26: 67-68]

Is it palatable?

Sometimes I wonder about the might of Judas who killed 'God'! Can I not presume that Judas is *a cut above* Jesus Christ (pbuh) and *cut out* to be a better God?"

The dagger-like query has gone deep into his flesh! Phillip hurried precipitately into the realm of silence.

"By the way, do you wish now that Jesus Christ (pbuh) should have lived longer on the earth all the way till his natural 'death'?"

"It was a Divine plan. It had to have happened," Phillip replied. He collected himself and appeared composed and temperate.

"Which one do you think is the right way to guide the human beings to the Path of salvation: by sending Messengers with guidance, or by sacrificing '*own begotten Son*' through a series of humiliations?"

"Everything cannot be achieved through words and actions. Sacrifice overpowers everything. Sacrifice does wonder and the time of Jesus Christ demanded so," Phillip hastened to add this.

"Was that the most productive way to convince the people of the world about the divine affairs of The Father?"

"Yes, it was," replied Phillip. He first shook his head and then uttered in a frail voice.

"Prophet Moses (pbuh) achieved more success during his life time than the success achieved by Jesus Christ (pbuh). Do you still think that the decision of the Father was sensibly correct?"

"Judaism had a very good head-start on Christianity, but it now lags behind. Christianity is the leading faith in the world supported by a strong-foundation. It has all been possible because of the crucifixion of Jesus Christ. Definitely the decision of the Father was sensible, and the plan was impeccable," Phillip stated assertively.

"I fail to understand why the same Father reacted kindly when Abraham (pbuh) was about to sacrifice his own son. The Bible says:

"*. . . . He tied up his son and placed him on the altar, on top of the wood. Then he picked up the knife to kill him. But the angel of the Lord called him from heaven, Abraham, Abraham!*

He answered, yes, here I am.

Don't hurt the boy or do anything to him, he said."

[Bible: Genesis 22: 9-12]

God even did not expect any sacrifice for Himself, so how could He sacrifice His own '*blood-related Son*' for the sake of heathens like us? Does it make any sense?"

"There is a huge difference between the son of Abraham and the Son of God. And I know you do know the difference.

The Father is not unjust, not even in the least sense. In the verse as mentioned earlier,

"*I am in my Father and that you are in me, just as I am in you,*"- the sacrifice, if you think from broader perspective, was actually a mutual one in the sense that Jesus Christ was an incarnated form of The Father in Heaven," Phillip narrated.

"If they are (The Father and Jesus Christ) 'One'; then, do you think, by way of reasoning, The Father in Heaven too was killed along with Jesus Christ (pbuh)?"

"They killed the physical body of Christ, not the incarnated soul," Phillip stated in a fainter voice. He was clearly *in a mood.*

"I am speechless, flabbergasted! Friend, if it is so, where did the incarnated soul go?"

"It came again as the Holy Spirit!" Phillip hastened to add.

"Suppose Judas and his team do deserve salvation. Then, what do you want to prove?" Kumaran inquired.

"That means Judas and the team carried out a divine-job by crucifying Jesus Christ (pbuh). The Plan of Father to sacrifice His own dearest Son was seamlessly executed by Judas. Jesus Christ (pbuh), himself being the Son of God, must be well aware of his '*sacrificial death*'.

Then, why did Jesus Christ (pbuh) call Judas a betrayer?

"*Get up, let us go. Look here is the man who is betraying me! Jesus was still speaking when Judas, one of the twelve disciples, arrived. ....* " [Bible: Mathew 26: 46-47]

Do you think Jesus Christ (pbuh) was against the Plan?

Before the alleged crucifixion, Jesus Christ (pbuh) was engulfed with grief. In the following verse, he expressed the same to his disciples.

"*And he said to them, the sorrow in my heart is so great that it almost crushes me. ....*" [Bible: Mathew 26:38]

Why did Jesus Christ (pbuh) call Judas and the team ignorant?

"Jesus said, "Forgive them, Father! They don't know what they are doing!"" *[Bible: Luke 23: 34]*.

This clearly indicates that Jesus Christ (pbuh) was not aware of the Plan drafted by his Father, neither was he happy being the target.

Friend, Crucifixion is a pure admixture of concoction and fabrication. Crucifixion of Jesus Christ (pbuh) did not happen at all. It's a formidable fiction concocted to *lead the Christian world down the garden path*!"

"Do you know what are you saying? -

You are simply challenging the root of Christianity! Perhaps sense has deserted you.

"It was nine o'clock in the morning when they crucified him." [Bible: Mark 15:25]

"At three o'clock, Jesus cried out with loud shout, "My God, my God, why did you abandon me?"" [Bible: Mark 15:34]

"With a loud cry Jesus died." [Bible: Mark 15:37]

"...He is not here –he has been raised!" [Bible: Mark 16:6]

The verses are sufficient to shut your mouth," Phillip reacted rudely. Then he snatched an aggressive glance at me.

"Friend, I'm in sense," I continued, "I want to know, who said, *"With a loud cry Jesus died"*?"

"It's informed by Mark," Phillip replied.

"Mark was not present there when the 'Event' was in progress. The Bible says:

"Then all the disciples left him and ran away." [Bible: Mark 14:50]

Mark too ran away from the scene to *save his own skin*. Then, how could he say that Jesus Christ (pbuh) was crucified?"

"Where is your problem exactly?" inquired Phillip curtly.

"How a man who fled the scene could detail the happenings of the event?

Show me the verse where God (The Father) himself said, '*Jesus died!*'"

"Seems sense has revolted against you.

"Pilate was surprised to hear that Jesus was already dead." [Bible: Mark 15:44]

He was 'dead' confirmed by the army present during the 'event,'" Phillip cited proof.

"Pilate confirmed the death of Jesus Christ (pbuh) from the source of 'hearsay'! He did not witness it. And the following verses do not strengthen the claim.

After the alleged crucifixion, Jesus Christ (pbuh) appeared before his disciples. The disciples demanded for a miracle.

"... . They ask for a miracle, but none will be given to them except the miracle of Jonah.

In the same way that the prophet Jonah was a sign for the people of Nineveh, so the Son of Man will be a sign for the people of this day" [Bible: Luke 11: 29-30]

Jonah (pbuh) was commanded by Lord to warn the wicked people of Nineveh. Instead of going to Nineveh, Jonah (pbuh) went to Joppa to board a ship for Spain. But the ship on its way faced a violent storm and was about to face a major catastrophe. Finally, Jonah (pbuh) was found responsible for the reason of the storm. The sailor threw him into the sea to get rid of the situation.

"At the LORD's command a large fish swallowed Jonah, and he was inside the fish for three days and three nights." [Bible: Jonah 1: 17]

"From deep inside the fish Jonah prayed to the LORD his God." [Bible: Jonah 2: 1]

"Then LORD ordered the fish to spit Jonah up on the beach, and it did." [Bible: Jonah 2: 10]

"Once again the LORD spoke to Jonah." [Bible: Jonah 3: 1]

What do you think, Jonah (pbuh) was dead or alive?"

"How can you say so confidently that he did not die and raise to life again?" Phillip stated.

"Then, should I get salvation through my belief in the sacrificial death of Prophet Jonah (pbuh)?"

"Jonah is not Jesus, -Jonah is momentous, Jesus is miracle," retorted Phillip.

"The fish did not chew Jonah (pbuh), -it just swallowed him. He was alive and he was praying to Lord. Does a dead man pray?"

"What do you want to prove, -Jesus was not crucified to death? Phillip asked with an ungracious harshness in his tone.

"Yes, Jesus Christ (pbuh) was not crucified to death!"

"The scuffling of the most sensible sense with the rationality gives birth to a distemper! The same seems to have happened to you!

Don't dare to shake the foundation of Christianity," Phillip sputtered. He was close to fuming.

"Friend, please tell me who raised Jesus Christ (pbuh) from death, -he raised himself, or the Father raised him?"

"The Father raised him," added Phillip after a little thoughtfulness.

"Was Jesus Christ (pbuh) crucified as a man or as a God?"

"He was crucified as a man, and the Father raised him from death and bestowed him again with divine glory!" Phillip replied glibly.

"Friend, the following verse could crash your dead habits of making dreary concoctions. The verse is telling aloud that neither was he God, nor was he raised from death. This part of the verse '*I have not yet gone back up to the Father*' means he did not taste death.

"*Do not hold me*," Jesus told her, *"because I have not yet gone back up to the Father. ....*" [Bible: John 20: 17]

A sick mind always tries to fabricate impure things to satisfy the cry of a treasured ego."

"The interpretation is thick with much insularity, and does not necessarily mean that it is right. This part of the verse '*because I have not yet gone back up to the Father*' means that he was not raised up to his Father who is in the Heaven. No way it means that he was not raised from death. Certainly, he was raised (resurrected) from death.

This is the foundation of our faith, the crux of Christianity and the *sum and substance* of salvation," replied Phillip with assertive confidence. He shot me a confident look.

"Did Jesus Christ (pbuh) himself ever say that your salvation solely depends on his crucifixion"? Can you show me any verse in the Bible?"

"Fools need clear verse! Wise mine out gems from the depth of obscurity," Phillip bawled. I found a layer of irritation fused with his tongue.

"Friend, I am entreating your intellect to ponder over the verse below.

"And he said unto him, why callest thou me good? There is none good but one, that is, God: but if thou wilt enter into life, keep the Commandments." [Bible: Mathew 19: 17]

Salvation is left floundering if dishonour shown to the Commandments.

Do you think Jesus Christ (pbuh) too was a fool who clearly told you about the way to salvation?"

"It is not easy for you to understand the Bible, -it's deep, profound and it needs an understanding mind and a collaborating heart," Phillip stated mixing a mystic bluff with his views.

"Does the Bible agree with a rational mind?"

"It does with those who discuss. It does not with those who argue," replied Phillip.

"The skewed nature of your salvation stands to be a clear dysfunction to the uprightness of rationality, and it is a bit joke about a drunk who is grappling under a lamppost for the key he lost on the other side of the unlit street.

You need to have had a sensible mind that understands the personality of Jesus Christ (pbuh) and realises the deep meaning of Salvation. Salvation is not a joke cracked by a jester, neither is an enticing dish served by others."

"Islam is radical and invites miseries to life. Islam is *a thorn in the flesh* of a rose," Phillip responded showing a mild tantrum.

"What are the new things that the Holy Spirit taught you? For, the following verse clearly says that the Holy Spirit will publish the consummation of all the truth.

The Bible says:

"I have much more to tell you, but now it will be much for you to bear. When, however, the Spirit comes, who reveals the truth about God; he will lead you into all the truth. ..." [Bible: John 16: 12-13]

Please tell us the truth that he revealed to you."

"He urged his disciples to disseminate the message of salvation. The Bible says:

"And in his name the message about repentance and the forgiveness of sins must be preached to all nations, beginning in Jerusalem." [Bible: Luke 24: 47]

It is now incumbent on us to take the message to the remotest corner of the world," replied Phillip. He appeared trim.

"After how many days of 'Crucifixion' did the Holy Spirit appear?"

"Why are you concerned about that? Do you want to precipitate a disaster on Christianity?" Phillip inquired in a lighter voice mixed with indignation.

"I do not wish to be unkind to Christianity. I want to understand the depth of the verse?"

"The Holy Spirit appeared in three days after the crucifixion. Now tell me what do you want to deduce from it?" Phillip asked curtly. He thudded his fist against the table.

"Does this part of the verse, *"...but now it will be much for you to bear"* suggest a time span of three days only?

Does your sense of logic agree to the view: 'Jesus Christ (pbuh) was raised from death only to deliver a message that consists of a few sentences only?'

Does it even meet the bare minimum requirement of a slender speech?"

Phillip offered a steady face almost inscrutable. Phillip observed silence and appeared reluctant to defend the 'weakly-concocted-theology' with logic that has already scattered the ashes of its dead soul.

"Friend, if you think that the so-called priests are *on the side of the angels,* then please ask them to clarify the queries lying unanswered on the table. I am offering you full liberty to call any priest of eminence to overturn my views with the might of rationality."

"Why are you so obsessed about this verse?" Kumaran inserted quickly. He pegged down his glance on me for a longer while.

"This verse can give a very bad shake to the foundation of Christianity!"

"Do you think that all that mentioned in the Bible are gibberish? Is it a disgrace to believe in Jesus and Holy Spirit?" Phillip responded.

He shot his left hand forward and after a quick while, he started to drum his fingers on the surface of the table and belched out a clear brusqueness in an infantile way.

"I have not yet sought support from the Qur'an. The reasons presented so far centre around the Bible.

Friend, you seem to have ducked down your head with eyes closed; you have refused to see the light! The Bible itself is a lie-bed that brims with concoctions of twists, distortions and dark fabrications. Besides, the priests have stuffed you with the drum-fire of lies that you would find nowhere even in the Bible. And unfortunately, you have stumbled blindfolded into the midst of these intricate lies.

Certain ulterior motive has taken the centre stage in designing such a vile plot!"

"Ulterior motive? What do you mean?" Kumaran inquired in an astonishment. He ran his right hand across the head to streamline the hair that rolled down to his forehead.

"Certainly he is going to create a suitable place for his beloved Muhammad," Phillip made a sober anticipation. He appeared *filled to the brim* with indignation.

"Exactly so. Because you have denied him his rightful place.

The Holy Spirit was supposed to tell many things as mentioned in the verse. Here I'm citing the complete verses:

"I have much more to tell you, but now it will be much for you to bear. When, however, the Spirit comes, who reveals the truth about God; he will lead you into all the truth. He will not speak on his own authority, but he will speak of what he hears, and will tell you of things to come. He will give me glory, because he will take what I say and tell it to you". [Bible: John 16: 12-14]

Do you find anyone who fits perfectly to the soulful interpretation of the verses?"

"Muhammad, the Holy Spirit!?" Phillip gawked. He cocked his eyebrows and shot me a glance that defied general descriptions.

"Certainly. Except Muhammad (pbuh), none can do the justice to the exciting precision of the prophecy. The Qur'an says:

"And when Jesus son of Mary said, "O children of Israel, I am God's Messenger to you, confirming what preceded me of the Torah, and announcing good news of a Messenger who will come after me whose name is Ahmad." [Qur'an: As-Saff 61:6]

The Qur'an has revealed all the truth and glorified mother Mary and his son Jesus Christ (pbuh) with high praise and sublime honour found nowhere in the world."

"But how can you believe that the claim made by the Koran is also from God Himself?" Phillip questioned. He looked at me with vague eyes.

"What do you mean?"

"Muhammad has played a very smart game in an underhand way. He is quite adept at doing such nasty things. -

Firstly, he declared Jesus Christ a Messenger of God but not God, and then cunningly, he declared himself as the last Messenger of God. He has *taken the wind out of Jesus' sail* and *made way* for himself!

So, how could you say with surety that the above verse too were revealed to Muhammad?

How could you say with confident assertion that the whole Koran was revealed by God to Muhammad only?" Phillip stated with a deft tongue. The pace of his speech was decently fast, voice was flowing and the tone was brimmed with towering confidence.

"Who discovered America?"

"Columbus," answered Phillip.

"Who discovered 'Washington DC'?"

My query gave him a bad shake and made him realise the preposterousness consists in his doubt.

"All right friends, for the time being, I agree that Muhammad (pbuh) was a union leader and the founder of a strange religion called 'Islam'. Then, -

To whom God revealed those scientific facts?"

"It may be to someone else and Muhammad plagiarized it," Phillip replied by way of argument. He *shot from the hip*. He gave me an oblique glance laced with a brag.

"Then why God did not take care of His chosen man? Why that man is not known to the world?

Friend, there is no power in the whole Universe that could scupper the intended plan of God.

Again, the below verse will help you clear the cloud of doubts. Prophet Moses told this verse in front of his followers:

"I will send them a prophet like you from their own people; I will tell him what to say, and he will tell the people everything I command. He will speak in my name, and I will punish anyone who refuses to obey him" [Bible: Deuteronomy 18:18-19].

Which prophet is like Moses (pbuh)?"

"Jesus Christ, he was born in Jew family," observed Phillip immediately. But, he instantly realised the brutal slip of his tongue.

"But according to you, Jesus Christ is God?"

His face was burning in a blazing embarrassment…a streak of florid blush was running frenziedly across his face. Seemed, he disowned his fallen tongue and beaten it up internally for the blunder. He *shot himself in the foot* and cut a sorry figure! His mood sank; his voice seemed to have been knocked out of him.

He brooded over the blunder and offered me a face overcome totally by dispiritedness. It was tough for me to look at his glum face more than a very short while. I bent my glance downwards.

"Friend, the Bible has distorted the facts and tried its best to hide the truth. This is nothing but an impure connivance that has been a conundrum for Christians! The truth is, you have trapped yourselves in a rudderless situation that commands control over nothing,…it is yawing aimlessly between the unrealistic references of concoction and crookedness. -

The scenario concocted in the Bible resembles a mid-air fuel crisis of an aeroplane flying from Tel Aviv to Los Angeles. The plane was supposed to be filled with fuel amounting to 1000 gallons, but mistakably was filled with 1000 litres. The crew member could not apprehend the impact of the "unit" and the pilot too overlooked the fuel level indication before the take-off.

Prophet Muhammad (pbuh) was the prophet like Moses (pbuh):

Both Prophet Moses (pbuh) and Prophet Muhammad (pbuh) had parents, but Jesus Christ (pbuh) did not.

Both were accepted as Prophets in their lifetime, but Jesus Christ (pbuh) was not.

Both died on the face of earth, but Jesus Christ (pbuh) was raised alive.

Both married, but Jesus Christ (pbuh) did not.

Both led a nation, but Jesus Christ (pbuh) did not.

Moses (pbuh) split the sea and Muhammad (pbuh) split the moon.

Admittedly, you have achieved almost a success in expunging the name of Prophet Muhammad (pbuh) from the pages of the Bible. But, have you achieved any success in preventing people from recognising the glory of Muhammad (pbuh)?"

"Which glory of Muhammad has been recognised by the people of the world?" Kumaran fired a taunt.

"He was the most influential person in human history.

American astrophysicist, Michael H. Hart proposed the name of Prophet Muhammad (pbuh) as the most influential person ever born on the earth. In his famous book, *"The 100: A Ranking of the Most Influential Persons in History*, 1978", he placed Muhammad (pbuh) at the top of the list arguing that only he achieved outstanding and unparalleled successes in both religious and secular fronts. No famous world figure could even match the excellence of his single feat."

"Michael H. Hart should have reviewed his selection process. How an 'illiterate' Arab could top the prestigious contest?" fretted Phillip. He appeared fairly normal as the blush of embarrassment almost drained from his face. This time his soft-bodied tongue did not wriggle but walked very slowly like a tardigrade!

"He did. He reviewed his selection process and reprinted in 1992, and much to your chagrin, he considered Muhammad (pbuh) again as the topper in the contest.

What is the educational qualification of God?"

"Why such inquiry all of a sudden?" asked Phillip.

"Because you just called Prophet Muhammad (pbuh) an 'illiterate' Arab."

"God is all Knowing. He does not need any education qualification," Phillip replied.

"Prophet Muhammad (pbuh) was divinely 'educated' by God Himself. He was not an 'illiterate' in that sense."

"God educated Muhammad! What an outrageous claim it is! Muslims are hardly unashamed of making such barefaced claim," Phillip sassed.

"Friend, look at the verse plucked from the Bible.

"*And the Book is delivered to him that is not learned, saying, Read this, I pray thee: and he saith, I am not learned.*" [Bible: Isaiah 29:12]

What do you think about the verse? Do you think the verse is outrageous?"

"It says about an illiterate person. That's all," Phillip made a linear reply.

"Then, why the Book was offered to an illiterate person? Can a wingless bird make a flight? Is the author of the verse sensible?"

"Wisdom gets perished in the locked libraries.

Someone will read the Book to him," Phillip replied in a righteously deceiving way.

"You have failed to find the insights in the verse. In the verse, the arch Angel Gabriel asked Prophet Muhammad (pbuh) to read, and in reply, he said that he was not a learned man. Though the Angel knew that the Prophet Muhammad (pbuh) was not a learned one, yet he insisted that he should read. Because the Angel knew that an 'institution of education' was about to come into existence in him instantly by the Permission of the Almighty.

Here I am citing a verse from the glorious Qur'an that corroborates the verse of the Bible.

"*He has been taught by one 'angel' of mighty power*"

[Qur'an: An-Najm 53: 5]

Collaboration of both verses dispel doubts and makes it indisputably clear that the Prophet was divinely 'educated'."

The Prophet's sublime qualities and his unconditional love for mankind were fully recognised and respected even in his lifetime.

He was noble by birth, munificent by heart, sweetest by tongue, effervescent by tone, humble by nature and magnificent in appearance. He possessed wide forehead, pointed nose and slightly curly hair that rolled down lushly to the shoulders. His chest bent in proportionately down the level of his famished stomach. His teeth, as if, were made of glinting quartz and his lips, as if, were carved out carefully from the frozen flesh of unblemished flowers.

He nursed a great reverence for the Almighty; he honoured his nomination as the final Messenger; he venerated the Qur'an; he showed deference for angels; he used to pay homage to previous Prophets and Messengers; he adored his attachment with the Archangel Gabriel.

He was kind to the poor, empathetic to the necessitous members, compassionate towards the weak, affable towards his wives, chivalrous towards women, gentle towards seniors, amicable with neighbour and merciful towards the enemies. His voice was flowing, soft, and his conversation was engaging and transporting…it impassioned winds of emotions for love, virtue and optimism. Smallness of means could not deter him from being generous in giving and outgoing in interactions. Maltreatment, resistance, harshness of opposition, cruelness of enemies failed to deter him from being the best in bearing the best pattern of conduct. His tongue always uttered fair, just and carved out words valued as pearls. He was a silent sink of pain, and a graceful pool of love; and his loving demeanour and enchanting smile scented the air with kindness and left everlasting impressions in the minds of the multitude. He cuts into a merciful and caring shadow upon the humankind like a great mountain standing tall against the wrath of the blazing sun.

He was orphaned at the age of six. He feared his life and experienced ever increasing hostilities from the fellow Meccan polytheists. He was forced to migrate to Medina, and later within a decade, he conquered Mecca without a bloodshed.

He was an army general and fought numerous battles against the worst odds and won many unbelievable victories ever registered in human history.

He transformed a state. As a statesman, he enacted many equitable, just and justly balanced laws that transformed the less important, divided and the squabbling race of then Arab into a nation to be reckoned with.

He executed the divine project with great deft and flair in his capacity as the last and final Messenger of God. He changed the outlook of the people about life and unfolded the mysteries of the Creation with the ultimate essence of truth revealed in the glorious Qur'an.

He used to wash his own cloths and extend helping hands to household chores. He used to stand in prayers for hours in night and handle the daily affairs of people in day.

In principle, he was the king of the world and the most beloved to God. He could have led life in the opulence of wealth and wide lap of lavish luxury. But he chose to fasten stone with stomach to subdue the pang of hunger. Barely was lit up the oven at his home even for a month.

His admirers were always ready to run on knees for him.

Such was Muhammad (pbuh), -the greatest human being ever travelled on the earth. The Qur'an has announced his high esteem:

"And raised high the esteem (in which) thou (art held)?" [Qur'an: Al Inshirah 94: 4]

He is serene in glory. His name stands tallest amongst all venerated heroic leaders of the mankind; he deserves to be called the saviour of the mankind."

"Would you please disclose the number of wives Muhammad did have? Is it also the part of his glory?" Phillip asked ridiculously.

"I did not because you do know it."

"But the world should know! You must disclose the number," Phillip burnt to dig out the 'number' and appeared insanely consistent in insistence.

He was out for my blood and became wild to hear the *number*.

"We need to correct the sight aberration of our psychological lens.

We use different lens to analyse different people. The nature of our discussion changes its colour, and veers its direction from person to person."

"Do not impart twist to the question. Just disclose the 'number'?" grunted Phillip.

"We suddenly become aesthetic lovers of intelligence if the name of Albert Einstein figures in discussion. We zoom the lens on his famous equation $E=mc^2$ and the theory of *General Relativity*. We do never barge into his marital life with sarcastic attitude as we used to do in case of Prophet Muhammad (pbuh).

But, now the time demands that I should peep into his marital life. Albert Einstein married twice and his first marriage was with Maric. When his first marriage fell apart, he married Elsa as his second wife. Einstein was surprisingly candid to Elsa about his extramarital affairs. Between the mid-1920s and his emigration to the US in 1933, there were several women in his life. Ballpark estimation says that he had extramarital relationships with four women.

But we trick our eyes by using ultra-conservative lens when the name of Muhammad (pbuh) trickles down in discussion. We immediately veer the focus of our discussion towards something 'unsavoury' allegedly linked to Prophet Muhammad (pbuh). We never look into or analyse him from the objective point of view. We never try to understand the grim situations he experienced and passed through.

When fanaticism blurs the eyes and befogs the mind, when rancour dwarfs the goodness of love and depresses the soul from opening up, and when chagrin chastises greatness in thoughts and prevents the heart from splaying its liberal wings, then only people deny the due credits to Prophet Muhammad (pbuh)."

"Both are famous for their respective feats!" Phillip replied with an insidious motive.

"Please clarify."

"Albert Einstein is famous for his $E=mc^2$ and Muhammad is famous for his $E_i= MC^2$!" Phillip *equation-ised* his views.

"Please elucidate."

I begged clarity from Phillip as the equation almost stunted the normal functioning of my mind. Though I could not expect anything soothing about Prophet Muhammad (pbuh) from Phillip, yet I was consoling myself to be positive. It welled up a curiosity and forced me to foster an obligatory optimism.

"E_i=Evils of Islam, M=Muhammad, C=Character of Muhammad, C= Conscience of Muhammad. ($C.C= C^2$)," Phillip illustrated the scurrilous connotations with his absolute cool.

The equation made me retch and I experienced a series of quick unsettling spasms capable enough to make someone droop to a faint.

I remembered a poem penned by Robert Frost. It depicts how the dusting of snow from a hemlock tree upon him by the movement of a crow changed his rueful heart instantly. The showers of snow transported him from the realm of ruefulness into the rival world of blissful feelings. He looked happy.

'The way a crow
Shook down on me
The dust of snow
From a hemlock tree
Has given my heart
A change of mood
And saved some part
Of a day I had rued.'

I almost tended to be happy and expected something agreeable when Phillip was busy in drafting the equation. My expectation suddenly became lofty and started expecting a celestial fragrance from the equation. But, Phillip dusted upon me extremely aberrant connotations of the letters that saddled me inwardly with a huge disappointment.

The doom-indicator crow and the poisonous hemlock tree together helped the poet come out of a bad mood, whereas a human being of sublime intelligence conspired to sadden my heart heavily. My heart ached, my muscles drooped, a painful numbness was spreading madly across every pores of my blood, and my sense almost collapsed to a faint as if I had drunk a beakerful of hemlock!

It was agonisingly mathematical! The present harrowing feelings reduced me to a benumbed stupor, and I wished I could nick my palm on broken glass! I experienced a regal pain that reduced my soul close to tears.

Muhammad (pbuh) is still a screwball to Phillip; he is scornful of Muhammad (pbuh).

Phillip detests Muhammad (pbuh) because of antipathy born out of misinformation crushed into him by the churches. Phillip abhors Muhammad (pbuh) because the name itself creates a sudden jerk of fear in him for some unknown reasons and unseen factors. Phillip abominates Muhammad (pbuh) because of his spiritual-union with Jesus Christ (pbuh) that does not allow him to mend his views towards Islam from moral grounds. Phillip loathes Muhammad (pbuh) because of sheer disgust that he nurses inwardly in his earnestness to downgrade the Prophet. Phillip hates Muhammad (pbuh) because Muhammad (pbuh) is the only figure whose reputation and honour are rising steeply to scale the summit and constantly throwing challenges to some mighty figures in the contest.

Edelweiss grows in the mid of crags of the wild Alps disdaining the intention of the snows that benumb. As time goes on, like a victor, the edelweiss jostles to prominence with grace-filled pose flaunting the wild blast of bloom enchantingly. It puts a stop to the reign of the beautiful snows and looks down upon the family of fading blossoms faithful to lower altitude. It illuminates the Alps' top with her animated blush and takes due pride in displaying rugged individualism. She celebrates her rugged individualism that endured silently the hard bites of the snows laid at her feet, the hitting of sleets that hailed down from the sky, the painful rubbings of frosts-carrying clouds that sifted through her petals and the wind that bent her unfeelingly and pebbled with the fury of drifting snows. Held high in esteem and hailed profusely by the generations of royals, the connoisseurs of beauty and the lovers who mortgage hearts to the demands of passion of no common worth. Many, overcome by craze, get wild and run on their knees to get a glimpse of the dainty blossoms for a special memory. Some scramble the steep cliffs to attain satisfaction that consists in offering the edelweiss to the happiness of their crushes! The snows finally pass the diadem to the edelweiss and become a scene worthy of common glances.

If 'E_i' were to mean the essence of Islam, then the equation would have been handsomely agreeable provided both the 'C' bear positive connotations. But the connotations are disparagingly distasteful, exceedingly poignant and could ruffle the calm of a mountain!

"Albert Einstein was one of the most renowned scientists of the 20th century. Now, for the sake of argument, I assume that Muhammad (pbuh) was a self-declared union leader and he authored the book called the Qur'an. I would now present a few comparisons between Einstein and Muhammad (pbuh). The final decision is left to the unbiased readers.

	Albert Einstein	Muhammad (pbuh)
1	He was forced to leave his native due to 'religious identity'.	He too was forced to leave his native due to 'religious identity'.
2	He never returned to his native.	He returned to his native with dignity and without any bloodshed.
3	He was one of the renowned physicists.	His talent is not confined to any particular field.
4	He published four papers (1905): [1]The photoelectric effect, [2]Brownian motion, [3]Special relativity, [4] The equivalence of matter and energy.	He published a collection of 'papers' in the form of the Qur'an (almost 1400 years ago). [1] ' Theory' related to cosmology: (1a) Origin and evolution of the universe.

	Papers were ignored by the physics community at that point of time.	(1b) The fate of universe. [2] 'Theory' related to astronomy: Motion of celestial bodies. [3] 'Theory' related to biology: Development of embryo. [4] 'Theory' on hydrology: Formation of water cycle. [5] 'Theory' on economics: Banking system & obligatory duty for the rich. [6] 'Theory' on philosophy: The Hereafter. The list is long. Some people still ignore it as religious dogmas!
5	He made 'blunder' in designing the '*static model*' of the universe.	Human beings are yet to find any fault in his theories.
6	He did not challenge the whole humankind to find any discrepancies in his papers.	He challenged the whole humankind to find discrepancies in his 'papers'.

7	He won Nobel prize in 1921 for his explanation of the photoelectric effect.	The Nobel Prize in Physics 2011 was awarded to Saul Perlmutter, Brian P. Schmidt and Adam G. Riess: *"For the discovery of the accelerating expansion of the Universe through observations of distant supernovae"*. They '*confirmed*' the view of the Qur'an on the expanding universe.
8	He wrote a letter to President Franklin D. Roosevelt (1939) to alert him of possibility of Nazi bomb. The letter is believed to be the key factor that motivated the United States to investigate the development of nuclear weapons. The result was Hiroshima-Nagasaki.	He too wrote letters to many statesmen inviting them to Islam.
9	Einstein deduced the well-known equation $E=mc^2$, suggesting that tiny particles of matter could be converted into huge amounts of energy, foreshadowing the development of nuclear power.	His numerous 'theories' can be utilised for the betterment of humankind. None of his theory, even if misused, can have any destructive effect.
10	During the war, Einstein helped the U.S. Navy evaluate designs for future weapons systems.	He did not help in designing any destructive weapons.

11	He was a strong supporter of Zionism and travelled on a lecturing tour to the United States in 1922 to raise funds on behalf of a new Hebrew University in Jerusalem.	He was a strong 'supporter' of Islam. He ordered the war captives of *Badr* to teach ten Muslims to read and write that won them freedom.
12	He did not prescribe any *art of living*.	The *art of living* prescribed by him is being practised by 25 percent of population of the world. His proposed art of living is sublime and second to none.
13	He had no records of nation transformation.	He transformed nations.
14	He had four notable students. Abdul Jabbar Abdullah, an Iraqi wave theory physicist, was harassed and arrested after the rise of the Baath party. Md. R. Siddiqui, an eminent Pakistani physicist, was instrumental in integrated nuclear deterrent development. Leo Szilard too was an eminent physicist in nuclear physics. Most of his students were engaged for the advancement of nuclear Physics.	He had four close disciples known as caliphs. The world has not seen yet another administrator like the second Caliph Omar Farrukh (RA). Other Caliphs too left everlasting impressions.

Now, I urge the readers to take decision being detached from unfairness."

"Only the sick and fanatics would laud the achievements of Muhammad. Better, you desist yourself from pulling up Muhammad to the level of Einstein; he cannot be elevated to that level.

By the way, why did not you mention that the Prophet of God has recommended in the Book to beat 'women'?" Phillip explored a point vaingloriously. He was brusque with me.

"What do you mean by the word '*women*'? Do you mean even a son can beat his mother?"

"You know better?" Phillip evaded the inquiry with a callous attitude. I did not know if he wished to sound callous!

"I can dissect your intention.

Friend, the statement is insensate and lacks decency. It can create menace in the minds of women; it can cause a shudder of fear!

"And We have enjoined on man (to be good) to his parents: in travail upon travail did his mother bear him,…" [Qur'an: Luqman 31: 14]

"And, out of kindness, lower to them the wing of humility, and say: "My Lord! Bestow on them thy Mercy even as they cherished me in childhood." [Qur'an: Al Isra 17: 24]

Such are the commands of the Qur'an! Nowhere you would find such vivid depiction about the esteem of a mother. At the zenith of reverence lies the sanctity of a mother; at the summit of honour lies the dignity of a mother!"

"But what about 'wife-beating'?" Phillip needled me again.

My tardiness in reply increased his insistence manifold.

"Yes, '*wife-beating*' is mentioned in the Qur'an."

"Menacing! Be glory to the author of the Book! One thing that can be said certainly that Muslims are cut out to be insane actors to act in diametrically opposite and ridiculously contrasting roles!

That means that the Muslim women are destined to bear the brunt of husbands and luckily, at the same time, can seek solace from their children! If I go deep into the dustbin, one can draw an easy inference that Muslim women, if deprived of children, destined to be tormented throughout the life, -a *raw deal* is reserved for them all the way to death!

Suppressed are their protests; oppressed are their physical bodies; repressed are their personalities; -are they 'female' or animal? 'Muslim women', 'defeated personality' or 'lower form of human beings' all three are synonymous and can be interchanged to construct a sentence of the same family," Phillip exhausted.

His tongue appeared scurrilous cutting hastily through the waves of defamation. He winged arrows of piercing criticisms that thrust into my heart badly!

"Now let us check what is written in the Glorious Qur'an.

"As to those women on whose part ye fear disloyalty and ill-conduct, admonish them (first), (Next), refuse to share their beds, (And last) beat them (lightly); but if they return to obedience, seek not against them Means (of annoyance): For Allah is Most High, great." [Qur'an: Nisa 4:34]

A good wife is supportive and harmonious with her husband. Presence or absence of her husband does not affect her principles. She is dedicated to protect the property and reputation of the family besides protecting her own virtue.

In case of something unpleasant and detestable occurrence on her part, the Qur'an has recommended corrective actions. Verbal advice or admonition tops the list. If that entails failure, then it must be preceded by severance in sexual relationship. If the problem still persists, then some 'slight' (as light as a feather) physical correction may be administered as the least preferred option in the sequence of actions.

Suppose you are asked to modify the above verse, how would you do it?"

"*Status and stature are equal to both men and women. Marriage is a social bond solemnised with the consents of two souls that admiringly and explicitly crowns equal rights to both. The manifold of integrity, love and mutual respect should front in every affair and find premium placement deep in the heart of the bond. The rights, so given or construed in the bond, should be the overarching principle and could be exercised by the either party with all fairness, transparency and appreciation necessarily when the fate of the bond seems to be threatened by a breakdown. In case of an unwanted occurrence, mutual discussion must be preceded by the event called the 'peaceful parting of the ways'. And, in the process of severance, one should not drag other in the mud'*," Phillip modified the verse.

He looked at me with a tinge of condescension that I had normally expected of him. His eyes glinted in satisfaction after bouncing the verse on the table.

"The verse resembles a '*new power balance*' equation that perfectly suits premiers of two powerful countries assembled across the table to solve a long pending border issue. Should the discussion fails to produce the efficacy, they should board immediately the next flight for departure.

The verse appears to have a tenuous hold on the future of the marriage. The efficacy of the verse is placed ambiguously somewhere between the precarious edges of brittle certainty and alluring uncertainty. The new verse lacks endurance essential to withstand the knocks of the breakdown.

Anyways, what is your confidence level that the issue will be sorted out at the first sitting?"

"The chance is high…," Phillip replied assertively and almost defended his confidence.

"What is the probability?"

"It is…it is 50 percent," Phillip replied after reducing the '*high chance*' to exclusively '*equal chance*' according to the law of probability.

If the first sitting *falls down on* the bleakness, and the 'bond' is poised about to be dissolved in breakdown, is it not wise to give a second chance to your married life?"

"What do you mean?" inquired Phillip in a feeble voice.

"What should be your next course of action?"

"I don't think that there should be any other viable ways," Phillip replied condescendingly.

"It's a defiance; it's a denial. Have you applied your search-engine to other viable options?"

Sensing his silence, I continued,

"But the Qur'an instructs that 'severance (for short period) in physical relationship' should be the next step."

"Why should I suffer for other's fault? The reason does not lie with me only," Phillip replied with floundering confidence. Phillip appeared quick to dispose of the 'bond' after the fiasco of the 'first step.

"'Suffer? What do you mean? Your solution seems to have been influenced heavily by an ulterior motive that denies access to a benign heart,' I began, 'Anyways, what is the chance that the issue will be sorted out at second attempt?'"

"Slim chance," Phillip said casting a bleak glance at me.

"Slim chance? How can you justify this? –

If mutual discussion can yield '*50 percent chance*', then how can you justify the '*poor outcome*' of mutual sacrifice? The efficacy of mutual sacrifice, I am impelled to say, can assertively surpass the outcome of mutual discussion; is not it?"

Phillip was silent and trying to supress the response.

"It does not need a seal of a great justice to assert that the mutual sacrifice is invariably bound to yield a greater result than the mutual discussion, and even if the mutual sacrifice yields '*50 percent chance*', then almost all the problems seem to have dissolved amicably in reconciliation before being threatened by the menace of family-breakdown. Friend, marriage is an institution founded on the mutual understanding and mutual sacrifice, -the former comes from the brain, and the later from the heart.

Like you said, 50 percent of issues will be solved through discussion, and for the rest 50 percent '*parting the ways*' is inevitable. Mutual discussion will certainly bring the issue from 'fire' to 'frying pan'. But for the rest 50 percent cases, the proposed solution will again throw the issue into 'furnace'. Your suggestion makes a closed loop like '*fire-frying pan-furnace*'.

The solution can provide a very good fillip to people like Salman Rushdie, -it shall pamper him to promiscuity! The perils called 'family-breakdowns' will intensify its presence manifold in the societies with enhanced might and augmented temper to shake every settled fabric of the family bond. The trend has already assumed a disproportionate form in many advanced countries of the world.

The first two competent steps seem to have had great qualifications to achieve the target that leads to reconciliation. If the disagreement does not stop there, and the collapse winks at inevitability, then only the third action, the least preferred option, is permitted by the Qur'an: a '*slight physical correction*' can be administered. It should be as light as '*beating with a quill*'.

If '*beating women*' were the only intention, then the Qur'an would have mentioned it as the first corrective action. '*Beating*' is not advisable, but permissible as the last option.

Friends, the divorce procedure stated in the Qur'an is second to none…it is the cream of the crop…it is the best."

"You have overreached yourself mentally. Better you can claim it in private when no non-Muslim is listening to you," Kumaran reacted. He frowned at my view.

"The whole parliament of a country had listened to the speech of a non-Muslim parliamentarian who openly and candidly stated that the divorcing process stated in the Qur'an is the most advanced one, and it is second to none. You can guess the name of the country…it's an easy guess friend."

The Qur'an is best interpreted through the deeds and the sayings of the noble Prophet. He himself was most affable to his wives and never did he utter a single word devoid of civility and chivalry. The Prophet did not even intend to admonish his wife Aishah (r.a) when a scandalous allegation was fabricated against her.

"Is it mentioned in the Koran that, if a woman is alleged for sexual disloyalty, then she has to gather four witnesses on her behalf to prove herself innocent?" Kumaran inquired swiftly.

"There are many barefaced mores prescribed in his Book! Exclusive prerogative given to masculine violence!" Phillip mocked being equipped with sophomoric knowledge.

"It's a load of tripe. The truth is just the opposite…!"

Both gazed at me with weird glance when I disabused the notion.

"What do you mean?" Kumaran asked looking at me directly.

"This is a piece of misinformation supplied by someone who finds pleasure in manufacturing slanders and suchlike against Islam.

"And those who launch a charge against chaste women, and produce not four witnesses (to support their allegations),- flog them with eighty stripes;…" [Qur'an: Nuur 24: 4]

Do you still think that barefaced mores prescribed in the Qur'an?

Certainly, this is not at all a masculine violence, rather a prescription designed to stop masculine violence against women. In other words, it is a boon for the chaste women but a bane for the slanderous men. You need to delve deep into the Qur'an.

Hope, now you are armed with the right information."

Slandering against a chaste woman has been taken seriously in the Qur'an. Allegations against women's chastity need independent corroboration of four unbiased witnesses. Failing to which, the slanderer must be treated as a wicked transgressor and subsequently be subjected to punishment. Our Creator has sent a strong signal to those who are in the habit of slandering women.

"What if a woman is proved guilty of adultery?" inquired Kumaran.

"Certainly punishment of medieval period is prescribed," Phillip cast aspersion. I stopped expecting cessation in his criticism.

"Request not to pin misinformation on Islam.

Friend, you will never be able to be a cut above Islam by just *dragging Islam in the mud* every time. I do know it is not easy for you to invest patience to delve into the Qur'an. I really find it very hard even to guess the reasons of your abnormal intolerance, real indecency and genuine outrage towards the Qur'an. Understandably, a moral mildew has delved a niche somewhere in your heart which always instigates you to collect mental food equivalent of a hard-drug through criticising Islam. A few drags of jimsonweed (thorn apple) could spark joy and lighten your heavy heart!"

"Are you begging grace for Islam?" Phillip added in a frivolous way.

"Grace is something meant for those whose foundation is shaky, - Islam has a granite-base. No intelligence has ever born that could give a bad shake to Islam.

"The woman and the man guilty of adultery or fornication, flog each of them with a hundred stripes:...." [Qur'an: Nuur 24: 2]

Prescribed is the equal punishment to both man and woman.

Now let me present a verse from the Bible.

"If a man commits adultery with the wife of an Israelite, both he and the woman shall be put to death." [Bible: Leviticus 20:10]

Now the ball is in your court to judge which punishment bears the resemblance to that of the medieval age.

Anyways, now I would ask you, what should be your stand against adultery?"

"But why do you call it 'adultery'?" Phillip reacted. His tantrum almost *hit the roof* having heard the word 'adultery'.

"Then, what should it be called?"

"You cannot snatch the freedom away. Once get married does not mean that you should fetter yourself forever to the nasty coupling of the wedlock. It's just a marriage, -not a complex labyrinth, neither a bottomless murky quagmire!" Phillip stated brusquely. I felt harshness in his voice.

"My query is evaded. Nowhere is mentioned in the Qur'an that a member once entered into a wedlock can never come out of it.

"O ye who believe! Ye are forbidden to inherit women against their will. Nor should ye treat them with harshness,…." [Qur'an: Al Nisa 4: 19]

The Qur'an has passed the caution to the right member. Being physically and economically 'mightier', men turn out to be instinctively inclined to exercise upper hand over women. Islam shows strong aversion to harsh behaviour towards women.

Woman too can exercise her prerogative to dissolve the relation solemnised in the wedlock. If she feels insecurity on her husband's part, she is allowed to come out of the wedlock through the dignified way as prescribed by the Qur'an.

"If a wife fears cruelty or desertion on her husband's part, there is no blame on them if they arrange an amicable settlement between themselves;…" [Qur'an: Al Nisa 4: 128]

Islam hates every form of compulsion. A woman can verily exercise her rights to sever the wedlock".

"How many wives did Muhammad have?" Kumaran asked in a great agility of his tongue.

Both were running after my blood for the answer. They became wildly off and made several attempts to bounce me into publishing the 'number'. I delayed the answer deliberately. I intended to put them off for a bulk of moments.

After a good while, I made my mind to place the disclosure to the party.

"Prophet Muhammad (pbuh) had eleven wives."

The '*number*' was greeted with much glee tightly coupled with furore that climbed unrestrainedly to an undisclosed height of rollicking zest. They celebrated the moment with an unusual rapture laced with trails of wild chuckles, streaks of impertinent smiles and mouldy sense of giddiness. The *number* indeed played an indispensable role in giving them the much-needed celestial mental food that helped them climb steeply to the highest precipice of rapture. They pinned themselves there and set *the new normal* of amusement whose madness just *went through the roof.* They brashly transitioned to the line of a joint conference showing common interest in criticising the 'dark' marital life of Muhammad (pbuh). Seemed it, a rude amusement slithered suddenly from the dark pockets of their hearts as they found a piquant zest for amusement in the number 'eleven'! I found them sodden with the flowing showers of zestfulness. I found them *shooting the breeze* for quite a longer while!

They stared at me hoping to see if some pain roiling my inner tranquillity and creating distressing wrinkles on my face. To disclose, the moment with its painful sharpness excruciated me badly and left me inwardly sore. But I tried to appear stoical immuring myself within silence. My sad soul was looking for a balm, and in its effort, it clasped a tender breeze and exchanged some private talks. It swapped itself with the breeze's soul.

"It frequently preys upon me, and no longer I could put back the query, -

Your beloved Prophet had more than ten wives, but the Koran has prescribed only four for you, -a sumptuously majestic meal for your Prophet, but an insipid dish for you! Is not it an injustice?" Kumaran lodged a complaint with a flippancy. He found easily an 'incongruity' in the holy Qur'an.

He added an extra swirl to the turbulence.

"Should the Qur'an prescribe eleven wives for the followers of Islam?"

"Yes...why not...if the quantity could *go through the roof* for your beloved Prophet, then why not for you?" Kumaran's tongue rustled. He held the Prophet to ridicule with his surface knowledge.

"Then, do you think the Almighty should prescribe for Muslims exactly the same '*marital life style*' (sequence of marriages must be honoured) of Prophet Muhammad (pbuh)?"

"The sequence does not matter much, what matters is the quantity –almost a dozen of wives! He just amassed women of his choice," lampooned Kumaran.

"Friends, no man on the earth could ever be willing to accept the *marital life style* of the Prophet Muhammad (pbuh) if offered to them. They will be damn scared to accept it.

The question might baffle many 'easy-to-be-misled' people if the true picture is not presented to them. People should be apprised of the life of the noble Prophet and his stupendous struggle in delivering completeness to the assigned divine project. People should know why Prophet Muhammad (pbuh) is called the most glorious person ever born on the face of the earth.

Prophet Muhammad (pbuh) led a very simple life supported by the bare minimum of necessities. His wives were not idly wasting away the hours in a lap of luxury, rather led a life of labour and sacrifice. Moreover, most of his marriages occurred at an age when carnal desire had lost its 'amorous' urge and was worn-out.

Now, let's have an honest analysis about the marital life of the noble Prophet:

He remained single until the age of 25. He was pure like snow and impressionable like a child, and maintained an utterly unblemished character.

From the age 25 to 50, in the prime of his life, he was faithful to his only wife Khadijah (r.a) who was 15 years older than the noble Prophet and had children from her two previous marriages. He remained in love with her until she died, and often the noble Prophet talked of his life with her with a great deal of love and nostalgia. It was his wife Khadijah (r.a) who offered him *a shoulder to cry on* when Prophet experienced mounting distress and pain at the initial stage of Prophethood.

Between the ages 50 and 52, he remained unmarried. He lived alone. He felt desolate without his wife Khadijha (r.a). Passing away of Khadijah (r.a) appeared to be a painful amputation for the Prophet.

At the age of 53, he married Sauda (r.a) who was too a widow. Between the ages 53 and 60, he married all his other wives for many pressing reasons evolved out of many harsh and hostile circumstances. It can be affirmed that a man could not suddenly turn hypersexual at this twilight age, -I can vow for this affirmation.

Now if I draw the summary, -all male Muslims have to marry (their first marriage at the age of 25) a two times widow (15 years older as well) having her children from the two previous marriages. After twenty-eight years of first marriage, he will marry second time again with a widow. During the third marriage, he may marry a virgin!

Now, I am asking you, -would you readily accept if the similar '*marital life style*' is offered to you?"

They both seemed in flight immuring themselves within wall of silence. They experienced a frostbite and appeared stone-cold like Siberian snow! I found them snugged in the quietude of a peaceful shell rebuffing my proposal internally.

"Can you show me any world known personality whose first marriage happened with a two times widow having children from her previous marriages? And the second marriage, after the death of the first wife, too happened with a widow?"

"I am calling up your maverick response. Please respond gentlemen."

My request did not call forth any emotion from them. Persuading them to respond seemed *like getting blood out of a stone,* perhaps their tongues were fettered tightly to teeth.

The Prophet was not chosen for leading 'king size' life but executing the stupendous task assigned to him. The unbelievers tried, more often than not, to influence the Prophet by the wile of trickery. He was offered many a time by the 'unbelievers' the chance of leading an extremely lavish and luxurious life marrying the most beautiful Arabian women on the condition that he must sacrifice Islam. But he denounced all that with an utter contempt. He knew, he was not chosen to celebrate 'carnal festivity' on the earth; he knew he was the Messenger of the Almighty and the life in this capacity was full of hardships and adversaries. He knew, things might not go well, and he was not destined to ride *on the crest of a wave* while confronting the unbelievers.

To cement relation and advance the nascent Islam, it was the demand of the situation to take some strong tribes into the fold of Islam. In a tribal society, it was customary to seal treaties through marriages, and in this regard, his marriage to one woman won all her people into Islam. Many believing women often approached Muhammad (pbuh) offering him themselves in marriage to become a part of the family of the noble Prophet. It was their irresistible spiritual desires to become a part of the 'divine journey' of Prophet Muhammad (pbuh).

Except Aishah (r.a.), rest of the wives of the Prophet were either widows or divorcees, and most of his wives were old and devoid of beauty. Aishah (r.a.) was the only young virgin amongst the wives of Prophet Muhammad (pbuh) and that too was a part of the divine plan. Prophet Muhammad (pbuh) is the only prophet whose speeches, teachings, lifestyle and all other minute details are preserved, and that were mostly possible because of the sharp and young mind of his wife Aishah (r.a). Contributions of his other wives and companions of the Prophet too were commendably huge. The books of authentic Hadith attribute more than thousands of narrations and Prophetic traditions to his wives alone.

The present world loathes marriage but nurses an untamed desire to strike physical relationship with widows and divorcees. They appear hell-bent to swindle the institute of humanity by exploiting widows and divorcees for mere carnal desires. A woman to them is just a pack of flesh and can be treated as the lower form of human beings!

"If I agree for the sake of arguments that Muslim can have eleven wives (virgin, widow or divorcee whatever may be) because their Prophet had the same number of wives. Then, do you suggest that Christians too shall marry seven hundreds (700) princesses and at the same time shall possess three hundreds (300) concubines?"

"What do you mean?" Phillip broke silence after being teased.

"The Bible says:

"Solomon Married seven hundred (700) princesses and also had three hundreds (300) concubines" [Bible: 1 Kings 11:3]

What would you say about the verse?"

"Solomon was the Prophet of Jews. You better ask them," replied Phillip.

"Then, do you think no Christian should ever marry a woman because Jesus Christ (pbuh) did not marry during his 'stint' on the earth?"

"Jesus Christ was Lord...marriage is not a normal for him; better you cut his name off the list," retorted Phillip.

"Then, how the Father in the heaven produced a '*begotten son*' in the form of Jesus Christ? Don't you think The Father is a Lord?"

A clear uneasiness ran across the face of Phillip. He tentatively blocked his ears as if my query produced loud reports of guns.

There are hardly any men living on the earth who in full consciousness would reject the marital life style of Solomon (pbuh) if offered on a platter. But I am doubly sure, they would reject downright, for the obvious reason, if the marital life style of Prophet Muhammad (pbuh) is offered to them. They would prefer to run on their knees in dreary ruts of scorching desert than adopting the marital life style of Prophet Muhammad (pbuh).

Now let us expand the deal of the logic. Let us take the consensus of women on the same matter. I am sure, no women living on the face of the earth, would prefer the marital life style of Solomon (pbuh), but definitely they would prefer the marital life style of Muhammad (pbuh). Every widow or divorcee would search a person who is like Muhammad (pbuh).

The noble Prophet employed his life to ameliorate the declining sensibility of human race, whereas we are instinctively resolved to exacerbate it further to the level of infliction. Contrast is clear; disparity is wide. We are 'fortunate' that our Creator has not reproduced the same prescription made for the Prophet Muhammad (pbuh).

"We sent thee (Muhammad) not, but as a Mercy for all creatures." [Qur'an: Al Ambiya 21: 107]

Muhammad (pbuh) was not a menace for humanity, but an unprecedented mercy sent by the Almighty. He was the saviour of humanity.

Status and dignity of women in Islam—if not studied thoroughly and objectively—can lead to brutal misunderstanding. Under those dubious assumptions, Muhammad (pbuh) is often accused of practicing and encouraging unjust treatment to women. But the truth is different and now it clearly stands out as opposite to the prevailing belief. In fact, the general rule in Islam is monogamy, not polygamy.

The Quran is the only Holy Book on the earth that openly stands for monogamy. Yes your read is right, -the only Holy Book on the earth that speaks '*marry only one…*'!

"If ye fear that ye shall not be able to deal justly with the orphans, Marry women of your choice, Two or three or four; but if ye fear that ye shall not

be able to deal justly (with them), then only one,....” [Qur’an: Al Nisa 4:3]

Polygamy is not recommended in Islam, rather permitted under certain guidelines and circumstances. Permission to practice polygamy is not associated with mere carnal gratification, rather it should be associated with compassion towards the widows and the orphans.

At the beginning of the above verses, the Qur’an has introduced a conditional clause about the ‘orphans’, -marry the orphans if you are sure that you can protect their interests and properties with perfect justice to them and to your own dependants if you have any. If not, make other agreeable arrangements for the orphans. Before the revelation of the Quran, there was no upper limit for polygamy, and men in Arab were in the habit of mingling indiscriminately with opposite sex, committing promiscuity and exercising masculine rights in committing indiscriminate form of polygamy.

Islam teaches to be compassionate not just to young, beautiful, lissom-leggy and petite women, but more so to women who are old, fading-beauties, destitute, widows, divorcees and orphans.

So, polygamy certainly is an exception in Islam.

Chapter 5

"Does Islam consider nationalism a dross?" Kumaran inquired with a raw seriousness.

He raised the temperature of the table a few notches. The caprice of his mood took me by surprise and shook me inwardly. A family of insane feelings were jostling to surface and ruffled the normal appearance of my face. I subdued it. I snatched a glance at him in disbelief.

"Why this question all of a sudden?"

"Do not be surprised by the suddenness…it is apposite.

What does the verse mentioned earlier mean: "*-and die not except in a state of Islam?*" Kumaran evidenced. He appeared way serious and was trying to tease from me the information that he was looking for.

"What could be the signification of the verse?"

"Here nationalism goes neglected. The verse hints that Islam must take the upper hand in your worldly affairs and be given obligatory prerogative to neglect nationalism. The verse says, if construed rightly, that your heart should beat for Islam and be imbued with the feelings and fervour of Islam. Islam, if I am not exaggerating, undermines the *raison d'etre* of nationalism!"

Kumaran deepened his voice accompanied by the charging tongue.

He suspended his breath, stopped the motion of blood and struggled much with the essential corporeal parameters of life to express that. He succeeded.

I wonder if he were bestowed with royal prerogative to rough up others on the subject of nationalism. He applied the prerogative to me and doubted my loyalty to the nation.

The verse that Kumaran was pointing to: *"O ye who believe! Fear Allah as He should be feared, and die not except in a state of Islam."* [Qur'an: Al Imran 3: 102]

"That does not mean that Islam subjugates the spirit of nationalism!"

"If you are asked to choose between Nationalism and Islam, - which one will you reject?" Kumaran tried to juice out my soft corner.

"Which one should be chosen?"

"I'm asking you, which one would you reject?" Kumaran insisted.

He appeared seemingly blinded by the fist of blatant chauvinism. I was contemplating to reply him in the tone of Samuel Johnson (English writer, 1709-1784) who once said:

"The patriotism is the last refuge of the scoundrel".

Or, through the voice of the great Albert Einstein:

"Nationalism: An infantile disease. It is the measles of mankind!"

I knew Kumaran was waiting eagerly in disguise to hear those kind of quotes from me that would make his path easy in charging me with sedition. But, I suppressed my protest as those quotes might have grafted me enough in sedition charge. I quashed internally the urges of quoting the voices of Samuel and Einstein.

Had the situation demanded to express those quotes in front of Mahatma Gandhi, or Nelson Mandela, I would have definitely expressed it, as I knew, they would not charge me with sedition, instead the two great leaders would allow me to express myself to exhaustion.

"Friend, you would definitely get the answer of your authoritative inquisition.

Which one will you prefer - living with two kidneys intact or with a single kidney?"

"If you sacrifice one kidney then surely your care and possessiveness for the other will increase manifold!" Kumaran replied with some unknown motive. But he looked confident.

Perhaps he intended to turf me out of the arena of nationalism!

"Are you living with single kidney now?"

"No. My view is just a logical inference and certainly not an aberration," Kumaran almost retorted.

"If I ask you to choose between oxygen and water -which one would you reject?

If I ask you to choose between the sun and the earth–which one would you reject?

If I ask you to choose between your father and mother –whom would you reject?"

"Please reply?"

"My question is evaded entirely. Could you submerge Islam by nationalism? If situation demands, could you sacrifice Islam for the sake of nationalism?" Kumaran forwarded his journalistic inquiry. He gave me a way cool stare.

"I too have not got answers of my questions; -it's blown in the wind. Why are you averse to answering?"

"My question is more relevant than yours. Islam has issued an ultimatum to Muslims: '*...die not except in the state of Islam...*". No religion in the world perhaps has issued such dire statement for his followers. Even not the 'Stalinist Communism'!

Does not it seem that the statement has depressed the spirit of nationalism?" Kumaran commented. Kumaran explain his views mixing refined acerbity with sharp.

"How have you been able to uphold nationalism by not sacrificing Hinduism?"

"For me, nationalism comes first and I'm very candid about that," Kumaran replied grandly. He then cast a niggardly glance on me, and then swerved quickly to avoid sight-confrontation.

"Why Hinduism does stand second to nationalism?

Which doctrine of Hinduism does prevent you from becoming a full-grown nationalist?

Or, does Hinduism contain any substance that discourages you from becoming a nationalist?"

"Hinduism does not say –'*you must die in the state of Hinduism*'. Nowhere in Hinduism would you find such disreputable religious doctrine," Kumaran stated in an agitated voice. He almost bawled at me.

"All right friend. What extra things you do for the progress of the nation that I don't?"

"Seemingly, your heart is caked with the thoughts of Islam, - nationalism is clearly *turfed out* of your heart. It calls into question the truthfulness of your nationalism," Kumaran criticised taking absurdity on his side.

Perhaps, he had done a vivisection of my heart and dissected it to finer grains to find out the mystery embedded in it. He placed the 'finding' on the table like a confident seer.

"Forget about the state of my heart for the time being. Just tell me –what extra things you do for the progress of the nation?"

"Do not bend the direction of the discussion. Come out of stubbornness and just answer my question," Kumaran appeared way insistent.

"Actions speak louder than words. Actions separates a patriot from a nationalist. So, please answer my questions."

"I work hard and pay tax to the development of the country. Now tell me –what extra things you do for the country?" Kumaran turned the question on me as if he turned a virtual gun on me.

"In principle, I'm paying almost double the taxes that you pay to the country.

Being a professional and good citizen of the country, I regularly pay tax to the government. Besides, being a Muslim, I am very much aware of my obligation towards charity (Zakah) as ordained in the holy Qur'an. Every year 2.5 percent of my savings paid in charity. Even the amount spent in charity does not get accounted for tax exemption. It is all done for the fellow human beings of my country.

Allah (swt) has solicited us to spend in charity.

"The parable of those who spend their substance in the way of Allah is that of a grain of corn: it growth seven ears, and each ***ear*** *hath a hundred grains…."* [Qur'an: Baqara 2:261]

"And the likeness of those who spend their substance, seeking to please Allah and to strengthen their souls, is as a garden, high and fertile: …" [Qur'an: Baqara 2:265]

Friend, look at the verses cited above. Are not they wonderful? This is the Holy Qur'an revealed for humanity.

If I sacrifice Islam that does not mean that it will jack my nationalistic spirit up. Rather, it will chip away at it. Friend, Islam is a massive Idea, and the nationalism, on the whole, is just a little element that can easily be subsumed in the greatness of Islam!"

"That's all fine, but what about your heart? Certainly it does not chant nationalism, for it is already overcome by the influence of Islam," added Kumaran.

Kumaran appeared insistent in the pursuit of knowing the elemental character of my heart. The tone of his voice was brutal, and he was almost adjacent to impose coercion and intimidation.

"Islam is blood for both of us!"

"What nonsense! It's for you only," Kumaran reacted and resorted to a mood almost freaky.

"Friend, you have failed to understand the insights of the remark.

Islam is blood for me means -it's a lifeline for me.

Islam is blood for you means -the colour of blood that frightens you!"

"It frightens not only me but the whole world. It gnaws away at the peace of the world. People hate Islam like plague!" retorted Kumaran. He put a spin on my view. Seemed, he was partially fused with fiery spirit.

Phillip's eyes glistened and he patted Kumaran's back admiringly. I failed to guess if he was endorsing his views or asking him to cool down. Finally Kumaran donned a fiendish smile and cast glance askance upon me.

"How much did you contribute to the making of the earth habitable?"

"It sounds out of the way now! Why are you asking this?" Kumaran inquired irritatingly.

"Can I not?

No one has so far brandished overpoweringly such nasty power on me like you.

It seems as if your forefathers did help God in making the earth habitable and in return God offered them the exclusive rights of ownership of the earth.

Tomorrow you may ask me –whether I do deserve to live on the face of the earth because my forefathers did not contribute to the efforts of God in making the earth habitable!"

"Did my view on Islam torment you?" Kumaran inquired mockingly. He knew very well that the comments directed at me had an intimate association with excruciation.

"Never! Yours is a small mocking. I have survived many of greater lethality and foulest, -yours is a moderate, mediocre and just a simple foul of average intensity!"

"How much did you contribute to the freedom struggle of the country?"

"Did you participate in freedom fighting?" Kumaran swung the query into my court quickly.

"So, we both did not help God in the making the earth habitable.

We both did not contribute to the freedom struggle of the country.

I spent more for the country –taxes plus 'zakat'.

Then, please tell me, which factor did force you to look into my nationalism?"

"It's Islam that always instigates me to call into question the delicate balance of your heart! Your heart is heavily inward with Islam; your tears trill for the sake of Islam and an intimate bond with Islam is winding in your veins! Islam tears apart the fabric that links your heart with nationalism and scatters its own fanatic grains upon the field making itself abundant in your flesh!" Kumaran *flew off the handle.*

"What Mahatma Gandhi did utter in his last breath?"

"Everybody knows it, – he uttered 'Hey Ram,'" Kumaran replied dispassionately and almost in a half-wonder.

"Was Mahatma Gandhi nationalist?"

"Have you achieved that exceedingly perfect synchronisation between religion and nationalism like Gandhi?

He took only two seconds to utter these two words. What do you utter during the last breath and how much time does it kill?" Kumaran inquired in an authoritative voice.

"'*There is no God but Allah (swt) and Muhammad (pbuh) is His Messenger*'.

But what do mean by saying Gandhi took only two seconds for the religion?"

"Gandhi took two seconds of his life for the religion and gave the rest for the sake of nation. What about you? -

Of prayer, five times a day is too much of a frequency! And, the world knows how callously and carelessly you do waste one full month in fasting! Do you have any surplus time left for the nation?" added Kumaran accusing me in an infantile way.

"Do you think Maulana Abul Kalam Azad (1888 -1958 CE) was a nationalist?"

He allowed nothing to escape from his lips but a poor silence! His tongue seemed undecided over whether to send down slander or sobriety.

Nationalism is not a submissive subject that one can trifle with! It's a delicate subject that demands deft handling!

He became diligent in finding out the 'true' feelings of my heart. He was wonderingly searching the reason how one could strike a perfect synchronisation between nationalism and religion! He was under the impression that Islam was monstrously discordant with nationalism, but during the discourse, he grew in disbelief as he gradually failed to find the same in me. To his dismay, the outcome of the discourse did not take his side, rather reshuffled his 'otherwise oriented' inner-self to the normal. The 'occurrence' transgressed all bounds of his parochial local logic. He swallowed it as pleasant surprise that *beggars belief*.

"Now I am presenting another verse from the Qur'an which is more encompassing, precise and incisive.

"*Say, my prayer, my offering, my life and my death are for Allah, the Lord of all the worlds.*" [Qur'an: An-Anam 6:162]

Does the verse confront with the spirit of nationalism?"

"Islam is a dark lair where absolute sense of fanaticism resides; it cuts off the subject from the link of the normal world affairs," Kumaran came out of the silo of silence and replied.

"What do you think of the Islamic prayer (Salah)?"

"It's just a ritual invented by Muhammad," observed Kumaran.

"Islam endeavours to cleanse its followers of unpleasant things and instils a sense of good conduct into them through various and varied spiritual means. Islam thinks seriously about the wellbeing of its followers, and in her eagerness to achieve that, Islam has prescribed the best physiotherapy available on the earth.

"*... and establish regular Prayer: for Prayer restrains from shameful and unjust deeds; and remembrance of Allah is the greatest (thing in life) without doubt. ...*" [Qur'an : Al Ankabut 29: 45]

The true prayer purges us of anything (act, plan, thought, motive, words) of which we should be ashamed of, or which would work injustice to others. Such prayer passes into our innermost self."

"The verse itself hints that prayer makes one a righteous person. So, for a righteous person the prayer stands as an option, right?" Kumaran placed the logic.

"Just look at the last line: "*...and remembrance of Allah is the greatest (thing in life) without doubt,*"

We pray to achieve proximity of Allah (swt)."

"Again, as the verse hints, for a good person the prayer is an option, -it just turns to be a form of exercise. You can remember your Allah during exercise also!" Kumaran drew some logic perfunctorily.

"If I agree for the sake of argument, I would request you to show me an exercise which can yield more benefits than the Islamic prayer?"

"Fanaticism prevents outlook from being wide and outgoing. Do not immure yourself within aberrations.

You have tricked your eyes, deceived your heart and cheated your soul by not knowing about some '*art of living*' ruling predominantly the world. Its acceptance is wide, and it has been grandly heaped with many high praise and sublime honours," narrated Kumaran haughtily.

"My rational mind does not permit me to make claim in vacuity. I know it jars on you, but the truth will publish itself in the due course of time."

"Yoga is magnificent and the whole world has shown full tilt towards it. Unfortunately, Muslims are still clung to obstinacy ignoring the benevolent calls and refusing the golden hands of Yoga. Seemed it, Muslims have sunk into the murky depth of religious quagmire and been languishing moronically there by adopting the medieval prescription of Muhammad. They unconsciously are sunk at the last depth of a sea where darkness rules. And above its surface, a violent whirlwind reigns that suppresses their cries for help forever," retorted Kumaran failing to resist a dig at Prophet Muhammad (pbuh).

"All right friend. Can you name any exercise which allows the heart to relax, but at the same time increases blood flow to the brain?"

"'Calf pumping Yoga' can increase blood flow upwards. Just stand on toes and ankles alternately and shake the calf gently. Besides, many other aerobic exercises can increase blood flow to the brain," Kumaran stated looking at me directly.

"Is my septuagenarian grandmother able to do the calf pumping and the aerobic exercise?"

"I hope you should not put a spin to my answer, -your query is justly answered," replied Kumaran.

"My query is not answered yet. You have failed to understand my query. -

Heart must relax during the exercise. Definitely, in calf pumping and aerobatic exercises the heart does not relax but works harder. Hope you got my point."

"What do you mean exactly?" Kumaran inquired in half-astonishment.

"The calf pumping and aerobic exercise increase blood flow to brain by dint of increased heartbeat. In fact, in this exercise heart beats harder, –it does not relax."

"Any example?"

"I can guess it. To cower in front of your Allah like – 'throw the face downwards and raise the hip upwards', right?" Phillip lampooned.

"A 'God' prayed like this!"

"Which God?" Phillip gawked at me.

"Jesus Christ (pbuh) prayed like this!

"He went a little farther on, threw himself face downwards on the ground, and prayed," [Bible: Mathew 26:39]

Friend, do you still want to throw satire? Just think, your 'God' prayed the way we Muslims pray!"

"It's just a way of prayer. It does not matter who prays—you or any God. Have you conducted any medical experiment to prove your point, or it's just a boisterous claim?" Kumaran inquired.

"It does! It matters who prayed the way Muslims pray. It adds pride and confers accolade to the 'prescription' of Muhammad (pbuh)! Just think the 'God' of Phillip prayed the way we pray!

I would like to draw your attention to the explanations. -

Blood flow is the single most important thing for our brain. Blood delivers glucose to the brain which is used as energy. Brain uses around 20 percent of the blood from every heartbeat.

Medical research says that there is no blood storage provision in the human brains and it makes imperative that blood needs always to flow into brain. It takes only about a fraction of a second to cause brain damage if blood ceases to flow into it! That's how important blood is for our brain! Running, swimming, aerobic or any exercise invented by human beings certainly increase the blood flow into the brain but by dint of increased heartbeat.

We know that the heart (blood supply pump) is located below the brain (human standing position). Blood, like other fluids, tends to flow downwards only (in favour of gravity). Extra energy is required if you want to pump blood above the location of the prime mover (heart). But if the position of the brain is lowered below the heart, blood-flow will increase (or will remain constant at least), and at the same time, the heart will relax. This posture is attained in '*Sajdah*' (bowing down). In Sajdah, increased blood-flow forcibly flushes the brain cells, replenishing oxygen supply and nutrients to the brain. Blood-flow to the pituitary and pineal glands in the brain is also increased. Sajdah increases the tensile strength and diameter of the brain arteries and makes it more resistant to haemorrhages occurred due to high blood pressure. It reduces clot impaction owing to the increased diameter of blood vessels.

It facilitates functioning of the brain stem responsible for regulation of cardiac and respiratory function, consciousness, and the sleep cycle. It keeps somatosensory tracts healthy.

Now, please tell me, which medical experiment have you conducted to prove that calf pumping and aerobatic exercises help heart relax?"

"You cannot see the exciting views of hills if a thick fog settles before your eyes," said Kumaran metaphorically.

"Can you name an exercise which can do better kidney massage than Salah?"

"Sit-ups can do the job. By lying flat on a floor in face-up posture and moving the upper body towards the bent-knees repeatedly could deliver the results," Kumaran cited example. Confidence was trickling in from his eyes.

"The exercise is for the able-bodied and meant for abdominal muscles development. I doubt if kidneys get delicately massaged the way they get pampered in Salah.

Kidneys undergo some sort of massage during and after the '*Ruku'* posture. During the *Ruku* some sort of squeezing pressure by the abdominal wall acts on the kidneys resulting in variation of blood flow. On standing (after *Ruku*) the pressure gets relieved allowing the kidneys to resume its normal blood flow. This helps kidneys retain its healthy condition for longer period of time."

"Can you name an exercise that regenerates spinal cord tissues?"

"The world knows '*Crunches Exercise*' enhances spine endurance. Lie down on a floor placing hands gently behind the head, bend the knees and keep the feet flat on the floor. By lifting the upper-body close to the bent-knees and exhaling

while you go up and inhaling while you come down. It makes spine stronger. Besides, you can practise '*Russian Twist*' to strengthen the spine against twisting impacts," stated Kumaran.

"I doubt if it does help maintain the good health of cerebral cortex. Hippocampus hardly gets any benefit from these exercises.

Spinal cord injuries (SCI) can cause widespread and sustained brain inflammation that leads to progressive loss of nerve cells with associated cognitive problems and depression. No drugs for early treatment of spinal cord injury have been developed so far. The Islamic prayer is the best method to regenerate tissues of spinal cord fluid. The different postures of *Salah* (*Ruku*, *Sajdah* and others) are very instrumental in regenerating tissues and keeping the spinal cord strong and healthy. The *Salah* helps spinal cord fluid retain liveliness that plays a crucial role in cushioning the spine against impacts.

Only the Creator of human beings knows the best about His creation. No exercise, or any '*art of living*' prescribed by a mere human brain could even stand distant-second to the '*Art of Living*' as prescribed by our Creator.

Friend, you have rightly said that Muslims are stiff enough to practise Yoga. Now tell me, why should I practise Yoga leaving the Salah?"

"Yoga has nothing to do with religion, -it's universal and secular. The whole world appreciates Yoga but Muslims. They have shown steep-fronted reluctance and blithe avoidance," retorted Kumaran.

"The answer evades the crux of my question. Anyways, never have I said Yoga bears association with any particular religion though. It might be secular, democratic, altruistic… and I am not going to dig into that. I affirm you that Muslims will reject the '*medieval prescription*' spontaneously if they find that something better at the other end is waving lovingly at them. Believe me, they will move away even there is death on the way.

Would you join me in prayer (*Salah*) if invited, –just to reap physical benefits?"

"Never!" Kumaran sputtered to an abrupt stop. He almost bawled.

"Why? Is not it universal?

Do you know that 25 percent world's total population practise this exercise five times a day?"

"It's Islamic Prayer as you have frequently mentioned in the discourse. But, never have I mentioned 'Hinduic Yoga'; -Yoga is secular and unlike *Salah*," Kumaran argued.

"Forget about the name, –what's in a name? Just reap the benefits of the *Salah*."

"Yoga placates mind, injects calming feelings and instils ethereal sense deep into the soul. It's sublimely soothing! It is still alive and rolling even after being frequently attacked by the predation of the times.

Yoga has spread its magnificent wings and been disseminating benefits to the people of the world. Many famous world personalities and statesmen practise Yoga to crush daily stress. Yoga has got some splendid wings and is being recognised by its majestic flight. But, what about *Salah*, –it is dark like gorge, confined like silo, narrow like conduit, –it attracts only Muslims!" Kumaran replied putting on military fatigues.

"Friend, I do agree that only Muslims pray the way Muslims pray. We pray the way Jesus Christ (pbuh) prayed, we pray the way Abraham (pbuh) prayed [*"Abram bowed down with his face touching the ground,"* [Bible: Genesis 17:3]. And the astonishing truth is that 1.6 billion people regularly and routinely offer the prayer five times a day!

Indeed, there is no high praise worthy to be conferred upon the *Salah*! Reputation of human praise appears pathetically dwarfed in contrast to the ethereal elegance of *Salah*! Prophets Abraham (pbuh) and Jesus Christ (pbuh) had already revealed the divine roots of *Salah*. It culminated with the coming of the last and final Messenger Muhammad (pbuh).

Islamic prayer is sublime, -it placates mind, soothes soul, rejuvenates resolve, perfects imperfection, enlivens hope, transcends common boundaries of mundane life to acquire bliss and rejigs the way we look at the Creation. Finding its replacement is like finding an alternative to God!"

"If you want to be Muhammad Ali, then you have to practise hard-exercise, not the easy *Salah*," Phillip quipped.

"If you want to be Jesus Christ (pbuh), you have to offer Salah, not the hard-exercise."

Phillip considered my reply as a swift riposte and swerved the glance from me.

Chapter 6

"Only jerks prayed like this!" observed Kumaran. He forwarded a dig at Muslims. His exasperation morphed into mild anger. I wonder how easily he could *take slander under his wing* and throw easily at Muslims.

"What do you mean?"

"Just think of the inventor (of *Salah*) Muhammad who was displayed as cartoon in the Charlie Hebdo magazine (Feb, 2006). In the front-page headline Muhammad was weeping and saying:

'It's hard to be loved by jerks!'

One can deduce from the references of the magazine that Muslims are jerks!" Kumaran mocked. His tongue intended to cut through the waves of invectives targeting the noble Prophet … but he stopped abruptly.

A tinge of redness flashed across my face nibbling away at the peace of my mind.

"Nowhere in the headline of the magazine mentioned – 'Muslims are jerks'. The comment is outrageous!"

"Do you think Hindus and Christians are linked to Muhammad? Do they follow Muhammad? Certainly not. In explicit sense, it indicates to Muslims!" replied Kumaran logically.

"I wonder how some people spontaneously impassion themselves to believe in satirically dross propaganda about a person? -

It pains me *in a big way* when I see some people surrendering their independent intellect to bondage and becoming easy prey to propaganda that features satires, caricatures, comedies and jokes. The Charlie Hebdo –is a satirical magazine and perhaps, the editor-in-chief of the magazine might be a satirical artist, comedian or a frivolous joker! How vulnerable your intellect is! I wonder how cheaply your rationality gets swayed by the bite of a cartoon manufactured by a person whose personality is perfectly balanced with the lowness of a joker? A joker's profession is, at its core, to hit the rational convictions of people, and the magazine has done that job perfectly and professionally. Watching the acts of a jester is an injustice to time!

Do you expect that I too should react to that cartoon?"

"Just think of the post publication incident. The magazine become the target of terrorist attacks that killed no less than ten people. The scene was gruesome and hell-like. Are you still not a jerk?" criticised Phillip. Phillip pushed me against a hard border.

"Muslims should not pick up violence against the perpetrators. The Almighty alone is enough to dispose the affair. Any deranged mind who dared to vilify Prophet Muhammad (pbuh) through vile portrait had always been rewarded publicly with an ignoble death."

"Really?" Phillip shrieked in a mocking way. He cast a sharp glance hoping to be offered with a moving experience.

"Please invest wiseness in analysing the history. It is clamouring for your careful attention.

Think about Abu Lahab! While nearing to death, his body was left decidedly by even his family members to rot in desolation. He fell into a torpor. His physical condition sank into a deranged state. The terminal phase of his life defies descriptions... it was not an easy-viewing!

Do you know Abu Jahl, the fiercest opponent of the Prophet? He was put down as the most uncouth member of the opponent camp by the vilest virtues of his tongue. He commanded the army of Quraysh in the battle of Badr. He faced an ignoble death in the battlefield as he was badly wounded and beheaded by a 'slave'.

Think about Swedish Cartoonist Lars Vilks! He drew an extremely unpleasant cartoon of the noble Prophet in 2007. The character of the cartoon surpassed the baseness of the lowest ignobility. His body was burnt to death in a car crash. The car that was transporting the curmudgeon was perfectly equipped with puncture-proof tyres and enshrouded evenly with a party of strong police protection. But, he failed to foil the foul of the death. The scene was so distasteful that devils jostled to relish it.

The consequence of vilifying the noble Prophet is extremely scary!

Anyways, I loathe violence and Islam too nurses an intolerance towards violence. Certainly, I support peaceful protest."

"Suppose if you were a protestor, how would you have protested?" Kumaran posed the question swiftly.

"I would have *turned the tables on* the magazine. I would have knocked its ignorance about Prophet Muhammad (pbuh). My placard of protest would have carried like:

"THE JERKS YET TO BE LED INTO THE TRUTH"-

"I have much more to tell you, but now it will be much for you to bear. When, however, the Spirit comes, who reveals the truth about God; he will lead you into all the truth." [Bible: John 16:12]

Or, I would have woven my protest as:

"WE CAN'T MAKE CARTOON OF JESUS IN REPLY,

FOR WE MUSLIMS ARE UNLIKE JERKS AND LED INTO THE TRUTH" -

"I have much more to tell you, but now it will be much for you to bear. When, however, the Spirit comes, who reveals the truth about God; he will lead you into all the truth" [Bible: John 16:12]

These would have been the slogans of my protests."

"Ridiculous indeed! I feel pity for you!

It departs from standard and descends into a farce when I see Islam advocating for peace, piety and normalcy! Because, at its core, Islam allows its religious fanatics to slither from the pockets of fanaticism and demolish statues of revered religious figures affiliated to other than Islam!" Kumaran bit me sharply.

"Please clarify..."

"In Afghanistan, the world still remembers afresh the scenes of pulling down of Bamiyan Buddhas (March 2001)! Do you remember that? Have you ever inquired as to why that had happened?" added Kumaran brusquely.

"All right friend. Tell me, then why do you support the cartoon of Prophet Muhammad (pbuh) published by Charlie Hebdo? –

As the world knows Muhammad (pbuh) is our beloved Prophet, and the morals of not conceiving him through any 'drawn physical image' has been no less than a civilisation for us. We respect that civilisation. But the magazine destroyed the very honour of that civilisation and injured badly the private feelings of Muslims across the world."

"Never did I say I support the cartoon. I, by way of arguments, just cited the cartoon published in the magazine. Moreover, Buddha is unlike Muhammad and regarded as Lord," Kumaran veered his stand apparently on cartoon and went farther afield to state '*Buddha is Lord.*'

"Who is Lord –Jesus Christ (pbuh) or Buddha?"

I just flicked the 'conundrum' on the table to be resolved. I kept on looking at them and was like being *a fly on the wall.* They both snatched at me a quick glance of ireful eyes as if I seemed to have consumed their shares of air to breathe. I sensed a riot for the post of 'lordship' was taking place between two mighty beasts loosed off in them inwardly. Both gyred and gyred but did not show the daring to grab the crown. Seemed, both were *thrown in at the deep end*!

Both were silent like snows and looking at each other with respectful eyes. Seemed, they were not interested to jeopardise the amicable relation existed between them. In mutual persuasion, their eyes met in *cloak-and-dagger* terms and inked an affable agreement refusing explicitly to introduce any *thorn in the flesh*. Their bloated confidence in respective belief appeared fickle, and I found them clumsier and poorly coordinated. They preferred not to invite mutual antagonism by announcing verdict on the contested 'lordship'.

My intention was not to pitch them against each other, rather I wanted to understand the presence of clarity and confidence in their respective belief. They preferred not to show ire at one another, neither did they dig themselves out of the confusion. They exchanged some obligatory glances and remained happy. They remained happy being equipped with the notions that take root in doubts, confusions and absurdity.

Even a packet of cigarette does suffer less confusion and is more inward with candidness than Kumaran and Phillip. Though the packet reads, '*honey dew smooth*', '*perfection protected*', '*taste balanced*', yet all these interest-arousing, carcinogenic statements perfectly balanced by a single heroic statement which outlines clearly the real character of the packet, and that is, -'*smoking kills!*' The packet exceedingly clears its stand notwithstanding through contradistinctive statements. But this is not the case for Kumaran and Phillip, -they dash away from disclosing theirs!

"Why did typhoon Trami bring down the 40-ton Buddha statue (the highest guilt statue in the whole Japan) in Okinawa, -the statue was lying face down and broken? Would you say, 'Jokes on the Typhoon'?"

"Wide and out of the way!

Both are poles apart as things. I'm talking about the Afghans not about the typhoon Trami, -are the typhoon and the

Afghans same to your knowledge?" grunted Kumaran. Irritation soaked through his mood.

"Buddha is Lord and the nature is controlled by none but Lord. Why did Lord Buddha pull down his own statue? Would you say, "Jokes on the Lord"?"

"The vein of my logic is misunderstood grossly. It has been misplaced from its due position. Buddha is revered as Lord, and the feelings associated with his statues should also be respected and preserved as the valued heritage of civilisation," Kumaran replied with sinking voice.

"Friend, your logic neither is misunderstood, nor mislaid. Actually, it *is not much of* a logic! If the Lord himself does not like his own statue, then how could you expect that the Afghans should?

Did 'Lord' Buddha asked his believers to erect his statue?"

"I have not read the Buddhist Scripture," observed Kumaran.

"Then, who did convert you to agree that Buddha was Lord?"

"This is the prevailing belief amongst the Buddhists," Kumaran replied.

"What does the word 'Buddha' mean?"

"The enlightened one," said Kumaran.

"All right. Then, do you think 'enlightenment' makes a person 'Lord'?"

"Just cut your lecture! It's *not much of* a good argument. It speaks much of your being too stiff in admitting the raw fanaticism behind the destruction of the statues. I find a fanatical obstinacy fettered inside you like a *big elephant in the room*. Birth of a sense in you seems a long way off.

The Afghans, in fact, deformed the face of the civilisation beyond recognition. What else could we expect from a bunch of jerks?" Phillip expressed sharps as usual. Nothing seemed to have kept him off his usual pattern of conduct.

"The 'last Buddha' did not allow even his physical image, then how the Buddha would have asked his followers to erect his statues?"

"Who is the 'last Buddha'?" inquired Kumaran in awe.

"Prophet Muhammad (pbuh) is the 'last Buddha'."

"I did expect that. It has almost been a quirk of the Muslim world to fit Muhammad into the prophecy of every religious scripture. Some sort of typical madness has made a deep seepage into their skewed psyche!" criticised Phillip.

Kumaran curved a crooked smile offering a tacit support to Phillip.

"All right! I am citing from the book 'Gospel of Buddha' as collected by Paul Carus in 1894. Ananda said to the Blessed One, '*Who shall teach us when thou art gone?*'

And the Blessed one (Gautam Buddha) replied, "*I am not the first Buddha who came upon the earth nor shall I be the last. In due time another Buddha will arise in the world, a holy one, a supremely enlightened one, endowed with wisdom in conduct, auspicious, knowing the universe,* ***an incomparable leader of men****, a master of angels and mortals. He will reveal to you the same eternal truths, which I have taught you. He will preach his religion, glorious in its origin, glorious at the climax and glorious at the goal. He will proclaim a religious life, wholly perfect and pure such as I now proclaim. His disciples will number many thousands while mine number many hundreds.*"

Ananda said, "*How shall we know him?*"

The Blessed one replied, "*He will be known as 'Maitreya'*".

[Gospel of Buddha by Carus, page 217 -218]

Now, please tell me, who, according to you, is the '*last Buddha*'? Who could fit perfectly into the prophecy?"

"You need to expand your heart, widen your outlook and extend supporting argument whenever demanded by the table. Do not be overhasty and brash in drawing conclusion.

Monk Xiang Haiming (613 CE) claimed himself he was the promised Maitreya;

Wu Zetian (690 CE) claimed himself he was the promised Maitreya;

Even, Bahaullah (1817 -1892) was believed to be the promised Maitreya.

Examples are galore. It is *not much of* a wiseness to fit Muhammad into every prophecy!" Kumaran replied. Phillip might have *thrown his weight behind* Kumaran.

"Are they as influential as Prophet Muhammad (pbuh)?"

"Muhammad known to you only. Myself and Phillip do not recognise Muhammad!" replied Kumaran in haughtiness.

"Tomorrow, every *Tom, Dik and Harry* would come forward and claim to be the promised *Maitreya.* Your principle of 'selection' does not include the 'test and trust' procedure; the least I can say, it is much of a farce!

Friends, gentlemen use knowledge to judge a person but legends use wealth of insights to assess a person. Legends mine deep to dig out the gems that possess lustre. Michael H. Hart stated:

"*My choice of Muhammad to lead the list of the world's most influential persons may surprise some readers and may be questioned by others, but he was the only man in history who was supremely successful on both the religious and secular level.*"

-Michael H. Hart, The 100: A Ranking of the Most Influential Persons in History.

He dared not to compare anyone with Prophet Muhammad (pbuh)."

"It's a controversial book and as for me, it lacks qualifications to persuade learned people of the world. That much I would say," Phillip stated assuming a great degree of sapience.

"All right friends, then Alphonse de LaMartaine (French author, poet and statesman) too was a jerk who mined the extraordinary success of the Prophet with his wealth of insight. He said:

"*If greatness of purpose, smallness of means, and astonishing results are the three criteria of a human genius, who could dare compare any great man in history with Muhammad?*"

-Alphonse de LaMartaine, Histoire de la Torquie (1854).

Do you think that he was robbed of his wealth of sense? Do you think that he was on the mission of appeasing Muslims?"

"Many renowned world personalities stated many great things about Jesus Christ also. That does not soak me, and unlike you, I do not pluck giddy happiness from these eulogies. H.G Wells said:

"*I am an historian, I am not a believer, but I must confess as a historian that this penniless preacher from Nazareth is irrevocably the very centre of history. Jesus Christ is easily the most dominant figure in all history.*" — H.G. Wells, British author (1866-1946)

He spoke about what Jesus is!" Phillip stated boastfully.

"A praise finds its sublime peak if it comes from your worst enemies. Many renowned personalities of the West, famous for nourishing disdain for Islam and throwing nasty slanders at Muhammad (pbuh), are praising Muhammad (pbuh) to the skies!"

"But, only 25 percent of world population converted themselves to believe in Muhammad. This is not the sum of the views of the world's population. The rest 75 percent do not find any exemplary thing in Muhammad. Which factor is putting off the majority? What would you say?" inquired Kumaran questingly. His quest was laced with thick mock.

"Islam tops in the contest. Islam draws strength from divinity and is poised to scale the summit. It has already *tipped the scales* of power-equation in favour of its dominance. I have already had much discussions on this and I think the topic is *at an end*.

You too do know that 'ego has a mania to deny the truth', and some will be left forever languishing in darkness draping the sheet of sheer denial. Ego is a polished form of 'superstition', and it demarcates the line where rationality perishes and superstition takes over."

"Cut! Stop behaving like a seer!" Kumaran interjected like a director. He appeared averse to listening to it further.

"Anyways, which is the most valuable and the oldest figure of civilisation?"

"I pass this to Kumaran," Phillip perhaps evaded the question.

"You better desist yourself from talking about civilisation. Civilisation does not fit you," remarked Kumaran.

"Reason?"

"I believe in the realisation of Margaret Mead (American Anthropologist, 1901- 1978) who once said:

'*The first sign of civilisation in an ancient culture was a femur (thighbone) that had been broken and then healed. In animal kingdom if you break your leg, you die. You cannot run from danger, get to the river for a drink or hunt for food.*'

The quote is profound and emerged from an intrepid and independent tongue.

Animals, for you, are merely a pack of flesh and meant only for food! Civilisation has made itself scarce for you!" Kumaran added assertively. Having stated, he kept on glancing at me for a while as if he were whispering into my ears about his distaste for the habit of meat-eating.

"Was Margaret Mead vegetarian or non-vegetarian?"

"My view is not person specific. The habit of meat eating does no longer seem attractive because it defies the moral call of civilisation," observed Kumaran.

"Well, there are few words in English like-elegant, attractive and best. Yours might be something but best.

I don't think the matter is worthy of discussion and I do not want to spend time *tilting at windmills.*

Well, I would suggest a way forward that offers a better means to survive on the earth without killing any life…neither plants, nor animals. Would you agree with me?"

"What's that?" inquired Kumaran curiously.

"We both should be like vultures…we shall survive on corpses and carcasses; it does not necessitate killing! Do you agree?"

Kumaran curved the lips stingily and began, "My food habit does not entail the necessity of bloodshed. Well, that much I should say."

"How do you benefit the animal kingdom being a vegetarian?"

"I save life. My intention slaps fetters on cruelty and imposes circumscription on violence. I honour the core purpose of civilisation," briefed Kumaran. He cast on me an oversensitive glance.

"Why do you drink milk?"

"The query is barren of insights.

Do you find any sort of violence in this food habit?" teased Kumaran.

"Don't you find any cruelty in the act of depriving a calf of her rights on having hundred percent share on her mother's milk? Do you share your mother's milk with others? Which civilisation has given you the prerogative of doing such atrocity?"

"A true civilisation refines itself with every stride. As it moves on, it develops more and more loathness to the action that brings about more killings and dishonours the honourable intentions of the civilisation.

Bloodshed *makes my skin crawl;* bloodshed is a complete absence in my food habit!" Kumaran censured my food habit indirectly.

"Regrettably, animals are not aware of your great intention. Your intention is oversensitive and melodramatic, and I think, *no way* it is going to benefit humanity.

The veins and the arteries of the deprived calf running contracted. Your food habit has snatched the share of the calf on her mother's milk! What will you say?"

"You have imparted a nasty spin to the discussion…the topic is drifting away," resented Kumaran. He snatched a glanced at me.

"I challenge, you will never be able to justify this 'atrocity' even if you call a battery of eminent atheists like Darwin, Dawkins, or Karl Marx.

Friend, you need to understand the purpose of creation of human beings. On the earth, human beings, being the supreme creation of God, could enjoy the prerogatives to rule the animal kingdoms. The following verses will give you further clarity on the prerogatives given to human beings by God Himself.

"*And He created the cattle for you as a source of warmth, food and many other benefits.*" [Qur'an: An Nahl 16: 5]

"*…; we give you to drink of what is in their bellies, from between digested food and blood: pure milk pleasant to drink.*" [Qur'an: An Nahl 16: 66]

Friend, do not squander the resources of your supreme brain on thinking about the dross stuffs like '*veg*' or '*non-veg*.' Do not behave like a goat or a cow who could not think beyond grasses and leaves. I have stopped thinking like a wolf or a lion who could not think beyond flesh and bones. Being human beings, we should think beyond grasses and flesh.

By the way, which is the most valuable and the oldest figure of civilisation?"

"Every artefact is valuable. And the age of civilisation hardly matters. What matters is its wider acceptance and refined evolution," added Kumaran fretfully.

"Human beings are the most valuable and the oldest figures of civilisation."

"What do you mean?" Phillip made a rapid inquiry.

"Why the USA is bombing and killing millions? Are they not destroying the living statues of civilisations? Which civilisation the USA is trying to preach to the world?"

"The country is famous for being the citadel of potential terrorists. The USA cannot stand back. The attack on the country no way can be considered as the aftermath of 9/11, rather the stand of the USA on Afghanistan can be fairly attributed to its efforts to eliminate terrorism from the surface of the earth. The USA has taken it seriously and redoubled its efforts to prevent the terrorism from taking root into formidable depth," Phillip replied like an army general and seemed his soul was angered with cruelty! He kindled the spirit of a debate.

"Who has given you the rights to destroy the whole country for the crime of an individual (if indeed that individual had committed the crime)?"

"It's not about an individual. The whole country directly or indirectly was involved and played a roguish role behind the nefarious plot. The country behaved like an axis of evils," Phillip argued with might and authority.

"Have you heard the '*Jesus Rifle*'?"

"How could you desecrate the holy name of Christ by associating him maliciously with a 'killer'?" Phillip reacted sharply. I could not read his face if he was truly astonished. His face shimmered in astonishment.

"Do you despise the '*Jesus Rifle*'?"

"Of course I do. I bear low opinion of anything that spills blood," Phillip reacted. His reaction was, perhaps, a cut out of an outwardly crafty appearance. I could sense a treacherous trait hidden in his acting facade.

"The telescopic sights of the '*Jesus Rifles*' are stamped with the Biblical verse *John 8:12*.

The zenith of 'fanaticism' should be redefined by analysing closely the ulterior motive deeply inscribed in the sober 'Jesus

Rifles'. I feel, this should be considered as the last murky depth of fanaticism one can find nowhere on the earth.

Millions have been massacred in the name of Jesus Christ (pbuh). The least to say, an evil dance orchestrated clandestinely with vile intention to kill millions in Iraq, Afghanistan and elsewhere with special rifles called the sobriquet '*Jesus Rifles*'. The verse says:

"Jesus spoke to the Pharisees again. "I am the light of the world," he said. "Whoever follows me will have the light of life and will never walk in darkness" [Bible: John 8:12]

The heart of every fallen soul in Iraq and Afghanistan is pierced with the verse *John 8:12* supposed to be the invoker of the blessing of 'Lord' Jesus Christ (pbuh)! Truly, parody does know no civility; crafty mind does value no conscience!

No amount of wonder is enough to wonder at the religious fanaticism stamped on the combat rifles. This poses a threat capable enough to deform the loving face of humanity. Do you still think that your heart is secular? No amount of fair arguments could exonerate you from the accusations.

"It's a war on terror!" Phillip replied. His tongue was striding with pride and executive authority. His heart seemed to have taken resolute stand on 'terror'.

"I remember the famous saying of philosopher Noam Chomsky:

"It is only terrorism if they do it to us. When we do much worse to them, it is not terrorism."

My soul laughs at you upon seeing the pitch of your argument- '*war on terror*'. The line '*war on terror*' bares the secret of your heart wherein malice grows and grooms. The line '*war on terror*' is but a smokescreen that hides the true instinct of your eyes through which demon relishes the spectacle of doom.

A four-line ode to the motive of your action,

'Massacred millions already,

And ready for thousands to guzzle;

To broadcast 'Lordship' of Jesus-- the parody,

Through the use of muzzle!'

I do know, even a small feather-light headscarf of a Muslim woman could create a tremor of wide terror in your secular heart! It did happen even in a civilised country like France.

The word 'terror' has given you much more salvation than the pure blood of Jesus Christ (pbuh)! -

Havoc is done in these lands. Millions of innocent civilians have been killed and mutilated in the name of 'terror'.

Do you think that the 'divine power' of the rifles could convert the country altogether to Christianity?"

"Disseminating the message of the Gospels is our main mission. Moreover, what is wrong if the country gets converted to Christianity? Is your stomach churning?" Phillip reacted. He almost assumed authority and reprimanded me.

"Never has it been a concern for me if someone willingly does something. It is not much of a character of my sensibility, neither is it aligned with my basic instinct. I do allow it to splay its magnificent wings!

Islam came to Afghanistan in 7th century (around 642 BCE) and still ruling the hearts of the people. The British, the USSR and the latest the USA invasion have hardly made any dent in that belief. Since 1838 (when the British entered Afghanistan) till today the country has almost been remained occupied by the foreign invaders. Till date, people of Afghanistan have been enduring all the onslaughts with unswerving patience and unflinching faithfulness towards Islam.

Do you still think the 'Jesus Rifles' will do the wonder?"

"Think of Spain. Muslim ruled almost 781 (711-1492 CE) years but was eliminated by Christianity. Islam had been pushed to that corner from where nothing returns," Phillip replied. He reminded me of that pathetic end of Muslims in Spain.

"I do agree Muslims were eliminated completely from the soil of Spain.

However, I do not agree that Islam was pushed to the point of 'no return'. You cannot obliterate an idea –Islam is a 'Divine Idea' revealed for the mankind by none but the Almighty Himself.

I was not definitely expecting such comment now as I had already explained the future of Islam. Anyways, I'm re-iterating:

"It is He Who hath sent His Messenger with guidance and the Religion of Truth, to prevail it over all religions, …)." [Qur'an: Al Tawbah 9: 33]

Islam is destined to prevail over every '-ism'. But the most surprising truth is that –it must prevail with Muslims or without Muslims!

"……. *If ye turn back (from the Path), He will substitute in your stead another people; …!*" [Qur'an: Muhammad 47:38]

This is a dire warning directed towards Muslims. So, preach or perish –is the unquestionable destiny of Muslims. History speaks profoundly about the veracity of the verse.

History is the Vision of Allah and is overrun with many such heart-breaking examples. Spain and Genghis Khan, -these two chilling examples are enough to understand the insights and resourcefulness of the verse.

The baton of 'Priesthood' is taken away from Jews and handed over to Muslims. The correctness of His choice must be respected, or else must be prepared to be 'replaced'! The verse *[Qur'an: Muhammad 47:38]* is hovering like a sharp-edged dagger and vacillating between the points of 'no-action' to 'dire action' to fix the fate of Muslims."

"Do you think Muslims are chosen people? Are you chosen by God?" Kumaran inquired. It seemed Phillip too was asking the same question through the tongue of Kumaran.

"Yes, we are."

"I am of the opinion that the chosen race must be a treasurable asset to God, and it must be guarded.

But the history disabused me of the notion," stated Kumaran.

"What do you mean?"

"Why are you so oppressed? Why are you getting killed everywhere in the world? Is God not willing to protect His chosen people," Kumaran forwarded the realistic questions.

"Which human race is the most oppressed race on the earth, and why?"

"Jews, am I correct?" Phillip answered.

"Yes, but why? -I would rather request Kumaran to answer."

"May be being the world's minority community," guessed Kumaran.

"Parsi, Sikh too are world's prominent minority communities but have never been oppressed like Jews. Why only Jews?"

"What exactly do you mean?" Kumaran inquired vacillating his glance between me and Phillip.

"An atheist will never be able to answer this."

Initially Kumaran flashed flair of confidence coupled with powerful intention to craft a reply. But his spirit subsided soon following some initial clumsy efforts. It made him upset …it *cut him to the quick*!

"Friend, Jews were the first chosen people of God. That's why they are the most oppressed race on the earth."

"God's first chosen people yet the most oppressed race, -it fails to convince me; I could not grasp," Kumaran said in a half-wonder. He could not make out the point.

"I would brief the history of Jews. -

Truly Jews were the first chosen people of God. The baton of the 'Priesthood' was given to them. Both the Bible and the

Qur'an have agreed unanimously on the favour of the Almighty that descended upon them.

"... The whole earth is mine, but you will be my chosen people," [Bible: Exodus 19: 5-6]

"Children of Israel! Call to mind the (special) favour which I bestowed upon you, and that I preferred you to all other (for My Message)." [Qur'an: Al Baqara 2:47]

The Almighty favoured them for the task of carrying forward the *Divine Constitution* to the people of the world. They were commanded to promote and promulgate the godly-message revealed to them to lead the fellow human beings from darkness to Light. But, they chose a deviated path instead of obeying the Divine Instructions. God showered boundless love for Jews and in the process, He exhausted His generosity in sending Prophets one after another to bring the Jews persuasively on the godly-track. But, they developed strong apathy towards correction. Eventually, the disobedience landed them in an uncouth tangle of braggadocio, insolence and depravity.

So low was the degeneracy of the Jews that they were unashamedly used to feel pride in the 'killing' of Jesus Christ (pbuh)! Depravity felt ashamed of being so degenerate when the degeneracy of Jews sank beneath it. The Qur'an says,

"That they said (in boast), "We killed Christ Jesus the son of Mary, ---." [Qur'an: Al Nisa 4: 157]

They hit the bottom of degeneracy when they started altering the God's revelation. In their unbelief and haughtiness, they corrupted the Revealed Book to the extent that matched perfectly the ignobility of the lowest form of depravity.

"Of the Jews there are those who displace words from their (right) places, and say: "We hear and we disobey"; but Allah hath cursed them for their Unbelief." [Qur'an: Al Nisa 4:46]

They set many unprecedented examples in the race of transgression being fully oblivion of the punishments prescribed by the Almighty. That precipitated the curse of the Almighty upon Jews. The perfidy will never go unpunished. The Bible says:

"If even after all of this you still do not obey Me, I will increase your punishment seven times" [Bible: Leviticus 26:18].

Indeed, a battle-axe is kept ready to crack a nut!

Just look into the mood of the verse and try to find the insights clearly inscribed here: '*seven times more punishment than the punishment allotted for the non-chosen people*'!

Muslims are the second chosen people of the Almighty and the second most 'oppressed race' on the earth. Muslims are the rightful receivers of this oppression! Hope, you got the insights!"

"Do you think Muhammad too was sent by God to punish Jews? Think of the battle of Khaybar (628 CE), –Muhammad was then the army general conquering forts one after another, and specifically, he brought the fort Qamus under the long siege that spanned for more than fifteen days. I really wonder, how a prophet of God could oppress people?" Phillip reproached the action of the Prophet. His tongue was striding irately.

"The fort was built to withstand a siege.

Friend, one thing you should inculcate into mind that prophets are sent not for oppression but for guidance, wellbeing and elevation of human race. They are but mercy to the people."

"He might be a Prophet to you, to me an oppressor. He was a brutal army general putting on falsely the patina of mercy," Phillip replied brusquely. I found rudeness resonating in his voice.

"If you want to enrich yourself, then just look into the massacre carried out by the Japanese Imperial Army when they captured Nanjing, the capital of China, in around 1937 CE. Here you would find the actual definition of brutality that consisted of the manifold of innumerable ignoble sights and gruesome scenes. The chillingly harrowing accounts will freeze your blood! Neither is it an easy reading, nor is an easy viewing! That brutality defies descriptions!

Anyways, Jews broke the Treaty of Medina (622 CE) and engaged themselves in conspiring against the fledgling Muslim community. They deployed all possible efforts to invoke obliteration to Muslims. That was the reason the Prophet led the army almost ten times smaller than the size of the enemy. The choice of his action is beyond reproach."

"This is unbecoming of a Prophet to wage brutality against dissenting voices. Of a Prophet, mercy should be placed at the top of the list. You must not get him to be seen beyond reproach," Phillip flung away the reason into the bin of denial.

"Jews religious leaders (Rabbis) knew from their scriptures about the final Messenger exactly the way a father knows his son.

***"Those to whom We gave the Scripture know him as they know their own sons. But indeed, a party of them conceal the truth while they know [it]".* [Qur'an: Al Baqarah 2:146]**

The Almighty offered Jews (after five hundred years since the Diaspora) the last mercy in the form of Prophet Muhammad (pbuh) sent for the whole mankind.

"It may be that your Lord may (yet) show Mercy unto you; but if ye revert (to your sins), We shall revert (to Our punishments):.." [Qur'an: Bani Israil 17:8]

Unfortunately, they squandered the great opportunity. They, not only disobeyed the Messenger, but left no stones unturned to harass the Messenger by creating a multitude of problems and security issues. The city of Medina was constantly reeling under the threats of conspiracies contrived by Jews.

Mercy was the second name of Prophet Muhammad (pbuh). The perfidious actions of Jews disrespected the *Treaty* and dishonoured the mercy repeatedly shown by the noble Prophet. Battle was left inevitably as the last option to invite peace to prevail in Medina and around."

"It is your spurious surmise that Jews harassed Muhammad. How would you convince people?" Phillip posed the question. A trail of disbelief streaked his face.

"Though Jesus Christ (pbuh) was closer to them in terms of kinship than Prophet Muhammad (pbuh), yet they showed ignoble behaviour towards Jesus Christ (pbuh). Pensiveness engulfs me whenever I conjecture the scene, -*they spat on him, they slapped him, and according to you, they even "killed" him*!

If they could have done to Jesus Christ (pbuh), then just think what they could have done to Prophet Muhammad (pbuh)!"

"They did not kill Muhammad as they did to Jesus Christ. Muhammad, being the 'final' Messenger must have had greater tolerance for the Non-Muslims," Phillip stated taking a welling of sympathy on his side.

"Friend, no power on the face of the earth that can kill Messenger (Rasul) of Allah (swt). I wonder how a person like you could squander intellectual resources carelessly into the pool of absurdity. It is purely an impure belief that Jesus Christ (pbuh) was "killed" on the cross. Yes, Jews killed Prophet Yahya (pbuh), and Yahya (pbuh) was not a Messenger but a Prophet.

Can you tell me, who oppressed Jews most?"

"First, you must admit that Muhammad too oppressed Jews, -a 'Prophet of God' oppressed people!" Phillip pressed me as if he were in a pressing need to tease from me an admission on the same.

"I do know you would not answer my question because it would certainly make you ashamed of your actions carried out purportedly on Jews. The world knows that the Idolaters and the Christians oppressed Jews the most. Just have a diligent glance at the pages of history:

1) King Nebuchadnezzar II of Babylon conquered Judah in 586 BCE and destroyed Solomon's (first) temple and exiled the Jews to Babylon. Jews returned to Jerusalem around 520 BCE and started the construction of second temple.

2) Roman emperor Titus captured Jerusalem and destroyed the city and the second temple (70 C.E). Jews migrated to the different parts of the world and the event was marked as Jews Diaspora. The Jews-Roman wars ended in wide-spread destruction and genocide in 132-135 CE.

3) The Roman emperor Constantine the Great (306-337 CE) converted to Christianity. The Roman Empire began to transition from Paganism to Christianity. And eventually, Christianity gradually became the dominant religion across the Empire. Oppression on Jews started with renewed vigour.

4) In1389, a pogrom began in Prague.

5) In 1492 an edict issued by the joint Catholic Monarchs of Spain for supporting the expulsion of Jews from the kingdom of Castile and Aragon.

6) In 1904, in Ireland, the *Limerick boycott* caused Jewish expulsion.

7) In 1911 *Tredegar riot* in Wales. Home Secretary Winston Churchill, described the weeklong riot as a "pogrom".

8) Pogroms in Russian empire:

Warsaw pogrom (1881), Kishinev pogrom (1903), Kiev pogrom (1905), Bialystok pogrom (1906), Lwów pogrom (1918) and Kiev pogroms (1919).

9) In 1919, in the Americas, a pogrom began in Argentina, during the Tragic Week.

10) In 1929, Jews were massacred in Hebron and Safed in the British Mandate of Palestine.

11) In 1941, the two-day Farhud pogrom in Iraq,

12) In between 1939-1941 pogroms held in Germany under Nazi rule.

13) Anti-Jewish violence in Poland, 1944–1946

14) Anti-Jewish violence in Eastern Europe, 1944–1946.

15) Anti-Jewish riots took place in Britain in 1947.

Friends, no longer you could sell to the world your fabricated craft of allegations against Muhammad (pbuh). Just look into the history …it clearly demands a sad and a shameful shake of your head."

"You have forgotten to mention the name of Muhammad in the list," Phillip instigated me. His voice sank a bit towards the end and it sank into barely above a whisper.

"Muhammad (pbuh) and oppression are poles apart. The list does not wish to include his holy name.

I would invite your sense to ponder over the bloodless conquest of Jerusalem by Caliph Umar in 637 CE. Caliph Umar was one of the four companions of Prophet Muhammad (pbuh). If a Caliph could not think of shedding blood of innocent people, then how the Messenger of God could afford to carry out bloody operation against non-Muslims without any valid reason?

Friends, call to mind the period of Muslim ruled Spain wherein Jews enjoyed their 'golden age of Jewish culture' during the diaspora. Do you still think Prophet Muhammad (pbuh) oppressed them? How could you easily utter such statement without knowing much about history?"

"How can you deny the fact that Christians helped them regain their land? I hope you can remember the '*Balfour Declaration*' (Nov, 1917 CE)," Phillip commented.

He threw in the infamous one-sided *Balfour Declaration.* Jews made it a solid springboard to claim the '*promised land*'.

"True! Christians fittingly paid off the long pending due to Jews."

"'*Long pending due*'? What do you mean?" Phillip shrieked. I found a vivid astonishment in his being surprised by my view.

"Jews offered you an easy Salvation by 'killing' someone of their own tribe. The act did not cost them politically anything but an innocent 'life'.

Countless generations of Christian's world found themselves enthused in receiving easily the 'sumptuous Salvation' born out of a devilish act of Jews. It truly entails a due to be paid off by Christians to Jews. Mr Arthur Balfour did exactly the same thing on behalf of the Christian's world by declaring Palestine as the national home of Zionists.

The blood of Jesus Christ (pbuh) was noble and deemed to be the flowing stream of Salvation. Blood of Palestinians are dirt and can be drained by the urges of hostility into a spent stream to fill the dry veins of an arid lands prospecting for Jews' settlement.

Devil was urged to celebrate the moment with a roisterous joy!"

"Be extra careful what you say and how you say. The remarks cut *close to the bone* of Christianity! Your attitude is dysfunctional to the broader sense of rationality," Phillip reacted casting a long raging stare.

"Did Palestine belong to Mr Balfour? Did it cost anything to him or his country?"

"Do not immure yourself within the walls of narrow outlook.

The world will laugh at you when you tell them that Muslims inherit Jerusalem because Muhammad set his foot on his way to the heaven. How ridiculous it is!" narrated Phillip. His voice trickled in soaring unpleasantness.

"'Balfour Declaration' has been the burning height of absolute preposterousness …a mere 'signature' of a distant person called Mr Balfour yielded an unequivocal rights to Jews to snatch the lands of two thousand years old inhabitants. Which law permits that?"

"Feeble argument!

Do you think that the 'touchdown' of your so-called Prophet carries more importance than the much awaited and politically justified historic '*Balfour Declaration*'?" stated Phillip with an assertion.

"The holy 'feet' of the Prophet marked a tremendous watershed in the history of Jerusalem. No Declaration suchlike the Balfour could ever outshine the divine legacy imprinted on Jerusalem by the glorious fleet of the holy Prophet.

Prophet Muhammad (pbuh) made a perfect touchdown that gave birth to a watershed in the history of Jerusalem!"

"A person walled within unconscionable logic could state easily such absurdity with gross insolence," sassed Phillip.

"How could you deny the fact that Palestine was the home of Jews' ancestors... it belongs to Jews. Are you against it?" Kumaran inquired bouncily. His gestures were overbearing that could command obedience from weak people.

"Do I sound like that? What do you think, who has the rights over your property –your first child or last child?

And suppose, if Prophet Adam (pbuh) returns tomorrow on the earth and declares that 'no one has the rights to live here on the earth except me, because I was the first one who came on the earth.'

What would you say?"

"Put your mind to the crux of the problem.

The history has clearly been bearing the witness that Jews' ancestors lived in Palestine for thousands of years or so. Naturally, and if logic is honoured, one can affirm without much presumptions that Jews have the first and the natural rights to live there. They hold the prerogatives," Phillip almost sassed me.

"The birth and the bringing up could cream possession and rights together over a piece of land, and in it consists the true legislation. No present Jews could pass this test.

By the way, do you think people presently living there should be eradicated?"

"All legal prerogatives are tilted towards Jews. Jews are rightfully poised to exercise that. Let them decide who would live there, and who would not," Phillip replied showing his absolute slant towards Jews. He gave me a wry smile.

He left the fate of the current inhabitants to the mercy of Jews. It does not injure his sense of logic, neither does it urge his human front if the current inhabitants are driven out or subjected to languish in ghettos for a beggarly life. His tone of voice can unnerve the rational sense of people; his advocacy for militant-like actions can appal the peace of mind. He supports belt-treatment to Palestinians!

"How could you be sure that the current inhabitants are not aboriginal? Do you have any proofs?"

"It hardly requires any proofs. When the Jews Diaspora started around 70 CE, people from neighbouring provinces started pouring into the land as interlopers. In a way, they were Arabs," Phillip stated.

"First prime minister of Israel David Ben Gurion wrote a treatise (1917 CE) wherein he said:

"…The greater majority and main structures of the Muslim Falahin in western Eretz Israel present to us one racial strand and a whole ethnic unit, and there is no doubt that much Jews blood flows in their veins –the blood of those Jews farmers, "lay persons", who chose in the travesty of times to abandon their faith in order to remain on their land."

Would you rebuke his views and dispose the rights of the people living there continuously for thousands of years?"

"I doubt if they could survive the modern DNA test!" Phillip replied looking at me obliquely. I found a fiendish curl in his otherwise insolent smile that disconcerted me a bit.

"Do you have the DNA structure of Prophet Abraham (pbuh) to be used as the reference?

The slant of your conscience is loud and clear.

I would request you to *call to mind* the fact that both Ismail (pbuh) and Issac (pbuh) were sons of Prophet Abraham (pbuh). And, if I go by your logic, then you have to agree with me that people living across the vast lands of the whole Middle East are the descendants of Prophet Abraham (pbuh), and certainly are entitled to exercise the provision of equal rights. They are equally privileged to live in the lands with peace and harmony.

Do you still think that the lands belong only to Jews?"

"A feeling of 'religious-link' has imbued your heart and given a wide way to irrationality. And that makes you nurse a blind fondness for the Palestinians," alleged Phillip. He blamed my religious identity for nursing a tilt towards Palestinians.

"My religion does not allow me foster partiality. Islam has influenced me with all its benign effects.

Why did Christians (Crusaders) occupy Jerusalem (1099 CE to 1187 CE)?"

"Silly question indeed!

Jerusalem is famed for being the birthplace of our Lord Jesus Christ. Does not this meet the competency of a rightful claim?"

"'Lord' Jesus is not your ancestor."

"Lord's wish is sacrosanct. Lord Jesus wished that His followers should be the proud owner of Jerusalem," stated Phillip. His tone was thick and frosted with haughtiness.

"Ironically, Jesus Christ, being the 'Lord', does not wish that Christians (& Jews as well) should rule Jerusalem."

"It is *out and out* frivolous. The comment befits a jester," retorted Phillip belting down my views.

"Friend, analyse the history and you will be completely jostled by a deep awakening.

History has witnessed that Christians ruled Jerusalem barely for 10 percent of the total period spanning between 637 CE to 1967 CE. Whereas, Muslims ruled almost 90 percent of the given period.

Do you think 'Lord' Jesus has betrayed Christians?"

"Jews were in exile. The invaders easily occupied the open ground," stated Phillip.

"Where were Christians?"

"The spiritual importance of Jerusalem has been realised bit late by Christians.

Anyways, Jerusalem is no longer in the control of Muslims. The occupiers have been vanquished. Christians have *turned the tide* by *tipping the scales* of the power-equation in favour of dominance.

Jerusalem is free now. Jerusalem is smiling like a flower of the Paradise. Roses are out now. Jesus, our Lord, has returned the lands to us and entailed the inheritance unto us forever," stated Phillip with a great degree of assertion. He snatched a haughtier look at me.

"Do Christians consider Jerusalem as their inheritance?"

"Of course," replied Phillip authoritatively.

"But, Jews too claim Jerusalem as their inheritance. Who is right?"

"We are the spiritual heirs. Jews claim Jerusalem being the descendants of the actual owners of the lands. We both inherit Jerusalem," opined Phillip like an executive.

"Jews did not like your 'Lord' Jesus and killed him. How they would react at your claiming of inheritance to Jerusalem?"

"You have failed to analyse the history properly. Christians and Jews both have a common target.

Crusaders drove away Muslims in 1088 CE. Jews started showing Muslims the door with the signing of the Balfour Declaration in 1917 CE. The malignant influence of Islam on Jerusalem has already been attenuated to a point of insignificance. We are due back to roll the idle stone covered much with mosses.

We are allies, merged in a confederacy, and we do have a common historic target," stated Phillip.

He hinted that much to be done along the offensive line! Phillip showed a half-hidden threat that urged fear.

"It was even bizarre to have imagined that one day [with the advent of Islam], Jews and Christians would forget the enmity between them and ally with each other for a common target called Islam. You have validated the truthfulness of the Qur'an once again:

"*O ye who believe! Take not the Jews and the Christians for your friends and protectors: they are but friends and protectors to each other.*" [Qur'an: Maidah 5: 51]

By the way, if all the current inhabitants of Palestine converted to Christianity, would you ask Jews to stop eviction?"

"The answer need to be earned by the performance of your merit," Phillip covered the answer with an obscurity.

"The spiritual merit of Muslims does not deserve to be conferred with the inheritance of Jerusalem. Only Christianity could crown you with the inheritance of Jerusalem.

Friend, history is the vision of Allah, analyse it deeply."

"Are you awaiting another Saladin?" inquired Phillip mockingly.

"The verse, I am citing again, is steeped in profundity.

"*Glory be to One Who took His servant by night from the Sacred Mosque to the farthest Mosque,*" [Qur'an: Al Isra 17: 1]

The Prophet was just a passenger in the journey. The journey was purely divine-inspired and full of purpose. The crown of inheritance of Jerusalem was given to Muslims.

Al-Aqsa is holy. A highly esteemed, honourable and spiritually guided leader like Caliph Umar (r.a), or Saladin (r.a) who freed Jerusalem in the past, shall appear again. The moment is approaching fast, and believe me Jews know that."

"Your infatuation with Islam has bred a fantastic distemper in you!

The future is no longer a formidable force for us...we render it duffer by our prowess! Fools wait for the actions of the future, but wise men manipulate the course of the wind. We make 'the times' tractable by connecting the present with the advantageous dots of the future and change the course of the future in our favour. We trap 'the future' in a complex labyrinth and force it to devise its own death! Think about Spain, the Ottoman Empire and the Balfour Declaration. The examples could even make the mountains lose determination to flaccidity!

Surprises are galore and waiting *in the pipeline*," stated Phillip with arrogance generally found in dictatorship.

Arrogance, abuse, neglect, foul words... all were found in his statements. It could make a weak soul feel the infliction of the resulting distress.

"The arrogance perhaps has relieved you from an obstinate pain that was excruciating your inmost for a long time! I remember the speech of Benito Mussolini delivered in 20 September 1920.

"When dealing with such a race as Slavic –inferior and barbarian –we must not pursue the carrot, but the stick policy."

Do you find any appropriateness in his arrogance?"

"The speech exposes his hatred for the Slavic. Mine is not hatred, but rather an argument full of rational logic," replied Phillip.

"I do not mean his hatred, rather his 'confident control' over his supposed 'future actions' on the Slavic. The world knows how 'the future' failed him and hung his dead body upside down in *Piazzale Loreto*, in 1945 CE."

"Not all devisers of 'the future' are deft and shrewd," replied Phillip tersely.

"Someone should offer you edelweiss to subdue your arrogance. Hitler too loved edelweiss."

"I love her ruggedness and tough individualism that subdue the bone-cutting bites of algid snows. I also love her beauty, furry petals, white blush and the ethereal feel that she exudes. My remembrance of her even overruns the due measure that she deserves being the cynosure of all eyes," retorted Phillip lovingly.

"It seems someone, sunk in lavish luxury of Hotel Monte Rosa, is emulating the feat of Edward Whymper by just reading his celebrated book '*Scrambles Amongst the Alps*'. Though driven psychologically to persevere to achieve the summit of the Matterhorn, but never endeavour to attempt physically. You look happy attaining a psychological amateurism! Exuberant imagination cannot execute anything as formidable as climbing the Matterhorn.

I wish you had delved deeply into the history of Jerusalem, especially since the time the holy Prophet set his foot. The fates of Christians and Jews have been written with limpid language in the clear pages of history. Endeavour to mine out the insights and you will realise that you both have been just two fallen logs badly mossed."

"Just tell us, are you against the Declaration or not? Are you against the idea that Jews should live in Palestine?" Kumaran made an inquest assuming a sense of authority. The voice appeared overmastering.

He disclosed his intention through the dark tone of his voice and alluded his slant to the cause of Jews. Seemed, he surrendered himself into the alignment that lies submissively at the feet of Mr Balfour.

"I nurse a distinct refusal to the rationality of the Declaration, for it tramples on the essential sense of rightfulness. However, I do wish sincerely that Jews shoud live peacefully alongside the current inhabitants.

Furthermore, I am announcing aloud my disposition that anyone, born on the earth, can live anywhere on the earth as long as no human logic is impaired or compromised. I love to see people living on the earth peacefully; I love co-existence; I love to see sapience prevailing across the inhabited landscapes; I love to see the scattered pieces of humanity get joined together and enlivened forever like a buxom bloom of a perennially flowering tree.

Jews diaspora started around 70 C.E. when the Roman emperor Titus captured Jerusalem and destroyed the city. A long passage of time has already passed witnessing successions of countless generations in the countries they had immigrated to.

Why, all of a sudden, they become hell-bent to come to their *ancestors' land* leaving the extremely well-off living conditions in the poshest cities like Brooklyn, New York, Moscow, etc.,? Why is the influx; is someone driving them out?"

"Does the influx cause consternation in you? Does it depress you?

Better you cut back these unnecessary worry, and inhale a lungful of fresh air. The fact is, they are just returning to the '*promised land*' as was promised to their ancestors by God Himself," Phillip stated in a lightning pace. His tongue fluttered. I felt, it hit me like a lashing of whip.

"Yes I am worried. The plights of the current inhabitants are very depressing and cut deep my heart. It arouses a deeper sadness in me and urges my reaction. It urges me to be a human being beyond prejudice.

I did know the Jews influx would happen when the Hour draws closer."

"Did God divulge the future of Jews in your dream?" Kumaran said half-mockingly. Phillip offered me an enigmatic smile. He looked at Kumaran and gave him an agreeable wink as if they both were locked in a psychological embrace.

"God has revealed many profound verses in the glorious Qur'an about Jews.

"And We said to the children of Israel after Pharaoh, "Reside in the land, but when the Promise of the Hereafter comes to pass, We will bring you all together." [Qur'an: Bani Israel 17: 104]

The verse is tremendous in stature and profound in insights. The '*promised land*' has been 'conquered' by Jews and the state of Israel has already *seen the light of day* where aspirations and fulfilment greet each other merrily. The settlement of Jews indicates that the Hour is quite near and almost on the doorstep."

"Do you foresee something ominous will befall upon Jews?" Phillip inquired.

"Yes, if they urge the Father's anger!"

"What do mean?" Phillip inquired rapidly.

"Jews not only denied the Messenger of God Jesus Christ (pbuh) but also humiliated him in an abominable way. They still boast extravagantly that they killed Jesus Christ (pbuh), the 'imposter'.

Moreover, they refused to accept the last and final Messenger Muhammad (pbuh) who was sent as the last mercy to Jews as well. Only repentance perhaps could save them from the repercussions poised to befall upon them. The Qur'an says:

"Perhaps your Lord will have mercy on you 'if you repent', but if you return 'to sin', We will return to punishment." [Qur'an: Bani Israel 17: 104]

The verse clearly indicates that goodness will be balanced with mercy, and wickedness will be perfectly weighed against punishment; what is sowed will invariably blossom into respective crop."

"Do you think doom is waiting for Jews?" Phillip asked almost in grim tone.

"*The writing is on the wall*! The verse is more transparent than the flesh of an unblemished crystal."

"Israel has made a resounding progress in the field of technology, and is constantly backed by the prowess of the superpower of the world. Nonetheless, do you think a great doom is poised to befall upon them?" Kumaran argued somewhat rationally. His glance was penetrating.

"Superpower will be proved paper tiger if pitched against God. You need to study the history of the world. The verse hardly needs any further explanations.

I do agree to a certain extent that Jews have been able to find a temporary political solution to their plights through establishing the State called Israel. But the real solution lies at the psychological level that needs an urgent correction.

Even the father of Zionist state, Theodor Herzl (1860-1904 C.E.) fell short of intelligence in apprehending the reasons behind the plights of his race. In *Der Judenstaat* he wrote:

"*The Jewish question persists wherever Jews live in appreciable numbers. Wherever it does not exist, it is brought in together with Jewish immigrants. We are naturally drawn into those places where we are not persecuted, and our appearance there gives rise to persecution. This is the case, and will inevitably be so, everywhere, even in highly civilised countries—see, for instance, France—so long as the Jewish question is not solved on the political level.*"

Theodore was looking for a solution to the plights of Jews in political level through setting up a Zionist State. He succeeded, to some extent or a great extent, but the real solution certainly lies at the mental level of Jews. Unfortunately, they have not yet learnt any lessons even from their pathetic past. They have failed time and again to realise fully the veracity of the Promise [*Bible: Leviticus 26:18*] made by the Almighty.

Pain soars when I find that the God's first chosen race has been reproducing the same vile treatments as they had exactly received from others in the past. It pierces the heart when I see Palestinians, standing in the defence line barely equipped with slingshots or blunt stones to stop the raging armour tanks, being razed and buried alongside the ruins of their homes. The scenes are harrowing. The helpless inhabitants have been constantly harried out of their lands.

The scenes resemble a pack of hunters standing midstream to wing arrows on schools of swimming fishes."

"Surgery pains...," Phillip commented. He uttered these two words and stopped abruptly. He looked at me raveningly.

I did not allow any words escape my lips. I cast a lugubrious stare at Phillip with eyes that do know no malice but cut an uncertain figure that lay enigmatically somewhere at the edge between conflict and confrontation. I suppressed my feelings and remained silent. I remembered the saying of Noam Chomsky (American philosopher, Dec 7, 1928 to living):

"See, people with power understand exactly one thing: violence."

"If power is given to you, would you drive out Jews?" asked Kumaran looking at me seriously.

"No power on the earth could drive out Jews, because it is the Almighty Who has brought them together here in Palestine.

You need to look into the verse *[Qur'an: Bani Israel 17: 104]*

again."

"The case is settled! God Himself has returned Jews their ancestors' land. At last, your melodramatic acting regarding 'Jews settlement' has seen its terminal phase. You should stop now and subdue your harsh voice that inflicts," criticised Kumaran. Phillip timed a flowing nod to honour the secret interplay between them.

"God did not tell them that they should eradicate the current inhabitants."

"I know your wound is deep and fresh, but I urge your patience, and like to say that it will be swathed by the finest balm of the time and healed…just while away few years," Phillip stated fiendishly. He cajoled me into agreement with soothing words that acted as sort of balm on my religious nerve.

"I know time is the nurse and remover of all scars!

I know that patience without grace is irritation. I will snug down in patience."

"What is the benefit of being chosen people of God?" Kumaran moved afield and fielded an insightful question.

"There is something really great being born in the family of the chosen race.

Divine bliss is at your easy reach as you are bestowed with the privilege of having direct or close acquaintanceship with the God's Commandments revealed to the community you belong to.

However, the favour directly entails a constant surveillance of God. The favour indeed is poised on a precarious ground. Any slip on your part in honouring the revealed Commandments will be compensated exponentially with the wrath of God. Undeniably, the chosen race is destined to be punished several times more than the unchosen race. And the degree of punishment is severer and always kept ready to fall lose upon. But for unchosen race, the punishment is linearly proportional."

"What was the reason that the curse in the form of Genghis khan descended upon Muslims?" Kumaran forwarded another insightful query.

"Muslims shirked responsibility. Muslims became oblivion of the sublime Duty of disseminating the Message of God to their fellow human beings to whom the Message of the Qur'an was alien. They did not honour the correctness of God's choice. People to whom Islam was a stranger eliminated Muslims. Genghis khan truly descended upon Muslims as God's curse."

Chapter 7

"Why do Muslims try to convert people?" Kumaran asked tersely. I found an apparent rejection of modesty in his voice.

"You should direct this question to Phillip.

Why did they use the "*Jesus Rifles*" in Afghanistan and Iraq and killed millions mercilessly in the name of Jesus Christ (pbuh)?

Why did they carry out mischief in the name of Christ (pbuh)?"

"The world knows the reasons of the wars. I do not want to repeat the same here. In short, *Islamic terrorism* have been the muses that constantly cater for determination to the mission '*war for peace*'.

The dividend in believing Jesus Christ is the 'Paradise'. Well, at least with this Bullet (John 8:12) in chest, -Afghans and Iraqis would get favour from Jesus Christ in the heaven. The bullets would advocate for them while negotiating for a place in the Paradise. The Paradise belongs only to the believers who live in the union of Lordship of Jesus Christ!" Phillip narrated the preposterous views with a temperate tongue and through an apparently virtuous voice.

I found him averse to looking at me, rather he kept himself busy staring reflectively at the shiny surface of the table. He kept on gliding his finger, and after a little while, started ticking constantly on the surface of the table that resembled the drumming of soft rain on a tin-thatched roof.

"He has replied. Now tell me why do Muslims try to convert people?" insisted Kumaran.

I stopped Kumaran for a moment as I wanted to reply Phillip.

"War departs from the line of intelligence, but murder departs from the line of conscience. In war, one can find a contest at least, but in murder, only the '*law of the jungle*' dominates burying the conscience in the barren land of virtue.

These are not wars but murders, -a widespread massacre imposed savagely in an unprecedented scale. The acts gave a nasty shake to humanity! You cannot be happy but *baying for people's blood*!

Anyways, are you sure Paradise is waving at you? Friend, please ask priests of highest eminence if they have *beaten a path to God's door* to receive the said 'divine confirmation'?"

"Jesus is our Lord and Saviour, -'*He is the Way and the Light*'. No need to reiterate the verses of the Bible. I do not want to *beat a dead horse*," Phillip reacted. He appeared enamoured of the 'Lordship' of Jesus Christ (pbuh) and found himself in a euphoric state.

"Do you know the smallest sentence in the Bible?"

"It's extraneous to the moment. What's the point? What do you want to prove here?" Phillip looked at me cantankerously.

"Do not try to fob me off please. Certainly, there is a relevance.

"*Jesus wept*" [Bible: John 11:35].

That much he would do for you on the Day of Judgement! He would feel a tender pity for you and weep because of your perverted belief that he had never preached! The Qur'an says:

"Christ the son of Mary was no more than a messenger;..." [Qur'an: Maidah 5: 75]

"... "But said Christ: "O Children of Israel! Worship Allah, my Lord and your Lord."..." [Qur'an: Maidah 5: 72]

Refined falsehood, posh imagination and polished preposterousness have been loosely integrated in designing the concoction to defend the alleged divinity of Jesus Christ (pbuh). Friend, you are standing on the brink of theological precipice because the concoction, by nature, is treacherous like quicksand, fickler like *shifting sands,* precarious like overhanging cornices and flimsy like spider web that cannot endure the bites of incisive rationality. You will never be able to cover up the overhang of the concoction.

No matter how much the concoction tries to be grand, imposing, polished and unctuous in dealing with the 'divinity' of Christ (pbuh), it will never be able to prevent debacle when put under the test of stringent dimensions. The concoction neither can rob the wealth of honesty, nor can deplete the power of truth. It will fail, time and again, to match the exciting precision of an impeccable truth.

It lends me an air to say that the whole scene of the concoctions was botched up in a haste to meet the demands of some pressing need. The scenes involving Jesus Christ (pbuh) were put inside an impure mould in a haste to manufacture an imaginative and transcendental figure of Jesus Christ (pbuh) that would necessitate the need of an intensely irrational sense to understand it. Blending of grandiose phraseology and shrewdness have been carried out purportedly inside the concoctions to lug readers into believing everything about Jesus Christ (pbuh) as true. The 'divinity' of Jesus Christ (pbuh) is counterfeited and installed on a shaky foundation comprising of four apocryphal pillars to offer a treacherous form to the so-called Christianity. And they are: '*God* is Jesus', '*crucified* was Jesus', '*resurrected* was Jesus', '*Holy Spirit* was Jesus.'

An obstinate poison has been injected into the hearts of millions from an unholy vial! The true personality of the mighty Messenger Jesus Christ (pbuh) has been tumbled into a pool of confused imageries. This is, no doubt, a great theological swindle against the person of Jesus Christ (pbuh), and would never be able to offer felicity to the hearts that starve spiritually. The concoctions have *led the multitude down the garden path*. The traitorous acts need to be stopped!

Friend, do not let your faith be in the hands of ruses lest it leaves you floundering in miserable crisis. How long will you delude yourself in believing this gross imperfection?

It now turns up that you must do some serious introspections about the easy availability of Paradise. The Paradise is much way beyond your narrow confines of vision."

"These are absolutely bizarre and hardly deserve any serious hearing. These are nothing but a tapestry of Muhammad's ravings. Dump it in the frozen chest of shrinking polar ice caps.

Things will be clear in the second coming of Jesus Christ. On that day the faces of people, who have distanced themselves from being in the Union of Lord Christ, will be daubed by a broader brush of mass disappointment. Most certainly, they will go berserk in search of solace and salvation. The Bible says:

"*But our citizenship is in the heaven, and from it we await a Savior, the Lord Jesus Christ.*" [Bible: Philippians 3:20]

On that day, every believing Christian will be offered the citizenship of the Heaven. The Bible says:

"*But our citizenship is in heaven, and from it we await a Saviour, the Lord Jesus Christ.*" [Bible: Philippians 3:20]

The heaven is ours," Phillip reacted evincing a solid faith in the union of 'Lord' Christ. His tone trickled in towering confidence and he grew too complacent over the verse.

"Who is actually coming Jesus Christ (pbuh), or the Father?"

"Of course, Jesus Christ," answered Phillip.

"As you stated earlier, '*God is One in three: the Father, the Son and the Holy Ghost and all three are equipoised and bestowed with equal divine power... Unicity of God is found in this Unity!*'

My simple questions are: Is there any 'physical difference' between Jesus Christ (pbuh) and the Father? Can you identify the Father if he comes in place of Jesus Christ (pbuh)?"

"It's Jesus; Bible has confirmed that. That much I would say," replied Phillip.

"Why would Jesus Christ (pbuh) come for the second time?"

"There are many verses in the Bible that speak about the purpose of his second coming. The following verse will still your brazen quest.

"He will appear a second time, not to deal with sin, but to save those who are waiting for him," [Bible: Hebrews 9:28]

That day will herald a merry moment for the Christians," stated Phillip.

"What Jesus Christ (pbuh) would say to you in his second coming?"

"I could not make out your point –elucidate it," asked Phillip reluctantly.

"I would like to draw your attention to the verses:

"When Judgement Day comes, many will say to me,

'Lord, Lord! In your name we spoke God's message, by your name we drove out many demons and performed many miracles!'" [Bible: Mathew 7:21-22]

Then he would respond:

"Then I will say to them, 'I never knew you. Depart from me, you wicked people!'" [Bible: Mathew 7:23]

Do not think that you would be rewarded with a shower of appreciation rained by the lips of your 'Lord' Jesus Christ (pbuh). Rather, you would be *on the receiving end* of his rebuke. The verse clearly indicates that he would rebuke you in public because of your ignoble practice of pushing him to the pedestal of 'Lordship'. You would be treated as a degenerate member of the noble family of 'Christianity'. It seems, you would be trapped in a dark corner and pummelled badly."

"He will snub the '*wicked*' people only. A clear indication lies in his statement," replied Phillip.

"Wrong! You can dump this belief into *Boomerang Nebula*, the coldest place of the observed Universe (-272.15 °C).

Friend, you should not wrong yourself. He will rebuke those moral degenerates who call him 'Lord, Lord!' The indication is *loud and clear* and denies the necessity of further clarity.

The verses loose an emphatically solid evidence to find out the real heathens! Do you still think that the people of Afghanistan and Iraq are heathens?"

"There is a huge doubt over the word 'Lord' on lips.

Just calling Jesus 'Lord' is not enough for the people who do not listen to him and do what he instructs.

The verses perfectly fit the heathens," Phillip retorted. He almost transitioned close to anger.

"Then, how the people of Afghanistan and Iraq merely carrying the shells of spent bullets inscribed with *John 8:12* inside their bleeding hearts will be offered Paradise instantly?

Is not it a logic-disorder on your part?

I remember the quote of Edward Gibbon (an English historian and writer, 1737-1794), -

"*In every deed of mischief he had a heart to resolve, a head to contrive and a hand to execute*".

The quote is highly condensed and profound!"

"What do you mean by the quote?" Kumaran inquired. He loosed a serious glance upon me.

"The reply can send a shiver down the spine of those who are unaware of the Bible! The urge of the verse is same as the fear that invites death. But, I am not surprised at all. His reply fits perfectly the cruelty of the following verses!

"So now kill every boy and kill every woman who has had sexual intercourse, but keep alive for yourselves all the girls and all the women who are virgins" [Bible: Numbers 31: 17-18]

"But when you capture cities in the land that the Lord your God is giving you, kill everyone. Completely destroy all the people: …, as the Lord ordered you to do." [Bible: Deuteronomy 20: 16-17]

Sometimes I wonder how God could have revealed such dread verses in a holy Book?"

"Think about the violent verses of the Koran? The roses are frightened to smell sweet since the moment the verses revealed their dreary presence. The verses will make the eyes clamped-shut in fear…," Phillip retorted precipitately.

"I know what the Qur'an is! Please tell me which verse frightens you?"

"Kill unbelievers, –wherever you find them kill them. How long will you *sweep the verses under the carpet*?" Phillip snubbed.

"Friend, your 'perception' about the Qur'an has long been trapped by the ruses of propaganda. I do know the verse you are indicating to. -

The verse encompasses the affairs exclusively related to the battlefield. The unbelievers unilaterally broke the *Treaty* signed between them and Muslims (of Mecca). The repetitive violations of the *Treaty* by the unbelievers led Muslims to resort to the last option that calls for battle. And, if you study exquisitely, you would find that the verse is thick with forgiveness. The verse does not overstep the line of civility and chivalry like the Bible that orders, -"*kill every boy and kill every woman.*"

"When the Sacred Months have passed, kill the unbelievers wherever you find them….. But if they repent, and perform the prayers, and pay the alms, then let them go their way, …" [Qur'an :Tawbah 9:5]

Besides, just look at the next immediate verse. -

"And if anyone of the unbelievers asks you for protection, give him protection so that he may hear the Word of God; then escort him to his place of safety,..." [Qur'an: Tawbah 9:6]

Look at the astounding nobility and profound humanity embedded in the verse, -unbelievers (if ask for protection) should be escorted to a place of safety. Every verse of the Qur'an lives in the thick of forgiveness and is rich in flowing mercy. The Qur'an and mercy cream together!

My good man, did you ever expect that such verses could exist in the Qur'an?"

"By the way, what was the sapience in quoting Edward Gibbon?" Kumaran asked curiously. The Quote of Edward Gibbon had triggered a welling of curiosity in Kumaran.

"The explanation is given by Bertrand Russel in his book, "In Praise of Idleness". He says:

"*The Jews first invented the notion that only one religion could be true, but they had no wish to convert all world to it, and therefore only persecuted other Jews. The Christians retaining the Judaic belief in a special revelation, added to it the Roman desire for world-wide dominion and the Greek taste for metaphysical subtleties.* ***The combination produced the most fiercely persecuting religion the world has yet known.*** *In Japan and China Buddhism was peaceably accepted and allowed to exist along with Shinto and Confucianism; in the Mohammedan world, Christians and Jews were not molested so long as they paid the tribute; but throughout the Christendom death was the usual penalty for even smallest deviation from Orthodoxy.*" [In Praise of idleness: Western Civilisation (page174)]

Phillip has disguised as a gentleman and presented himself as if filled with an unbelievable measure of benevolence poised to be utilised for the wellbeing of humanity. But, Bertrand Russel has dug out his true nature remained so far wrapped in dark obscurity. He has beautifully delineated that nature through his superfluously candid statement, '*The combination produced the most fiercely persecuting religion the world has yet known*'. His views perfectly fit Phillip."

"Falcon does not snack on fly!

We want to top the list. We do always carry the unswerving resolve for world domination and that very notion is inherited from none but our great Roman ancestors. The Bible is just a theoretical visage of our religious facet that hardly adds any weightage to the side of our realistic thinking. Frankly, we are less concerned about the purity of theology, and almost immune to the scam purportedly carried out deep inside the Book. It hardly hinders our plan; it hardly offends our motive; it hardly disgraces our morality. We do use religion just as a *duffer stamp* of self-identification, and our real recognition is, -we want glamour, glitters, multi-dimensional sensuality and above all the overpowering world domination. We must *stop at nothing* to achieve it.

We believe in Edward Gibbon's famous saying:

"*The winds and the waves are always on the side of the ablest navigators*."

The albatrosses travel miles over the deep ocean not for tiny krill but majestic lobsters! In the quote consists our contentment; the quote vocalises our grand plan.

The rest left to your ablest guesses!" Phillip loosed off the entirety of his ulterior motives.

Finally, he exposed the undercoat of his true instinct. He cracked the hard crust of obscurity, and let the core of his instinct take wings and fly in public. I lauded the way he opened up copiously and presented the disclosures trampling down general hesitation that most people pamper secretly beneath the acting facade. He bared the secrets!

"Notorious bullet does not follow linear path!

By the way, who is the biggest obstacle in your path?"

"It does not require further analysis nor any meritorious guesses, –it is Islam! Islam is the toughest opponent," Phillip disclosed his secret mind.

Phillip sloughed off the overcoat that acted defiantly as camouflage in the face of 'secularism'. For a long time indeed, he tried to sweep the 'secularism' under the carpet, but could no longer succeed in keeping it lurking in the dark shadow of concealment. I looked at him and kept on looking as long as the sullen silence allowed me to. His reply was savagely hard on me as if he loosed a hail of bullets whose reports frightened my soul. But his candour deserved a great laud.

"Friend, hundred years ago, an event that snubs your secularism, turned up when the French army General Henry Joseph Eugene Gouraud had conquered Syria in 1920 CE. The French seized Damascus and Henry Gouraud entered the tomb of great Saladin. He kicked the tomb and said:

"Saladin, we are back."

This line recounts the past of secularism! The event that transpired on that day still coursing afresh in memory. The line is afresh and haunting the soul of 'secularism' since then. He loosed the evil hidden in his heart. The malicious line has still been hovering over and mocking constantly the untrustworthiness of the so-called '*secularism*'. It is announcing aloud that the 'secularism' never did contain any honest substance, -it is vain, dubious and fraudulent. It is but a thick smokescreen of cruel deceptions that spans multitude of ignoble things!

Secularism: its appearance takes the allure to new heights; its handshake is flaccid; its conversation is outgoing; its demeanour is appealing; its voice is supple; its conversations ooze pools of springs but it nurses a dreadful motive with a stone heart! It hides toxic cyanide under the patina of cocoa!

Your actions do not jibe with your speech; the smoke screen is pierced wide!"

"He did not say that. You happened to have read some malicious article," grunted Phillip.

"Then why did he enter the mausoleum of Saladin? For what?"

Phillip did not respond but dragged a long deep sigh that produced a suppressed sound.

"How would you convince me that Muslims are naïve and do not intend to convert people forcefully or forcibly to Islam?" Kumaran brought up the question again with a renewed interest.

"Friend, have you ever invited your inquisitiveness to investigate the real drive behind it? -

The Instructions of our Creator have been the real drive. It has been made obligatory for us to share the Message of the glorious Qur'an to the people still living life unaware.

"Invite (all) to the Way of thy Lord with wisdom and beautiful preaching; ...." [Qur'an: Al Nahl 16:125]

To make someone believe in Islam is not our aim, neither is it under the purview of our entitlement. We can only preach the Message to the people in the best way possible. There stops our duty, and honestly, we never intend to overstep the line drawn by the Almighty. Even the Messenger no way is permitted to arrange the affairs of an individual. It is Allah (swt) and only He disposes the affairs.

"We sent down the (Qur'an) in Truth, and in Truth has it descended: and We sent thee but to give Glad Tidings and to warn (sinners)." [Qur'an: Al Isra 17: 105]

Islam does not believe in compulsion, neither does practise coercion. The verse below clears the cloud of suspicion.

"Let there be no compulsion in religion: Truth stands out clear from Error: ...." [Qur'an: Baqara: 256]

Religion depends on faith and must not be induced with force, else it will lose lustre. Religion founded on falsity is bound to shrink in acceptance and eventually slips into concealment for forever. It loses its appeal and stops thriving.

We preach the Message as our obligatory duty commensurate with the divine instructions given to us by none but the Almighty. We are ordained to invite people to the Truth revealed to us. We are not instructed to 'convert' the heart of the people, neither are we instructed to introduce the word 'convert' in our preaching.

I think you have misplaced your understanding."

"But while conveying the Message, the world knows that Muslims adopt the trick of making the word 'convert' *conspicuous by its absence.* The skilful speech, deft use of certain words that bear blazing similitude to the word 'convert' make one to *toe the line* of conversion," Kumaran stated making direct eye contact.

"Should I make a small request, Kumaran?"

"What's this?" Kumaran looked at me.

"How do you feel about the Message of Islam?"

"Fanaticism is abundant in your flesh and plaguing your mind with a rare contamination. The attitude displayed so far is emblematic of what is going on in your mind. Please never try to fit the defeated device called Islam into my psychology. You know, a cowpat cannot distribute the smell of a cowslip! I don't think lotus could bloom at the tip of landfills," Kumaran stigmatized me being powered with military attitude. He flicked my inquiry off the table with a vehemence.

I had failed to anticipate the tempest my proposal could have bring about.

"Reason?"

"It is simple, loud and clear... I do not want to be radicalised. Islam threatens to cut off the delightful flight of the life and reduces one to the level of a gauche. It strips down the pleasure of life to spiritual rigidity. The majority of world population is still away from Islam, and so far, I have aligned myself with the majority. I cannot relegate myself to live in airless colony, and neither do I ever think that I should make Islam an overarching principle of life entailing unnecessarily *a chip on my shoulder.* My freedom consists in the absence of Islam. I cannot bear the drag of Islam. And yes, I avoid Islam like the plague!" Kumaran criticised with a clipped military tone.

Kumaran gave me a glance of distaste, -the glance was very dissecting and as sharp as a chip of glass.

"What do you mean by '*airless colony*'?"

"We have already exposed the true nature of Islam through countless illustrations, and the cover has been removed from its brute undercoat.

As damp collects mildew, Islam invites rust. We have watched Islam for a long time and it seems *as dull as ditchwater*. Islam has heaved its ideology on easier section of people having tenuous hold on intellect. Islam has entangled itself in a complex of untidily harsh boundary conditions and looks like a caliginous night contrasting perfectly with a sunshiny day! Islam appears to be an unwanted mass of morbid substance that slaps fetters upon life and confines one to the axis of reduced freedom…the life with Islam is a long siege," Kumaran's tongue overshot the line of average billingsgate.

"These are psychogenic fears and can be ameliorated by positive cast of mind! Friend, it's nothing but a medley of mere conjectures and misinformation…you seem to have been swollen with it!

For argument's sake, I agree that Muslims are living in lower form of environments and coerced to languish in deplorable mental conditions. Now, please tell me, how much does it affect Muslims mentally?"

"Islam stifles! It fills the mind with countless abandoned clutter!

Islam casts tenebrific shadows over its followers and forces them to live in tenebrous trench that stretches from the affair of circumcision to the affair of circumambulation. It imposes a plethora of circumscriptions on the freedom of choice. The life of a Muslim is like a forlorn baby confined to a toyless room! The '*art of living*' that Muslims morbidly adopts cannot offer them anything better than an overmatch. The truth is that Muslims have foregathered themselves happily on the brink of mental precipice …blinds drawn on their eyes!" Kumaran scathed Islam with deft flicks of tongue and presented lugubrious reports on mental health of Muslims.

His prowess in this field seems could turn a benign medicine into poison! I wonder how he carries secretly such ample stock of abuses in deep pockets of his heart!

"Well. Why is Thailand your favourite touring destination? Reasons?"

"Thailand is a great place! It is a turf of positive vibes, progressiveness, delight, amusement and social sass. Here one can find extended freedom of mind resonating in and around the ambience injecting a merry sense that is, of course, resoundingly refreshing. Mind relaxes here and finds itself clear of clutter. Here, life finds its true meaning of existence; here the sun does not set in; night appears ethereal; amusement and entertainment jostle with each other; and here millions of splendid wishes find easy fulfilment! In short, here you are celestially off! I remember one of the celebrated quotes of Buddha:

"*The secret of health for both mind and body is not to mourn for the past, nor to worry about the future, but to live the present moment wisely and earnestly*."

The quote seems to have encompassed all the quintessence of life…in fact it is the embodiment of life," Kumaran continued unweariedly with triumphant voice. His voice trickled in the dreamy contents of his enamoured heart.

"Friend, do you know, in Southeast Asia, Thailand tops the list in suicide rate? The rate is astonishingly high and increasing agonisingly with each passing day. Why Thailand is grappling with mental health challenges? Are you aware of the *other side of the coin*?"

"Suicide is omnipresent, it happens across the world. What do you mean exactly?" Kumaran inquired brashly.

"Like you said, they do have everything for enjoyment including innumerable sex workers, unhindered sense of mingling of opposite sexes, colourful night clubs, great expanse of romantic beaches, amazing amusement halls vibrating with gyrating pole dancers wrapped in transparent corsets, drink-sodden couples performing quadrilles in enjoyment, ...and what not. Then, why Thailand is the top suicidal country in Southeast Asia? Why do they end life out of depression?

Truly, Afghans are deprived of all suchlike modern amenities to spice up lives. Moreover, Afghanistan has been constantly reeling under the threats of foreign occupations and oppressions for some unrelenting decades. Extreme poverty, lack of basic health facilities and utterly insalubrious physical living conditions have been some of the deeper reasons for the deplorable conditions. Violence and bloodshed have left much of the country in ruins. Here mountains cast tenebrific shadows, landscapes are barren, streams are spent, infrastructure is wretchedly poor, economy finds no pedestal, light dims, bloom faints, blossom droops, roses do not smell sweet, mercy is scarce, fear is scary, knowledge is robbed, understanding is plundered, people prowl like beasts, here hope crumbles, freedom falters, poverty laughs, opulence taunts, banks do not disburse, disaster befalls, hardship mocks, religion gags, health sinks, meagreness collaborates with smallness, nonchalance partners with insensitiveness, hearts sink *in the throes of* hopelessness, attacks lunge forward frequently, bickering grows into quarrel, and quarrel into fight, and fight into skirmish and skirmish into battle ... and the *straw to break the camel's back* were the wars,...and what not! They lead lives in bondage to the worst forms of every necessity. None can deny the fact that Afghans do have every reason to end their lives out of disconsolation; they do have every reason to plead suicide! But surprisingly, they have been slicing through the waves of darkness and responding constantly to the calls of promising life. Nothing has caused them *to bite the dust!* They have *tipped the scales* against the cruel adversities!

Why the suicide rate in Afghanistan is amongst the least in the world? Which factor has prevented them from committing suicide?

Just imagine, what could have happened had the same grim geo-political situation been imposed on Thailand? I would request you to search top suicidal countries in the world…and verily, there you would find even Japan and Russia waving at you!

Are they not aware of the sagacious quote that you mentioned? After all, why do they end lives?"

"The quote is magnificent by appearance, munificent by heart, golden by hand and admiringly philosophical by nature,…it gives epitomical meaning to life. It arouses optimism, and it frees you from the bondage to avarice and lust. Simply put, the quote is a bliss and I carry it in the deep niche of my soul," stated Kumaran brandishing a victorious attitude.

"Buddhism is much closer to them and unquestionably they do possess greater acquaintanceship with it than you do. It is widely preached and accepted 'religion' in Thailand. They understand Buddhism much better than you and verily they know where the sapience lies.

Where do they fail?"

"Reasons are galore and I do not want to go deeper into the socio-political situation of the country.

But, I do believe that entertainment and spirituality must form a tight coupling and go hand in hand making their way to the same collective destination. Entertainment is attractive and spirituality is desirable…they must shake hands and be always together to produce the best of things."

"Who would teach spirituality?"

"Spiritual gurus," Kumaran said in a tender voice.

"They would *lead the country a merry dance!*

Anyways, Afghans, Syrians, Libyans, Palestinians, Iraqis do not have *spiritual gurus* and neither do they have the infrastructure for the so-called entertainment and amusement. But, they lead the way in showing the world being the countries where the suicide case is rare and buried deep in obscurity.

Friends, the answer lies in a very simple sentence. It is very light and easy even for a dying person; the lips do not move when the tongue utters it. And it is: '*La-ilaha illaAllah*' meaning 'there is no God but Allah'.

This is the most 'prized' line ever existed on the earth, and this is the only '*celestial verse*' that could still the morbid hunger of soul.

The line bears a lovely relation with the following verse and together can create a wonder.

"Every soul shall have a taste of death: and We test you by evil and by good by way of trial. To Us must ye return." [Qur'an: Al Anbiya 21: 35]

The verse offers a divine succour to depressed soul, placates tumultuous mind and enables life to see a beaconing *light at the end of the tunnel*. The verse indeed is towering in stature that instils unique character into followers to face unweariedly the extremes of hardship and adversity with unfading grace and gratitude."

"Be happy being in the *airless colony*. Scarcely anything else could be so depressing as to watch Muslims being happy being a bellhop! Stick to bellhop's job as none is enforcing you to become a Steve Jobs," grunted Kumaran.

He evaded my question and moved afield giving a tight embrace to ego. Ego does never sublimate its contentious fronts into wisdom, rather it clasps contention and swirls up. Ego should learn a wiseness from the diary of a vice President who sublimates ego and dedicates himself to implement the agenda of a President, hoping never or fruitlessly for the top post.

"Profit making in lawful way is not prohibited in Islam, but unlawful way of amassing wealth, flattening up profits exorbitantly, profiteering or avarice is. Stagnation of wealth into the dreary hands of a handful of people is a distaste to Islam...Islam disapproves of it. Islam stands strongly for even circulation of wealth and loathes the insane disparity between opulence and penury, and therefore urges the rich to spend for the people deemed less privileged in the society.

Neither does Islam encourage extravagance the way Steve Jobs (American business magnate, co-founder of '*Apple Inc.*') astonished the world by changing car in every six months. He infatuated himself with the extravagant passion of being 'different', and in this effort he chose to drive a car without affixing number plate. He chose to replace his car with brand new one in every six months without violating the legal 'registration law' that allows plying of six-month-old new car without a number plate. That passion brands a weird impress on the minds of people. It's an excess; it's an extravagance ...it does not fit into the vein of Islam.

Wealth brings luxury and makes happiness scarce. But Islam makes happiness abundant relegating luxury to the class of '*the least wanted*' in the life. A meagre meal, a decrepit living room where he beds down on the floor, little possession, penury, reduced social interactions all these cannot prevent a bellhop from being friendly, impressionable and outgoing with people. Nothing like indigence, frustration, hopelessness could make him to think that 'he is a nothing'. For, he knows a bright ray is waving at him from the other end of the life called the *Hereafter,* where he shall spend his magnificent eternal life. He knows the life on the earth is full of dull events and futile rigmaroles, and the stint here on the earth is just a tiny fraction compared to the never-ending eternal life in the *Hereafter*. His face gleams when he turns to Islam because he finds a hope-filled light that glimmers through the thick of hardships. A caliginous night can never slap a termination on his hope of seeing the bright sun in the next morning.

Should the bellhop stick to the principles of Islam, Islam will promise him Paradise, and nothing can threaten to destroy that belief in him."

"I am mystified by your passion for Paradise that overruns the bound of an extravagant infatuation! It is but a report of a drink-sodden reporter, or a filibuster of a stubborn, lugubrious member of a parliament!

I know billions of stars trickle through fine rose the mass of perfumed mists that descend gently upon Muslims to wash them with divine bliss! After all, Muslims will be sent to Elysian Field[5*] where God would confer them immortality!

Be happy being a bellhop!" Kumaran shot the scathing reply.

He nipped the skin around the left cheek perfunctorily with fingers and cast a glance devoid of grace.

"All right friend, what do you think of Prophet Muhammad (pbuh)?"

"The name itself arouses a distaste and *makes my skin crawl*!

I do not find even a suspicion of Prophethood in him. He might be a Prophet to you, but is a '*mlechch*' to me! He is turned completely out of my appreciation and good thoughts," grunted Kumaran. His tongue sliced through the sheet of contempt.

"What do you mean by '*mlechch*'?"

"A lowborn, -devoid of nobilities! We do know him by this 'meaning'!" observed Kumaran. He expressed his excitingly precise belief.

"I think this 'meaning' born out of desperation! It clearly accuses you of appeasing ego! Is it your personal 'connotation' of the word?"

"What, according to you, the meaning of the word '*mlechcha*' should be?" probed Kumaran.

Seemingly, he was not eager to hear anything that would alter his standing notion about the Prophet, or anything that would bring repute to the noble Prophet. He pledged his belief to a torpor.

"I do know Muhammad (pbuh) by repute. Here, one of the meanings of the word is 'foreigner'."

Kumaran snorted at my reply foretasting clearly of his disapproval. It seemed he was overpowered by an obstinate insensibility!

"No,…not at all. The word connotes 'lowborn', and many acclaimed Hindu scholars have nodded in total agreement," Kumaran stated taking self-approved authority on his side.

Seemed, he swore blind allegiance to the view of the scholars.

"All right my friend. Please read the following *sloka* (Sanskrit transliteration):

"Atosmitrantare mlechcha acharyana samannita,

Mohamad itikhyata sishyasakha samannita"

[Bhavisya Purana:Pratisarg Parv 3:Khand 3:Adhya 3:Sloka 5]

Just look at the *sloka*—here, both the words *'mlechcha' and 'acharya'* appeared side by side in the same verse. *And,* needless to say, *'acharya'* means a good teacher, a teacher who is enlightened and full of knowledge. And it names none but Muhammad (pbuh) whose name is also mentioned in the same sloka.

Do you think an '*acharya*' is a *'lowborn'*?"

"I don't know the full *sloka*," replied Kumaran candidly.

"Then, how did you pin your faith on the wall of the market-sold interpretation of the word *'mlechcha'*? Is not it a lapse of intelligence?"

"The meaning has been massively heralded by the societies I live in. I have just tilted myself fully towards the plane that amalgamates me with the pulse of the societies," observed Kumaran.

The pitch is deliberately curated for a fun amalgamation of falsities, fictions and a family of spurious things. A nasty tortuousness has been imparted to the straightness of the '*slokas*'! The mess is not tractable, and nothing can sublimate the complex tangle into a transparency!

"Don't follow the flocks. If you are endowed with a brain then use it independently –just apply it. Here, I am citing another *sloka* (Bhojraj Ubach),

"Namaste girijanath marusthalnibasine,

Tripurasurnasaye bahumayaprabortine"

[Bhavisya Purana:Pratisarg Parv 3:Khand 3:Adhya 3:Sloka 7]

Here, *Rajabhoj* is paying obeisance to the resident of the desert by calling him *'girijanath'*. Here *'girijanath'* means one who holds elevated place amongst the human race, -he is the pride of humankind; he destroys the devil '*Tripurasurnasaye*'.

Question arises, how a devil-destroyer could be ignoble?"

"I am actually least bothered about the *connotation* of the word, or as to how it is construed. I have found a comfortable niche in the society by conceding to the widely accepted meaning of that word," replied Kumaran looking at me enigmatically. He shot me a mysterious glance that a few can apprehend.

"Would you support me if I preach the above *shlokas* to the people? I believe that it would help enhance bond, create amity and edify deeper understanding amongst us."

"It's hard,...well, actually it's harder and the chance is slim and might fades away into the inviting arms of failure. It would perhaps never be able to produce the intended fruitfulness of your efforts...it would *go belly up*...better not to overstep the line," Kumaran issued a half-stark caution.

He wounded the bell of 'actions'. He wrapped the signal in spoken-pushbacks that indicated possible foretaste of happening of something harsher and worse. He gave me a sly smile curving lips very stingily.

The distorted meaning of the word *'mlechcha'* literally betrays the truth and derogates from the beauty of the *sloka*. The connotation (*'lowborn'*) is a pernicious connivance of the minds habituated in praising devils in idleness. Kumaran, perhaps, has become willingly a prey to it. I cannot afford to wonder much as I do know that the negative things about Muhammad (pbuh) speeds alongside the light, or even faster!

"It suits the moment to quote the British historian Thomas Carlyle:

"The lies (Western slander) which well-meaning zeal has heaped round this man (Muhammad) are disgraceful to ourselves only"""

"Cut…cut! I am least attracted to the dreary way of life that Islam prescribes," grunted Kumaran.

He was not himself and his tongue simmered again. He dropped away the morose weariness that crippled his tongue only for a brief moment. I found a thickness in his voice resulted due to excessive exertion of his tongue.

After a short while, Kumaran made a significant cut in emotion and showed almost a stone-cold serious face that I had ever observed in our friendship. Finally, he curved out his lips for a graceless obligatory smile. I gave a grace-filled one in exchange.

"Well, I have plucked with great care and soulful devotion the brightest bloom of the Vedas and Puranas…and it is no one but the greatest human being Prophet Muhammad (pbuh)."

"The world has had already much of Islam. We know the blush of the bloom that exudes nothing but perfume of total fanaticism. You seem to have over-reached yourself in blind devotion to Islam," derided Kumaran.

He drew a breath quite long and deep, and sighed looking at me with eyes that blinked out an uncanny expression. He stopped the further advancement of his tongue and settled reluctantly to an artificial calm.

"Friends, please remove the blinds drawn on your eyes and look at Muhammad (pbuh) …the greatest creation of your Lord.

Friends, Islam is the only *'-ism'* on the earth that nurses a great sense of deference for the spirit of questioning, arguments, debate, discussions and criticism. And believe me, if your ego does not overpower the flair of rationality, if your biasedness does not overthrow the justice of conscience, if your narrowness does not overshadow the fairness of outlook, then you will never be able to defeat Islam in logic-driven confrontation. Friends, Islam is not a religion, but a Divine Idea born to outshine all.

Muhammad (pbuh) is not a person whom you can *trifle with*. -

The Universe was persuaded to come into existence on the promise that Muhammad (pbuh) would be created and brought to the earth. Creation drew nearer to its full realisation when Muhammad (pbuh) set his foot on the earth.

I penned a small poem as an ode to my beloved Prophet. I see him speaking through my poem,

'Life is deceptive as the shape of water,

And as treacherous as the kiss of wine,

I'm promising you the life in the Here-after,

In the tranquillity of Kingdom Divine.'

Muhammad (pbuh) is taller than the collective height of the mountains, vaster than the collective vastness of the skies, deeper than the collective depth of the oceans, more generous than the collective generosity of the selfless hearts, more magnanimous than the collective magnanimity of the greatest forgivers, more truthful than the reflection of the most truthful mirror, more honest than the pure echo of the most honest hill, more trustworthy than the promise of a sure death, more unblemished than the pure flesh of the most virgin crystal and more dearer than the collective dearness of the dearest kinship.

Prophet Muhammad (pbuh), a man than whom there is none better! The purpose of the Creation cannot be happy with anything less than Muhammad (pbuh)!

Friends, I feel Prophet Muhammad (pbuh) and the Qur'an are still much for you to bear. I am citing again the verse that Jesus Christ (pbuh) told to his disciples about the coming of the noble Prophet Muhammad (pbuh).

"I have much more to tell you, but now it will be much for you to bear. ..." [Bible: John 16: 12]

I feel the verse still finds its relevance in you. That's all gentlemen."

"We know how Muhammad has led you unto the all truth! The world is running on her knees to pay obeisance and shower glory, laud and honour on Muhammad! The sky is trickling bliss, the night is no longer sunless, peace is coursing in the veins, souls are dripping copious mercy, generosity running in flesh and all these happened with the arrival of Muhammad," Kumaran threw sarcasm.

"Yes it's true that Muhammad (pbuh) has led us unto the all truth.

Friends, suppose we are stuck in the dreary ruts of a scorching desert, and we do have only a glass of water to still thirst. A housefly falls into the drink. What will you do?"

"Drain out the tops of water along with the fly," replied Kumaran glibly. Phillip dripped a quick nod on Kumaran.

"I was expecting such presence of imperfection in your knowledge.

I would like to cite a simple yet incredibly important *hadith* of the noble Prophet. The holy Prophet said:

"*If a fly falls into the drink of anyone of you, he should dunk it all the way in and then remove it. Because on one of its wings is disease and on the other is its cure.*" [Sahih al-Bukhari: 3320]

So, before I drink the water, I would dip it completely and let it fly away. No knowledgeable person with his extent of knowledge *can hold a candle to* the level of knowledge given to Prophet Muhammad (pbuh).

Friends, a common fly carries pathogens of many diseases. It is also true that it carries parasitic bacteriophages that fight the germs of the diseases.

Friends, the Qur'an is the epitome of revelation, Muhammad (pbuh) is the embodiment of mercy and knowledge and Islam edifies the meaning of life and the way we lead our lives.

Could Darwin, Dawkins, Marx, Newton or Einstein guide you unto such truth?"

I kept on shrieking for their attention on the *Hadith* only to be replied later with silence complete with character-filled fugitive smiles. Their lips were clamp-shut and dragging a response out of them seemed *like getting blood out of a stone*!

The moment gave way to silence that started conspiring to depose the air of discussion in an underhand way. The sound of the silence was merrily tinkling in and deepening its presence further speedily. The silence was uncharacteristic but prolific in giving birth to distance, dissension and disenchantment. As instants became moment, the air of discussion seamlessly crumbled and dissolved into the flesh of silence much in the same way as sight sinks wearily in the vast countenance of the farthest horizon. They lethargically leaned on the chairs inhaling a lungful of air at least twice and looked impassively sedate dissimulating the true feelings. The implosive winds of the present feelings were gagged rudely down somewhere in their inmost selves and prevented repeatedly from being blown on their faces. The moment seemingly tore apart our mutually respectful shared-relation and the very delicate fabric of secular outlook that we had been selling to one another for a long time.

The silence morphed into a frozen state deforming grotesquely the fragile facet of our superficial perspectives on modernity, tolerance and secularism. As moments became duration, the ambience worsened further and sank into staid state collaborated by the silence that constantly stood by it. Meanwhile, we exchanged some slender glances perfunctorily with one another for a longer while. The soul of the discussion receded from the table as if the silence asked it to skedaddle fast. We could not find a decent substitute for silence and the stop came much sooner than I expected. We were caught in a weird moment that appeared *out and out* barren. The moment wept itself to sleep clinging firmly to the inviting lap of the frosted silence. An uncouth uneasiness was performing its gory dance on and around the table ringed tightly by a teasing silence. We remained downhearted amid the festivities of the silence.

Our relation morphed into a wound that wept blood. The relation experienced the pain of an amputation.

Conversion by force lowers the repute of a civilised society. Kumaran is a free citizen and entitled to choose his faith freely by way of freedom. Meanwhile, it is our obligatory duty to take the Message to him in the most adorable way possible. Islam hates compulsion like oppression; -and it is something to which Islam puts up the highest degree of aversion.

"Ye are the best of people, evolved for mankind, enjoining what is right, forbidding what is wrong, and believing in Allah…." [Qur'an: Al Imran 3:11]

The verse is brimming with august praise from none but the Lord of the worlds. The praise is celestial, extraordinary and can never be substituted for anything. It teaches some humongous lessons to Muslims to behave with appropriate sensitivity and proper delicacy deemed befitting to the towering calibre of the verse. The baton of Priesthood has been handed over to Muslims. In the pursuit of Priesthood, Muslims have been bestowed with two marvels as guides -the unchallenged holy Qur'an, and the unblemished noble Prophet. And most importantly, '*being the best of people*', the significance of the verse implies that we must *see the errors of our ways* before taking up the onus of disseminating the Message to the people of the world.

The 'authentic teachers', though outwardly ardent and fervent about Islam, but are actually slouching in backbenches being heedless to the Duty of sharing the Message to the world. The pride of being *'the best of the people'* seems to have been doubtful and receiving constantly apocryphal echoes from an honest hill.

In the following verses, the Almighty has presented Himself in a different mood. It reveals that He is in 'unprecedented pain' as His Pure and Majestic facets have been adulterated with the animal instinct called 'sex'! The excruciating pain has been described here grippingly; --it could force a true Muslim to conceal his embarrassment in a shell of shame. Here the lesson is wider; here the wisdom is profounder.

"They say: "((Allah)) Most Gracious has begotten a son! Indeed, ye have put forth a thing most monstrous! At it the skies are ready to burst, the earth to split asunder, and the mountains to fall down in utter ruin, …" [Qur'an: Maryam 19: 88-92]

The verses are a decent equivalent of an apocalypse! The 'ignominy' is blazingly so deep that the three massive creations of the Lord are ready to plunge into ultimate collapse: the sky to burst, the earth to split apart and the mountains to fall down. A burst of deep wailing emerges from the verses and entreats Muslims to disseminate the Message of the Qur'an to the people who, out of dreary ignorance or cognisance, ascribe the '*sexual instinct*' to God. The Message should reach its intended recipients who say: "Jesus Christ (pbuh) is the begotten son of God".

A depressing mood bursts into my inmost and ruffles insolently the peace of mind when I find that the Cry of the Lord fails repeatedly to awaken Muslims to a serious realisation about the implications of the verses. Entreaty of the Lord matters a little to them, and they, out of insolence, feel little indignity of not minding to pay a serious heed to it. Rather, with great inadvertence alloyed with indolence and indisposition, the last chosen race of the Lord seems to have adopted a habit of threatening to dislodge the Duty from the front page of obligation. Should Muslims dislodge the Duty from the frontline obligation, God would too invite a cause that will lead to their deposition from the post of the chosen race. God would replace them with another stead of people should Muslims become oblivion of the Duty.

The teachers of Islam have not learned any worthy lessons from the history of Jews, neither any even from the life of the Holy Prophet Muhammad (pbuh). –

Before the revelation of the Qur'an, the prophet, *off and on*, visited a cave called *Hira* where he used to make a quiet retreat into the realm of meditation. It was his routine activity before the revelation of the Qur'an. Post revelation, the account says that he did never visit the cave in his life time, instead he entered the field, he entered into discussion and he confronted people to whom the Message was alien and absurd.

Abu Jahl too stepped out of his lair with ranks of steep-fronted resistance! He stepped out to execute his mission of dire opposition and dissension towards Muhammad (pbuh). He stepped out to spoil every move of the Prophet with tongue sharper than sword, words more malignant than plague and intention ranker than evil! He had swapped his every human sense with devil! He sold out his soul in accommodation to lowness of behaviour and deployed his vilest intentions to belittle the Prophet. He became frenzied in his efforts to plant a blemish in the Prophethood, but ultimately all his pernicious schemes made nose-first landings.

The camps of Abu Jahls are still rocking! -

The enemy camps with ulterior motives have set out to teach the people of the world about 'Islam' in a distasteful manner alloyed with a rank of misinformation and disinformation. The camps, most certainly, have slipped into a routine to depose Islam in underhand way. A plague of wrong information campaigns are being relentlessly waged against Islam to distort its true image to the degree that makes Islam calamitously abominable. The world is being subjected constantly to compulsive over-feeding on the multitude of misleading information about Islam. The outcomes of the campaigns are extremely disturbing and can send a shudder of wide fear through the hearts of innocent non-Muslims.

We are at a crossroads, and we do have indeed a little of time to relax in the shrunk shell of idleness *turning a deaf ear* to the earnest cry of the divine cause. Rather, we should *go into overdrive* shrugging off the insouciance to make the Message reach faster to the farthest horizon of the earth with its splayed wings of inclusiveness, mercy and benevolence. It demands that Muslims should *bend over backwards* to ensure that the Message should reach its intended recipients wrapped in an ornate coating of love and altruistic compassion. Our main vocation as apostles is to pull up the Message from obscurity and offer the podium that it deserves the most. We should share with our fellow human beings the core purpose of life on the earth and the great news of the glad tidings that the glorious Qur'an has brought for the whole humankind. I wish Muslims had made it a dear wish to their hearts. Our main guiding principle must be, for now and ever, imbibing a great degree of compassion and tolerance, -

'Men you are my brothers entitled to know the purpose of the Creation from your Muslim brothers'.

Hobson's choice[1]*: The term is actually an illusion of choice where very limited options are offered. You take it or leave it is the basic rule of the Hobson's choice.

Lagrangian Points[2]*: Those are stable points in space where satellites are placed. In these points the gravitational forces of two orbiting bodies balance the centrifugal force.

Oymyakon[3]*: The earth's coldest inhabited place in Russia.

Sputnik Moment[4]*: In Oct' 1957 Sputnik 1 was launched successfully into earth's orbit by the USSR. It gave distinction to USSR but shocked the USA. The USA was surprised by the moment.

Elysian Field[5]*: Paradise in Greek mythology.

About the Author

S F Rahaman did his master's in mechanical engineering. He works as a research engineer in an organisation of high repute. His professional career spans more than sixteen years.

Printed by Libri Plureos GmbH in Hamburg,
Germany